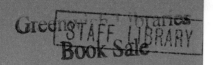
Greenwich Libraries
STAFF LIBRARY
Book Sale

D0296747

LONDON BOROUGH OF GREENWICH

GREENWICH LIBRARY

Woolwich Road, SE10 ORL Phone: 01-858 6656

	DATE OF RETURN	

Greenwich Libraries
Book Sale

London

Borough

of Greenwich

WE GOVERN BY SERVING

STAFF LIBRARY

Reference

Library

Greenwich

Greenwich Libraries
Book Sale

Greenwich Libraries
Book Sale

LIB.129

£15-50

School Librarianship

SCHOOL LIBRARIANSHIP

edited by
JOHN COOK

PERGAMON PRESS

SYDNEY · OXFORD · NEW YORK · TORONTO · PARIS · FRANKFURT

Pergamon Press (Australia) Pty Ltd,
19a Boundary Street, Rushcutters Bay, N.S.W. 2011, Australia.

Pergamon Press Ltd,
Headington Hill Hall, Oxford OX3 0BW, England.

Pergamon Press Inc.,
Maxwell House, Fairview Park, Elmsford, N.Y. 10523, U.S.A.

Pergamon of Canada Ltd,
Suite 104, 150 Consumers Road, Willowdale, Ontario M2J 1P9, Canada.

Pergamon Press GmbH,
6242 Kronberg-Taunus, Hammerweg 6, Postfach 1305, Federal Republic of Germany.

Pergamon Press SARL,
24 rue des Ecoles, 75240 Paris, Cedex 05, France.

First published 1981

Copyright © 1981 John Ralph Cook

Cover design by Allan Hondow
Typeset in Australia by S.A. Typecentre Pty Ltd
Printed in Singapore by Singapore National Printers (Pte) Ltd

National Library of Australia Cataloguing in Publication Data:

School librarianship.

Bibliography
ISBN 0 08 024814 4
ISBN 0 08 024813 6 Paperback

1. School libraries—Australia.
2. Library science. I. Cook, John, ed.´

027.8'0994

Greenwich Libraries
Book Sale

SBN 1	2	3 LOC. COP
08	024814	4 G STAFF 1
EDITION DATE	1981	
CLASS NO.	027·80994	

All rights reserved. No part of this publication may be reproduced, stored in
a retrieval system or transmitted in any form or by any means, electronic,
electrostatic, magnetic tape, mechanical, photocopying, recording or otherwise,
without permission in writing REFERENCE

INVOICE PAR 29 MAR 1985 £15·50

Contents

Introduction

School libraries in Australia have developed greatly over the past fifteen years. In New Zealand, school library development is being planned and implemented. Elsewhere in the South Pacific region, teachers and school administrators are looking towards school libraries and school librarians to provide the facilities and expertise for a greater emphasis on resource-based student-centred learning.

School library development has been often associated with large new buildings. Now there is a change of emphasis, towards the skills and practices of school librarians, rather than the physical premises from which they operate. School librarians now emphasise their role in providing information and in curriculum planning in the school, as well as the more traditional and accepted acquisition, organisation and provision of books and other materials.

This book aims to fill a need for school librarians in our region, by providing a practical handbook of procedures, for much of the content of the British and American texts is not relevant to conditions here. In addition, the book provides a description and analysis of the present state of school library development in Australia and New Zealand, which will be useful for people both here and overseas who wish to understand our situation. The best of our school libraries stand comparison with any in the world; it is hoped that our experience, as reflected in this book, will be of interest and value to people working in this field in other countries.

Note should be made of one point of terminology. The terms 'school librarian' and 'teacher librarian' are virtually synonymous in Australia. There is general agreement that for appointment as a school librarian or teacher librarian a person should hold qualifications in teaching and librarianship, as well as having undertaken tertiary study in a general teaching area. There is not general agreement, however, about the preferred name for such people. I prefer 'school librarian' as it correlates with overseas terminology and can accommodate differing levels of qualification in teaching and librarianship. On the other hand, Roy Lundin, for example, in Chapter 1 of this book, prefers to use 'teacher librarian' as he believes it gives greater emphasis to the teaching and educational role of the librarian in the school. Jan MacLean, in Chapter 2, explains that in New Zealand there is a clear distinction between the two terms.

The contributors to this book are all eminent practitioners and teachers of school librarianship in Australia and New Zealand. I am very grateful to them for giving the time and energy in already busy personal and professional lives to contribute so willingly and ably in this way to the development of school libraries. I also wish to record my thanks to my wife, Nancy Lane, for her help and encouragement throughout this project.

John Cook

The Contributors

The editor, *John Cook*, BA (Hons), DipEd (Adel.), DipT (ATC), DipLib (College of Librarianship Wales), ALAA, is Principal of Infotech Library and Information Consultants, Perth, Western Australia. He has been a teacher and school librarian in South Australian secondary schools, and from 1974 to 1978 was Lecturer in School Librarianship at Adelaide College of Advanced Education (now Adelaide College of the Arts and Education). He was President of the School Libraries Section of the Library Association of Australia 1976–77, and in 1979 was elected a member of the LAA's Board of Education.

Joan Brewer, BA, DipEd (Adel.), FLAA, FACE. Originally a secondary school teacher, Joan Brewer subsequently had experience in school, tertiary and technical libraries in Australia and in England. She is Principal Lecturer in School Librarianship at Adelaide College of the Arts and Education where she has been Head of Department since 1970. She has been active in the Library Association of Australia, particularly as a member of the Board of Education, from 1973 to 1979, and is a member of the Libraries Board of South Australia which is responsible for public libraries in that State. In 1976 she was awarded a Fellowship by the Australian College of Education for her work in the development of school libraries, and her work in this field and in education for librarianship was similarly honoured by the Library Association of Australia in 1980 by the award of its Fellowship.

James G. Dwyer, Teach Cert, BA (UWA), ALAA, FACE. Jim Dwyer has taught in primary and secondary schools, and his library experience covers the National Library of Australia, public libraries and school libraries. Since 1964 he has been responsible for school library development in the South Australian Education Department. He has been overseas on three occasions to examine school libraries and school/ community library developments and has served on many national and State committees on education and librarianship. He was elected President of the Library Association of Australia for 1981, and is the author of two publications on school/community libraries, *Co-operation or Compromise* and *Consolidation, Compromise or Conquest*. The honour of Fellowship of the Australian College of Education was conferred on him in 1980 for his work for school libraries.

Joe Hallein, BA (Wyoming), Teach Cert (Dickinson), MSc (Western Michigan), GradDipEdAdmin (Newfoundland), ALAA, is Senior Lecturer and Director of Post-graduate Studies in the School of Library and Information Studies, Kuring-gai College of Advanced Education, Lindfield, NSW. He is also Consultant for Library Development in Tonga and Western Samoa, a Counsellor for the Innovations Program of the Schools Commission, and Past-President of the School Libraries Section, Library Association of Australia (1978–79). He has previously been a Lecturer in the School of Library and Information Science, University of Western Ontario; School Supervisor and Consultant for School Libraries in Newfoundland; Media Specialist for the Government of the Virgin Islands; and Consultant in School Library Development in the Caribbean area.

Roy Lundin, BEd (Br.Col.), MEd (Qld), PhD (Monash), ALAA, MACE, is Head of the Department of School Librarianship at Kelvin Grove College of Advanced Education in Brisbane. He came to Australia in 1968 from Canada, where he had been a school teacher and principal for ten years. In 1970 he became one of Queensland's first teacher librarians. He has been Research Officer of the Commonwealth Secondary School Libraries Project at the University of Queensland and Research Fellow on the School Libraries Research Project established by the Schools Commission at Monash University in Victoria.

Jan MacLean, BA, Dip NZLS, FNZLA, is Principal Lecturer of the new School of Library Studies at Wellington Teachers' College. Before this she was a Senior Lecturer at the New Zealand Library School, and specialised in library services and literature for young people. She has been involved in much of the work during the past ten years on school libraries, serving as a member of the study group on *Libraries in Education*; the Survey Organiser for the Fenwick Report; and was the NZLA representative on the Working Party on School Libraries (the Foley Report).

Maureen Nimon, BA (Hons), DipEd (Adel.), DipT (ATC), GradDip ReadingEd (ACAE), ALAA. Maureen Nimon began her tertiary education by studying concurrently for a university degree and for qualification as a secondary school teacher. After gaining a first-class honours degree in history, she taught for some time in a secondary school, and then became a lecturer in history at Adelaide Teachers' College. She retired for several years; then, having qualified as an Associate of the Library Association of Australia, she worked as a reference librarian. In 1974 she was appointed as a lecturer in the Department of School Librarianship at the institution now known as the Adelaide College of the Arts and Education. Since that time she has completed a Graduate Diploma in Reading Education, and is at present engaged in study for a Masters degree in education.

Anne Simpson, BA, DipEd (Adel.), ALAA. Anne Simpson has had wide experience in schools and libraries. She has worked in the State Library of South Australia, Children's Section; a local public library; a primary and a secondary school library; the History Faculty Library, Oxford University; and the cataloguing section of the Barr Smith Library, University of Adelaide. She has been in charge of cataloguing at the School Libraries Branch of the South Australian Education Department; and since 1977 has been a Lecturer in School Librarianship, specialising in bibliographic organisation and children's literature, at Adelaide CAE.

Beryl Turner, BA (Vic.-Well.), Dip NZLS, ALAA. Beryl Turner has taught at infant and primary levels in urban and rural schools in New Zealand and the United Kingdom. She is a graduate of the New Zealand Library School and has worked in School Library Services, and children's and adult lending divisions of a municipal library. She ran a children's book department in a campus bookstore and was also engaged in bookselling in the United Kingdom for a short time. In 1968 she was appointed Acquisitions Librarian at Wattle Park Teachers' College in Adelaide and became the Librarian there in 1969. A year after the college moved to Murray Park in 1973, she took up her current position as Lecturer in School Librarianship, specialising in children's literature, at Adelaide CAE. During 1978 she attended courses on children's literature at Simmons College in Boston, USA, as both student and guest lecturer.

CHAPTER 1

School Library Development
in Australia

Roy Lundin

School libraries in Australia have for many years been the subject of special attention, but it was only in the late 1960s and into the 1970s that actual development took place as a result of special funding. The history of school libraries is, therefore, relatively brief and recent; but in a very short time most schools in Australia received buildings, staff and resources which have brought their libraries up to a standard equivalent to the best in the world. This chapter traces these developments, highlighting the major stages, and then discusses some of the things that have been learned from research and experience.

A brief history

In 1935 the Munn-Pitt report stated that in a national survey there was found a great variation of library facilities in schools, but that

> No secondary school was found, even in the largest cities, in which all of the elements of satisfactory service exists.[1]

Nothing seemed to be done until the 1950s when there was, apparently, a surge of interest in school libraries that led to the establishment of a few respectable libraries—especially in large private schools. The interest soon waned, however, because of lack of government support, and these libraries deteriorated and in many instances became trophy rooms.

A version of this chapter was delivered as a paper at the New Zealand Library Association Conference at Wanganui, 14–18 February 1977. Another version appeared in the *Australian Library Journal* 26, 13 (1977).

New stirrings came to the surface early in the 1960s, when work began on a set of standards for school libraries. In South Australia, Ernest Roe completed in 1963 a doctoral study of the influence of libraries on education[2], and it was from this study that came his very important book, *Teachers, Librarians and Children*.[3]

The foundation stone of Australian school library development was the Fenwick Report, *School and Children's Libraries in Australia*, which was the outcome of a six-month visit in 1964 by Sara Innis Fenwick as a Fulbright lecturer at the invitation of the Library Association of Australia.[4]

The Fenwick Report was published in 1966, and in the same year the Library Association of Australia (LAA) published its *Standards and Objectives for School Libraries*[5], a document that had taken about four years to produce. These 'standards' drew attention to the educational value of adequate school libraries and set quantified target standards. This gave everyone something to aim at.

There did not appear to be much activity for the next two years, but a doctoral study by Smart[6] revealed that this was a time of intense lobbying directed at the then Minister of Education, Senator Gorton, who became Prime Minister in December 1967 after the death of Mr Holt. Put in its crudest terms, the lobbying seemed to convince the appropriate politicians that there was political mileage in granting funds to school libraries. One difficulty in the plan was that education in Australia is a State responsibility, and federal intervention is, therefore, not always appreciated. However, a precedent had been set by former Prime Minister Menzies who started a program of direct, special-purpose federal grants for secondary school science laboratories in 1964.

The LAA also turned its attention to a campaign of public awareness by making a public submission to the Prime Minister on 8 December 1967, setting out specific recommendations for a plan of action.[7] The submission examined briefly the changing role of the school, the teacher, the school library and the teacher librarian. Then it recommended the introduction of federal grants for school libraries to be implemented in three stages. Stage 1 was to include the establishment of a school libraries section within the Commonwealth Department of Education and Science, the formation of a Commonwealth advisory committee, and the invitation of an overseas specialist to advise on the project. Stage 2 was to involve financial aid being granted for demonstration or pilot school libraries and the training of teacher librarians. Stage 3 was to be the full implementation of the federal aid program to all schools. In retrospect, if the federal government had, in fact, followed this program, many of the problems that did arise could have been avoided.

The Australian Library Promotion Council (ALPC) got into the public awareness act shortly afterwards, in 1968, by commissioning Margaret Trask to write *School Libraries: A Report to the Nation*.[8] This report not only echoed some of the statements of the Fenwick Report and the LAA Standards but also presented some new and startling facts about just how shocking school library funding and provision were in Australia.

The breakthrough came on 14 August 1968, when the then Federal Minister for Education and Science, Mr Malcolm Fraser, announced that an initial grant of $27 million would be provided for buildings, furniture, equipment and resource materials relating to *secondary* school libraries for the 1969–71 triennium. In 1971 a further grant of $30 million was provided for the 1972–74 triennium. These funds were for all secondary schools—government and non-government.

The Minister also appointed a Commonwealth Secondary Schools Libraries Committee of well-qualified and experienced educators and librarians, and he asked them to implement the program. This Committee in 1971 produced *Standards for Secondary School Libraries*[9], which was not so much a set of target standards for adequate school libraries as it was a set of guidelines for the program of government spending.

UNESCO made a contribution in 1970 when it sponsored a seminar in Sydney on the role of libraries in secondary education, a report of which was published in 1971.[10]

In these early days, also, even though there was an active School Libraries Section of the LAA, new school library associations began to be formed in various States and these banded together in 1969 to form a new national body, the Australian School Library Association (ASLA).

The good things about the federal grants of 1969 to 1974 were (a) that money was coming in, and (b) it was promised on a triennial basis which allowed for planning. But the library world was not completely happy because there were no funds for *primary* school libraries, and only about $100 000 for short, one-to-two-week crash courses for teachers on how to run a library. Some State departments of education stepped in and tried to rectify these omissions. ASLA, LAA, the ALPC, State governments and several other groups and individuals made many submissions to the federal government concerning these needs.

Another good feature of this federal program was that the need for early and continuing evaluation was recognised. A research team in the Faculty of Education of the University of Queensland was commissioned in 1970 to evaluate the impact of improved library provision on the quality of secondary education in Australia. A tall order, but the project's first report in 1972, *Secondary School Libraries in Australia*, was able to report, among other things, that in the first four years of the program:

> There is still a great deal to be done before the full consequences of the Commonwealth grant can be laid out, but the evidence from a variety of sources (observations, opinions of students, opinions of teachers, analysis of questionnaire data and the like) tells a remarkably consistent story of the Grant making available a greatly enriched stock of facilities which are supporting and making possible, if not coercing, new patterns of teaching and learning. These new patterns include more individualisation of instruction, more opportunities for learners to participate in their education, to be enthusiastic about it, and to be more responsible for their progress. There is already evidence to show that many students are responding positively to these opportunities . . . there are, however, at least two things revealed in this study which seem to blunt the impact of the Grant to some extent: the lack of properly qualified school library staff and the lack of inservice training for all teachers in the use of libraries.[11]

This project was terminated in January 1975, and a new expanded School Libraries Research Project established at Monash University.

The ALPC 1972 report by Cohen, *Primary School Libraries: A Report to the Nation*[12], reinforced the pressure for federal funding for primary school libraries, and in that year both the Liberal and Labor parties made election promises to provide such grants.

In 1973 the new Australian Labor government, in accordance with the recommendations of the Interim Committee for the Australian Schools Commission, provided for 1974–75 a further $21.28 million for secondary school libraries, and $3.78 million for training teacher librarians and for their replacements in classrooms. Also, a Primary Schools' Libraries Committee was established to implement that part of the program and draw up *Guidelines for Library Services in Primary Schools*.[13]

At this point, the development of school libraries in Australia had gained a dizzying momentum and it was believed this would continue until every school in Australia had a library equipped and stocked at least up to published guideline standards. But, complications soon arose: first, the money began to run out and be worth less; second, the policy of the Schools Commission shifted, so that the needs of the school as a whole were considered, rather than selected elements for special funding.

In any event, there was enough pressure on the Schools Commission to continue special funding for school libraries in 1976 and 1977. In 1976 schools received $13.05 million for library buildings and resources, and about $2 million for the training of teacher librarians. In 1977, amounts were much more difficult to isolate but grants for school libraries and related projects exceeded $13 million for library buildings, about $1.5 million for training teacher librarians, and there was an undefined amount for books and audio-visual resources. From 1978 non-government schools and State education authorities have been able to determine how much of the total federal grants for education can be spent on these specific resources—and considering this, the total federal money spent on school libraries in Australia is estimated to exceed $20 million each year.

It is also safe to say that federal grants have stimulated State and local (school-level) spending. Indeed, when all the elements of school libraries—buildings, resources, staff and central support services—are considered with respect to government schools, the States are now bearing up to 80 per cent of the total cost. It costs money to accept money.

This stimulation has been referred to as 'incentive funding'. Part of the Schools Commission's program for non-government primary schools was to give grants according to needs to bring all their bookstocks up to 25 per cent of the 1974 *Guidelines* standards. In a 1975 survey of 203 of these schools, it was found that:

A considerable percentage of the schools (31 per cent) were prepared to spend local funds on further improving their bookstock to meet 50 per cent or greater of the *Guidelines* bookstock standard. Sixteen schools (7.9 per cent) have reached the *Guidelines* basic bookstock.

School initiative has not been limited to increase in bookstock. Substantial improvements have occurred in other aspects of library and resource service in the schools. Schools have been prepared to spend local money, time and effort in processing, organising and housing library materials and equipment. In addition, principals and teachers have shown willingness to attend seminars and courses associated with the organisation and use of library resources.

There is much evidence that the rate of activity and local initiative has quickened since the Book Grants were received. In fact, the great proportion of changes in library and resources have taken place in 1974–75. There seems little doubt that the Substantial Book Grants have acted as an incentive to many schools to provide a more adequate library service now, and encouraged some to make considerable plans for 1976.[14]

Growth of school libraries

In the twelve years 1969–80 inclusive, about $200 million of federal government funds will have been spent on school libraries. Add to this the

State and local spending modestly estimated at about the same amount again, and the figure is over $400 million. What has been achieved in tangible items from this expenditure?

Buildings

The most recent statistics with regard to buildings were obtained for 1977. At the end of that year it was estimated that about 1200 new secondary school libraries had been built up to *Guidelines* standards. In addition to these, many libraries had been extensively refurbished, so that about 65 per cent of secondary schools, serving about 80 per cent of secondary students, had libraries of a substantial nature.

The 7200 primary schools in Australia have not experienced such dramatic development because of the size of the task and the later start. Of these schools, more than 3000 are too small for separate library buildings. Of the remainder, the Schools Commission selected 41 in which to develop 'pilot libraries' as demonstration units in a variety of school types. These were the subject of intensive evaluation by the Monash University School Libraries Research Project.[15]

Since 1977, the building program in primary and secondary schools has slowed, but by no means has it ceased. Future surveys will reveal the details of library provision, but it is safe to say that every school in Australia now has a library, and almost all of them are of recent origin.

The new libraries are very impressive features in the schools in which they have been placed. In most schools, the new library is the most luxurious facility in the school. These libraries provide for individual, small group and large group activities, through such facilities as carrels (individual study booths), discussion rooms, production booths and annexes. In most schools, these facilities did not exist to any satisfactory extent before the libraries were built.

Staff

Before 1970 there was little opportunity in Australia for teacher librarians to obtain adequate preparation. In 1963, for example, McGrath found that 'teacher librarians' were essentially teachers who were placed in charge of libraries in addition to their other duties. This was mainly because little specialised training existed.

> With the exemption [sic] of the full year post basic training course for primary school teacher-librarians at Melbourne Teachers' College leading to the 'Trained Teacher-Librarian's Certificate', there is no *adequate* provision for the training of school librarians in Australian Teachers' Colleges.[16]

It was possible, however, for teachers to become qualified librarians by achieving a Registration Certificate from the Library Association of Australia, through its external examination system which was established in 1944. It was not until the mid-1960s, however, that these external studies began to cater for a specialisation in school librarianship.

In an attempt to assist those teachers being placed in charge of the new school libraries, some funds from both federal and State governments were provided for short in-service courses of a few days to a few weeks. It was soon recognised, however, that such 'crash' courses were inadequate and ·that the lack of qualified staff led to considerable concern about obtaining value from the capital investment. The first report of the Commonwealth Secondary School Libraries Research Project concluded that the lack of properly qualified school library staff tended to limit the educational impact of the federal grants.[17]

Attention was also focused on the problem of the supply of adequately prepared teacher librarians at a national workshop held in Canberra on 1–4 August 1972. It was reported that the national survey of the Commonwealth Secondary School Libraries Research Project found:

> Of the 577 people reported in charge of libraries full time or part-time, only 168 (29%) achieve the state of teacher-librarian . . . only 32 of these people have library qualifications recognised by the Library Association of Australia, and of these only 14 have degrees.[18]

At the same workshop, Hughes reported on courses of training for teacher librarians. Although he found that in 1972 there were 433 potential teacher librarians in training, he qualified this figure as being too generous. By eliminating those who were enrolled in various 'crash' courses, he concluded that the figure would be more accurate if it were half the original.[19]

To rectify the situation, some State departments of education had initiated their own training programs. Then, the Interim Committee of the Schools Commission recommended in their 1973 report, *Schools in Australia*, special grants of $3.78 million for the training of teacher librarians and for other teachers to replace them in the classrooms.[20] It was expected that these funds would provide at least the equivalent of six months' full-time training for 500 teacher librarians per year in 1974–75. These funds were supplemented by State funds and, as a result, during those two years 932 teachers received specialised training, many of them for a period of one year full-time.[21] Similar support was provided for these programs in 1976[22] and 1977[23].

The basic training programs have all been established in colleges of advanced education; and in 1977 there were at least 13 courses in Australia specifically for prospective teacher librarians, at undergraduate and graduate levels, and a total of approximately 900 students (equivalent full-time) were enrolled in the courses.[24]

Substantial government support for the training programs produced fairly dramatic results. The table below is an attempt to bring together all the known data relating to the increase in numbers of 'teacher librarians' in Australian government schools from 1969 to 1978. This information was obtained from a survey of all State and territory supervisors of school libraries, and from published documents. No comparable statistics exist for Australia's 2138 non-government schools.

'Teacher librarians' are somewhat variously defined in the table, and there is no indication of how many of them work on a part-time basis. Those in Western Australia and the Northern Territory tend to have only a one-term in-service course in school librarianship. In New South Wales there is no information about the state of their qualifications in librarianship, but they are all trained teachers. Those in Queensland have only one semester of training in school librarianship, and this is approximately one-half of the Graduate Diploma in Teacher Librarianship available in that State. The definition of 'teacher librarian' for this purpose is therefore considered to be: a qualified teacher with a significant amount of training in school librarianship—that is, not less than the equivalent of one term full-time, and presently recognised as adequate by the employing authorities. Qualified librarians without teacher training are excluded.

Given all the problems with missing data and definition of qualifications, it is clear that the number of teacher librarians has been growing steadily. By December 1978, there were approximately 3500 qualified teacher librarians in Australia; and this number is almost ten times that in 1971.

The present national target standards, generally accepted, have been put forward by the Schools Commission in *Books and Beyond: Guidelines for Library Resource Facilities and Services*.[25] Essentially, the recommended staffing standard is for one 'Head Teacher Librarian' for every school with enrolment above 100 students. In addition it is recommended that there be 'Other Professional' staff, who may also be teacher librarians, at the rate of approximately one to 500 students. To meet this standard would require between 9000 and 15 000 teacher librarians for Australia's 9444 schools. Thus, there is a shortfall of more

Teacher Librarians in Australian Government Schools, 1969–78, by State

Year	Vic.*	Qld	NSW	SA	WA‡	Tas.§	NT	ACT
1969		2						
1970		25		238				
1971		52		346				
1972		165		397				
1973		288		437				
1974	385	327		455			29	
1975	623	360		493	114	61	35	
1976	741	431		512	149		42	
1977	1 205	519	1 348†	521	189		44	76
1978	1 425	541		549	314		49	99

*Source: *Statistics Bank* (Library Branch, Education Department of Victoria), and a letter from Mr B. Sheen, Supervisor of School Libraries.
†Only about 20 per cent of these teachers can be assumed to have significant education in school librarianship.
‡Source: *Education Library Service Bulletin* (Education Department of Western Australia).
§Source: W. L. Brown, *Libraries in Schools, Colleges and the Community*. (State Library of Tasmania, Hobart, 1976), p. 28.

than 5000 teacher librarians, if the minimum standard is to be met.

Attention has recently been focused on the provision and training of school library support staff.[26] It soon became obvious that there was a huge number of clerical tasks in a school library that were a waste of a teacher librarian's time. Many, if not most, school libraries now have paid assistance. Also, in several States, courses have been established to train middle-level 'library technicians' or 'library assistants'. *Books and Beyond* sets out some standards for the types of support staff a school library may require, and the number of hours per week such staff should be employed.

Resources
While it is held that nothing can or should completely replace books, it is now recognised that all carriers of information can be considered legitimate library material. The school library is now universally accepted as a multi-media resource centre. Some infant and special

schools have carried this to the point of having 'toy libraries', and it is not uncommon to find animals in school libraries—live and stuffed.

It has been calculated that in 1964 the average State government subsidy on school library materials was 32 cents per child per year, and that in 1968 the average was up to 37 cents.[27] Most of these funds were spent by only 10 per cent of the schools—the ones that could 'raise the first dollar' to attract subsidy. During 1969–75, more than $20 million was spent on print and non-print materials and related equipment, from federal grants alone, for secondary schools. This represents a condition-free expenditure of approximately $3 per secondary student per year. To this must be added the expenditures of State government and school funds on materials, and this would amount to approximately the same rate again per student. In all States the subsidy scheme has been abandoned and a direct grant scheme implemented. Generalisations are difficult here. For example, in 1975 secondary schools in Victoria spent about $8 per student for materials, and the New South Wales government spent $15 per primary student for materials. One of the side effects of this has been the impact on book publishing and selling, and on the retailing of audio-visual materials. Another factor that must be considered here is that funding has not increased at the same rate as the cost of materials; for example, the average price per book has risen from $3.50 in 1969 to something over twice that amount. The rate of collection building has been seriously affected by this. In any event, the national bookstock in secondary schools is well over 10 books per student, and primary schools are fast approaching that figure. All schools are being systematically funded.

One case demonstrating collection development is that of a primary school of 700 students which had in 1974 a total of 50 library books of doubtful quality and a couple of old radio-tuners; by 1978 it had a new library building, more than five books per student and a considerable collection of audio-visual materials and equipment. Another case is that of a secondary school of about 1500 students, which during the period 1969–76 grew from a classroom-sized library of 100 m² to one of 750 m²; from 5500 books to 20 000 books; from a few reel tape recordings to about 1500 cassettes; from 15 periodical subscriptions to 80.

Support services
All six States and the two territories in Australia now have central support services, mainly for government schools. Services that are offered include:

administration of grants;
school library advisers in local regions;
bulk buying and distribution of some resources;
continuous in-service training programs for teachers and teacher librarians;
advice on copyright;
selection aids for print and non-print resources;
production of materials;
media-mobiles, that is, vehicles carrying collections of software and audio-visual equipment;
professional materials collections;
technical services.

After two studies by Down and Young[28], a computer-based cataloguing service is being offered by the Schools Commission, based on the South Australian Education Resources Information System, to an increasing number of schools throughout the country. The Australian School Catalogue Information Service (ASCIS) is the fulfilment of a dream of many teacher librarians, whereby cataloguing information is supplied on microfiche to schools, with a card supply service also available at minimal cost.

Things learned from research and experience

When federal government money started pouring into State education departments and schools in 1969, there was a rather dazed lull for almost a year, because it was suddenly realised that the expertise to spend it effectively was lacking. Yet, there was political pressure to spend the money by certain dates and to account for the expenditure. This lack of expertise, plus pressure, resulted in a considerable number of mistakes—especially in building design and selection of equipment. As far as learning about school library development was concerned, it appeared that planners and practitioners were either too late to implement their discoveries or they had trouble convincing the decision-makers and designers to put the new ideas into practice. Over the years, however, some of the mistakes have been corrected and deficiencies made up. Needless to say, there is still much to be learned.

Buildings

One method used to make rapid progress was to use a standard design for the library building in many schools. It is now realised that each school may require a tailor-made library space.

In all the new libraries the space needed for audio-visual storage and production was underestimated. Not only did no one know the kind of space needed for this type of media but neither did any one expect such rapid growth of audio-visual collections. The resulting problems have been very difficult to overcome.

Indeed no one really knew how big a school library should be. It was not until 1975, when hundreds of libraries had been built, that evidence was found to reveal that library space of 0.6 m^2 per student, based on total school enrolment, was perceived as adequate by teachers and teacher librarians.[29]

In the old, established, egg-crate-design schools the location of the library was another problem. Many of the first libraries were built on the fringe of the school, out by the road—perhaps so that everyone could see what the government was doing for our schools (but also because there was talk of having libraries open at night). It is now realised that if there is to be a centralised library it should be centrally located, even if it means converting existing buildings and then adding more classrooms in another part of the school.

There is also considerable questioning of the value of big, separate, free-standing libraries; especially, for example, when it has been observed that an effective library service has been operated from such places as a condemned medical room measuring 4 x 4 m—not that this is desirable.

During the first six years of federal funding it was calculated that 75 to 80 per cent of the funds were spent on free-standing library buildings, which seems somewhat out of proportion when one considers the relative educational value of buildings, materials and staff. Consider, for example, that in a school of approximately 1800 students the new, very large library carries an average of 241 class groups per week, representing about 7000 student visits. Because they are booked into the library by the teachers, rather than regularly scheduled, it means that there are 241 periods when classrooms are vacant. The cost-benefit of such poor use of space may be open to question. Consider also that the cost of a large free-standing library has risen from $90 000 in 1969 to about $250 000.

These considerations, among others—including changes in ideas about school library organisation, school design and education—have led at least one leading school library expert in Australia to comment:

> I think our buildings are going to become immeasurably smaller. I think we will find that eventually school libraries will not have one function of

providing working space for students and staff. The library would become the focus for the acquisition, the organisation, production and dissemination of information but not necessarily for its use. It may not necessarily even store materials in that part of the school-building we call the library.[30]

At least, library buildings will need to allow for internal and external flexibility.

There is no doubt that resources and services require spaces, and these have been accurately calculated, but to try to get everything and everybody into one place is not feasible—especially in large, existing schools. New schools are a different matter.

It is now felt that as school resource services develop, a school-based planning committee should continually define space needs and apply for funds, and then the governments should provide the money *as it is needed*. Such an approach will usually be more economical because it will require adaptation rather than a completely new facility, and it will avoid wastage because the results will be much more relevant to the needs of each school.

Staff

Perhaps the most important element of a school library program is the cadre of qualified staff employed within it. To determine the numbers and kinds needed for optimum results continues to be a problem. One of the most definite things we can say is that staffing needs depend on what the school is trying to do.

At first it was believed that schools needed one full-time teacher librarian for each 240–300 students.[31] It is now known that all schools require the services of a teacher librarian, but that in large schools one teacher librarian for 400–500 students is adequate to meet present needs *if adequate support staff and central services are provided* to relieve the teacher librarian from the middle-level and clerical tasks.[32] For example, in the large school referred to earlier, with 241 classes attending per week, consider the number of man-hours it takes to re-shelve the 4000+ items removed from the shelves each day. Support staff is needed for this.

Recent considerations of staffing standards seem to indicate that up to three or four support staff are needed for each professional staff member. Some of these support staff may be required to have professional or semi-professional skills in specific areas—such as, for example, educational materials, design and production.

One aspect on which evidence has supported an early discussion relates to the insistence on *teacher* librarians being placed in charge of school libraries. In 1972 at a national workshop in Canberra, the consensus of the educators, librarians and educational administrators present was as follows:

> Programs of education for teacher-librarians should be designed to enable participants to achieve competence in the fields of teaching, librarianship and administration, so that they can organise effectively and exploit the school library and its resources, and in so doing form their own professional attitudes concerning the role of libraries in resource-based, research-orientated teaching and learning.
>
> In addition to the three areas of education, librarianship and administration . . . it is important that tertiary education should be undertaken to the level of a 3rd year major within another academic field.[33]

This notion was supported by research:

> . . . the person-in-charge [of a school library] performs better on the job if he has training and experience in both teaching and librarianship, plus a tertiary degree.[34]

And it was supported by experience. Where librarians without teacher training have been appointed to schools, the library tends not to become an integral part of the educational program; teachers tend not to communicate with the library staff nor do they trust the library staff to supervise students; and the collections tend to reflect public library rather than school library needs. Even librarians who have been given a brief course in education have not proven successful in school libraries mainly because they lacked teaching experience. This same lack of experience has been the downfall of teachers who took library training immediately after teacher training.[35]

This is not to suggest that there is anything *wrong* with librarians. It is just that (a) teachers will not accept non-teachers as equals in the school setting, and (b) a teacher librarian must be qualified and experienced in teaching to be able to take part in the planning and implementation of the educational program in a school—the most important aspects of the practice of school librarianship. In addition, because school libraries are rather new, teacher librarians have had to take on the responsibility for the in-service training of teachers concerning the role of resources in teaching and learning. Such involvement would be difficult for a non-teacher.

The importance of the role of the teacher librarian is now being recognised throughout Australia, in that every State Department of Education has established 'subject master' status for teacher librarians in large secondary schools. In some large non-government schools this status has existed for several years, and in at least one school in Australia there is a Deputy Principal (a teacher librarian) in charge of 'curriculum development and resource services'.

One other decision that was correct was to make teacher librarians 'media generalists'. This avoided the evolution of 'audio-visual co-ordinators' and the possible American-style split between book people and audio-visual people. What is happening now is that teachers and teacher librarians are evolving as specialists—in bibliographic organisation, children's literature, television production, film-making, and so on—and all feel that they can contribute to a total, integrated, school resource service. A good teacher librarian must be a resource generalist who knows and understands content, regardless of the container it comes in.

Resource collections

All Australian school libraries have become multi-media centres. At first, there was considerable emphasis on the containers for purposes of acquisition and organisation. It is becoming increasingly common for schools to acquire 'items', and less distinction is made among media. All types of media are being acquired for programs or units of work, rather than the acquisition of one medium at a time.

In an increasing number of schools audio-visual materials and equipment can be borrowed as easily as books. In 1969 and 1970 this was very rare, and only a few people thought it was ever possible. The prevalent feeling now is that equipment and materials are for students, and that 'hands-on' is important to learning. It has been observed that a short initial 'play period' exists until these 'newer media' are taken for granted by students and teachers and used educationally.

Some schools have experimented with various degrees of open access. Some have even integrated all media on the shelves in Dewey order—'supermarket shelving'. The general conclusion is that parallel shelving (of, for example, outsize books) is best in terms of both economy of space and efficiency of organisation. Also, some materials and equipment are best made available on semi-open access—that is, visible but available only on request. It has been found that borrowers rarely steal items, but if some materials are on open access the non-borrowers are tempted!

Further on the topic of audio-visual media it has been learned that:
(a) commercial materials are often unsuitable; therefore they must be adapted before use;

(b) teachers and teacher librarians usually have not the time nor the expertise to produce original materials of sufficient standard; therefore it is necessary for them to compile and adapt existing materials and for the Education Departments to set up high-standard production centres to meet local needs;

(c) a system of maintenance services must be established early in the program if the full value of expensive equipment is to be realised;

(d) various kinds of equipment should be completely compatible to avoid wasting money;

(e) portable audio-visual equipment is far superior to fixed, built-in systems in meeting the variety of teaching and learning needs and it is also more economical;

(f) it is necessary to intelligently anticipate new (and rapid) developments in technology; for instance, one State wisely waited for the colour video-cassette equipment before making large investments in television production and reception; now there is concern because of the video-disc development.

Bulk buying of resources has always been an attractive proposition because considerable savings can be gained—up to 47 per cent in one instance. The effect can be disastrous on some local booksellers—and if school library people are trying to create a book-reading public they will create a book-buying public, and so keep the local bookseller in business. Bulk buying has been found very beneficial for remote schools and for basic collections, especially of reference materials. Generally, however, schools must always be permitted to select to meet their own needs, otherwise they find much irrelevant material arriving and gathering dust on the shelves because 'nobody ordered it'.

Also, there have developed a few school library co-operative buying schemes—one involving about 60 schools—to take advantage of cheaper overseas purchasing. But, even more important, local networks of five to ten schools have sprung up of their own initiative all over Australia. At times these 'neighbourhood groups' can include an education/teacher centre, a college, a university, or a public library. Many of these networks have begun by producing union lists of periodicals and some have progressed to well-developed inter-library loan schemes. Usually, one school becomes the 'hub' that co-ordinates the services.[36]

At this stage, there is no empirical evidence concerning the standard number of items, books and other, required per student to give adequate service. Estimates range from 10 to 40, and more. What is known is that small schools require more items per student than large schools.

Quantitative standards, therefore, follow a log-curve formula. The most basic collection for schools of up to 200 students should be 3000 books and 3000 other items. The most definite guideline evolved is: Select carefully to meet needs.

In fact, in the recent economic climate, selection is a critical issue. It is no longer possible to buy everything seen in bookshops just because someone thinks it would be nice to have. The pressure of economics tends to force schools to avoid luxuries and stick to the essentials to get the best and most for their money. It may well be that not only library buildings, or spaces, but also resource collections will be smaller than one would have thought they should be. The emphasis will, then, shift from quantity to quality, more duplication of titles, more turnover, larger collections of paperbacks, pamphlets, and periodicals, and more sharing among groups of schools. Selection will be absolutely critical, and therefore it will be important for central support services to put out reliable selection aids.

Hand-in-hand with the ideas of smaller library buildings and, perhaps, smaller collections is the observation made of the stages of development in the organisation of resources. From observation and reports it appears that there are three developmental stages in this respect and they can be shown diagrammatically as follows:

Decentralised → Centralised→ Decentralised
(fragmented)   (co-ordinated)

There is a fine line, or rather several fine lines, between the final state of decentralisation and the first. These lines are the organised services, procedures and communication links which characterise an effective library program.

There is no question of the necessity of centralised controls and keys, but in this final stage there may be, as a result of physical necessity, the need for certain materials and equipment to be located, *not* scattered, throughout the school, but all need to be co-ordinated centrally so that they can be retrieved by the library staff, at least when needed.[37]

School resource services have, then, moved from fragmented collections, to 'school libraries', to 'resource centres', to 'school resource services', which now permeate the whole school and flow in and out of the school and the whole community.

This discussion cannot explore the whole list of what has been learned about school libraries. The whole area of usage patterns, for example, remains untouched. Briefly, some further findings are:

new library buildings have a positive, dramatic impact on the quantity of student usage, but it is the teacher who has the greatest influence on the educational quality of student usage;

whereas the new library facilities affect student usage, it is the teacher librarian who most influences teacher usage;

teachers lack pre-service and in-service training in the increased role of resources in teaching and learning;

students show greater satisfaction, motivation and independence in learning when library provision improves and usage increases;

a combination of some fixed and some flexible scheduling of the school library is necessary for optimum results;

there is the need for constant evaluation and monitoring of school library development, not only at the State and national levels, but also at the school level, to continually improve services to meet real needs.

One finding that requires a brief description is that relating to the concept of *readiness*. It could have assisted in better spending of funds if it had been applied early in the programs. Stated very simply, it was found that some schools were more ready than others to receive new libraries or *large* grants for resources. That is, in some schools the principal and teachers recognised the need for change, a library and increased collection of resources, and they had the knowledge, expertise and plans for spending the money; in other schools this was not the case. As McArthur reported:

> Indicators of this internal recognition in particular schools were reported by the researchers to be the establishment of representative education committees to plan for utilisation of the new resources, involvement of teachers and pupils in the selection and acquisition of materials, reconsideration of their methods of teaching and curriculum content by teachers, and visits by the principal, librarian and teachers to other newly established school libraries for ideas and advice. Although it was impossible to quantify these indicators, the visiting researchers felt sufficiently confident to categorise schools on a global factor of 'readiness' with three levels: ready, moderately ready, and unready.[38]

Which is not to suggest that some schools should not receive any funds for school libraries, but that they need something else first. That something else is stimulation in the form of advice and in-service training at the school level. If this had been realised in 1969, program implementers could have ensured that the federal grants would have had a greater and more rapid impact than they did on the quality of education, and the number of white elephants could have been reduced.

Conclusions

Planners do not have the benefit of the 20:20 hindsight that reporters have. But if such reporting can assist in future programs, then it is of some value. Furthermore, there are many questions yet unanswered, and, of course, changing conditions require new solutions. One thing on which there is universal consensus is expressed in the first of the 'Principles of School Librarianship':

> Every member of the school community needs close and immediate access to an organised collection of resources and services appropriate to his educational, informational, recreational and cultural needs and interests.[39]

In meeting such an aim, planners should carefully consider needs, then set priorities as follows:
(a) staff—advisory, then teacher librarians, then aides;
(b) resources—upgrading, then development, then maintenance;
(c) space—support for expansion as needs become evident to school-based planning groups.
Any national program should incorporate these into a strategy for implementation which should have flexibility as its keynote.

Finally, with regard to change, Professor Ron King has said: 'When you think in terms of educational change you must think in terms of decades.'[40] The dramatic development of school libraries in Australia in little over one decade is a demonstration of what can be done with interest and support from governments. But this tangible outcome of an educational investment is only part of the change process. The impact of these improved school resource services on the quality of the teaching/learning process is just beginning to be felt and will continue for several decades to come.

References
1. Ralph Munn and Ernest R. Pitt, *Australian Libraries: A Survey of Conditions and Suggestions for their Improvement* (Australian Council for Educational Research, Melbourne, 1935), p. 105.
2. Ernest Roe, An Examination of the Influence of Libraries on the Education of Secondary School Children in South Australia (unpublished Ph.D. thesis, University of Adelaide, 1963).
3. Ernest Roe, *Teachers, Librarians and Children: A Study of Libraries in Education* (2nd edn, Cheshire, Melbourne, 1972).
4. Sara Innis Fenwick, *School and Children's Libraries in Australia: A Report to the Children's Libraries Section of the Library Association of Australia* (Cheshire, Melbourne, for the LAA, 1966).
5. *Standards and Objectives for School Libraries* (Cheshire, Melbourne, for the LAA, 1966).
6. Donald Smart, Federal Aid to Australian Schools: Origins and Aspects of the Implementation of the Commonwealth Science Laboratories and Libraries Scheme (unpublished Ph.D. thesis, Australian National University, Canberra, 1975).
7. Library Association of Australia, Committee on Federal Aid to School Libraries, submission to the Prime Minister (LAA, Sydney, 1967).

8. Margaret Trask, *School Libraries: A Report to the Nation* (Cheshire, Melbourne, for the Australian Library Promotion Council, 1968).
9. Commonwealth Secondary Schools Libraries Committee, *Standards for Secondary School Libraries* (Australian Government Publishing Service (AGPS), Canberra, 1971).
10. UNESCO, *The Role of Libraries in Secondary Education*, Australian UNESCO seminar held at the University of New South Wales, August 1970 (AGPS, Canberra, 1971).
11. Commonwealth Secondary School Libraries Research Project (CSSLRP), *Secondary School Libraries in Australia: A Report on the Evaluation of the Commonwealth Secondary Schools Libraries Program* (Department of Education, University of Queensland, Brisbane, 1972), p. 215.
12. David Cohen, *Primary School Libraries: A Report to the Nation* (Australian Library Promotion Council, Melbourne, 1972).
13. Schools Commission, Primary Schools' Libraries Committee, *Guidelines for Library Services in Primary Schools* (Schools Commission, Canberra, 1974, mimeo).
14. Neville Johnson, *Needs, Incentive and Initiative: A Report on an Evaluation of Substantial Book Grants to Non-government Primary Schools* (Department of School Librarianship, Kelvin Grove College of Advanced Education, Brisbane, 1978), pp. 18–19.
15. John McArthur, *Implementation of an Innovation: The Pilot Library Scheme in Non-government Primary Schools* (Department of School Librarianship, Kelvin Grove CAE, Brisbane, 1977).
16. Lawrence H. McGrath, *Central Library Services of the Education Departments of the Australian States* (Libraries Board of South Australia, Adelaide, 1965), p. 71.
17. CSSLRP, *Secondary School Libraries in Australia*, p. 215.
18. Roy Lundin, 'Why bumble bees cannot fly: an examination of the workload of teacher-librarians', in *Education for School Librarianship: Proceedings, Findings and Recommendations of a Workshop held in Canberra, 1–4 August 1972*, Australian Department of Education (AGPS, Canberra, 1973), p. 28.
19. Phillip Hughes, 'Courses for school librarianship', in *Education for School Librarianship*, pp. 36–9.
20. Schools Commission, Interim Committee (P. H. Karmel, Chairman), *Schools in Australia* (AGPS, Canberra, 1973), p. 85.
21. Roy Lundin and John McArthur, *Impact and Inadequacy: A Report of an Evaluation of Government Post-primary School Libraries in Victoria* (School Libraries Research Project, Faculty of Education, Monash University, Clayton, Vic., 1975), p. 22.
22. Schools Commission, *Report for 1976* (AGPS, Canberra, 1975).
23. Schools Commission, *Report: Rolling Triennium 1977–79* (AGPS, Canberra, 1976).
24. Neil Radford, 'Education for librarianship and the manpower problem', *Australian Library Journal* 27, 13 (1978), 197–202.
25. Schools Commission, *Books and Beyond: Guidelines for Library Resource Facilities and Services* (2nd edn, AGPS, Canberra, 1979), p. 9.
26. For example, *A National Seminar Workshop for the Education of Resource Support Staff*, papers, proceedings and recommendations of a seminar-workshop held at Shearwater, Tasmania, 8–13 June 1975 (draft only).
27. Trask, *School Libraries: A Report to the Nation*, p. 8.
28. Douglas W. Down and Wesley A. Young, *Cataloguing for Schools: The Feasibility of Catalogue Card Services for All Schools in Australia*, a report to the Australian Schools Commission (Melbourne State College, Carlton, Vic., 1975, photocopy); *Australian Schools Cataloguing Service*, a report to the Australian Schools Commission (Melbourne State College, Carlton, Vic., 1977).
29. Lundin and McArthur, *Impact and Inadequacy*, p. 12.

30. John Ward, 'Current trends in school libraries', *Australian School Librarian* 13, 1 (1976), 7.
31. *Standards and Objectives for School Libraries* (Cheshire, Melbourne, for the LAA, 1966).
32. Lundin and McArthur, *Impact and Inadequacy*, p. 11.
33. *Education for School Librarianship: Proceedings, Findings and Recommendations of a Workshop held in Canberra, 1–4 August 1972*, Australian Department of Education (AGPS, Canberra, 1973), p. 43.
34. Roy Lundin, *On Establishing Standards: Theory and Research* (Commonwealth Secondary School Libraries Research Project, Paper no. 2) (Department of Education, University of Queensland, Brisbane, 1973), p. 28.
35. Graham P. Corr, 'Some patterns of education for school librarianship', in L. H. McGrath (ed.) with M. J. Walker, *Planning and Development of School Library Services: Proceedings of the UNESCO Regional Seminar on School Libraries*, held in Perth, 12–17 August 1976 (Churchlands College, Perth, for the Australian National Commission for UNESCO, 1976), pp. 169–76.
36. Peter J. Pegg (ed.), *Be Prepared for Networks*, proceedings of the seminar held at Kelvin Grove CAE, Brisbane, 6–8 May 1975 (School Library Association of Queensland, Brisbane Branch, 1976).
37. CSSLRP, *Secondary School Libraries in Australia*, p. 65.
38. McArthur, *Implementation of an Innovation*, pp. 4–5.
39. *Journal of the School Library Association of Queensland* 8, 2 (1975), 5.
40. R. C. King, 'Open education and other educational innovations: implications for libraries', in *Proceedings of the 18th Biennial Conference of the Library Association of Australia* (LAA, Melbourne, 1976), p. 196.

CHAPTER 2

School Libraries in New Zealand: The Long Haul

Jan MacLean

When describing the development of school libraries in New Zealand in what is to be largely an Australian publication, I am conscious of having something of an inferiority complex. In comparison with the notable achievements over the past two decades in Australia, New Zealand has only partial success to offer. Despite much activity during the 1970s, school libraries in New Zealand have yet to reach what could be considered to be a recognised minimum standard in staffing, resources, facilities or buildings. Nor, as it will be seen, are they universally recognised as being a vital and integral necessity in the development of education. While much has been slowly, and at times painfully, achieved much more needs to be done if New Zealand school libraries are to play an important role in the future.

It is not difficult to describe school libraries before 1945 in New Zealand:

> School libraries . . . scarcely exist in New Zealand. With one or two exceptions, library facilities in both secondary and technical schools are extremely meagre, and in no case do they reach an approved standard of library service . . . Most elementary schools have collections of books which only by courtesy can be called libraries, the stocks having been badly selected, poorly housed and in bad physical condition . . . Under the existing conditions the schools are practically without funds for library purposes, money having to be taken from the small grant for incidental expenses which the Department of Education allows boards for this. The consequence is that the schools have to depend almost entirely on their own efforts to provide library facilities.

Such were the grim conclusions of Ralph Munn and John Barr in their report, *New Zealand Libraries*, published in 1934. Their recommendation on the subject was brief and deceptively simple:

Efforts should be made to improve the libraries of primary, secondary and technical schools and to establish small permanent collections of reference books. Improved financial provision should be made by the Education Department with this object in view, by increasing the grants or subsidies for the purchase of books and better equipment. More co-operation between library and school authorities is advised.

Before discussing the developments since the 1930s, however, it would be as well to describe the school system in New Zealand and outline the present conditions in which school libraries exist. New Zealand has a national educational scheme, and although control of the schools is based on ten regional boards for primary schools and local community boards for individual secondary schools, there is strong direction and control from the central state organisation, the Department of Education in Wellington. Finance is provided from national taxation, and educational policy planning and curricula are decided on a national basis. This ensures a great degree of uniformity throughout the country and although private schools operate more independently, they too tend to follow the state pattern. Primary schools in New Zealand take children from 5 to 12 years of age, a special category being intermediate schools that take some of the school population of the ages of 11 and 12, and secondary schools take pupils from 12 to 18 years of age. Within this framework, then, school libraries exist on a national basis and, with a few notable exceptions, are governed by the sketchy and fragmented policy of the Department of Education. A brief outline of it is important in understanding the state of school libraries in New Zealand and the events that have led to the present situation.

All schools, secondary, intermediate and primary, have some kind of library room or space. This is now provided for in the building codes for new schools, though this provision has only been in force for primary schools during the past few years. Secondary schools, on the whole, have adequately housed libraries, the standard design being a free-standing rectangular building of one level with space for a mezzanine floor. Primary schools have much less adequate library space. New schools have a library multi-purpose room, but in the older schools library space may range from a 'bookstore' of 3 x 3 m to converted classrooms or spare space anywhere in the school. The size of all school libraries is regulated by the size of the school enrolment.

All new primary and intermediate schools receive a setting-up grant of up to $2100, and secondary schools a library setting-up grant of up to $13 000 spread over three years. In addition, library furniture, such as shelving and catalogue cabinets, is supplied. Education boards receive library grants of up to $2.20 per pupil which they then pass on to their intermediate and primary schools. There is no fixed grant for secondary school libraries, and the average amount per pupil allotted from the general-purpose grant is approximately $2.00. Most schools raise money locally for their libraries, and this usually adds 50 per cent or so to the amount received from the Department of Education.

As regards the provision of school library staffing, in primary schools there are no positions or time allowances for teacher librarians. Secondary schools receive an allowance of two weekly teaching half-days to give the teacher librarian time to manage the library. There are no full-time positions for school librarians. Most primary schools are entitled to ancillary staff for non-professional work, the principal deciding how much, if any, of this ancillary staff time is used in the school library. Secondary schools are entitled to library assistants, in addition to their other ancillary staff, and have an allowance of hours per annum according to the size of the school roll.

Such then is the present condition of school libraries in New Zealand. From 1934 and the gloomy statements of the Munn-Barr Report, to today, it has been a struggle to develop school libraries.

The first significant step, and one that was to have far-reaching results, was the establishment in 1942 of the School Library Service. This was a national service, attached then to the Country Library Service and remaining today as part of the National Library of New Zealand. Like the Country Library Service, which had been established to provide government aid in the form of stock and support services to the neglected smaller public libraries, the School Library Service was to provide recreational reading to country children by placing long-term loans of high-quality children's books into schools. Up to this time, the major public libraries of Wellington, Auckland and Dunedin had provided classroom libraries for many of the city schools, but clearly no scheme of support for school libraries could continue on this small foundation. The initial success of the School Library Service ensured its rapid expansion and by the early 1950s the service had broadened to cover book supply to all primary schools and a similar service to secondary schools. The basic plan behind the service was to send out long-term loans of mixed collections of books for recreational reading for the whole school, except the primer classes, the size of the loan collection being dependent on the number of pupils. It was clearly established at an early stage that these books, selected and bought by the School Library Service, were to be the best available, so that not only would an economical use of funds be made, but also standards of quality, long missing in school libraries, would be established as well. This basic service was supported by a request service of individual titles and special collections so that, in theory at least, any school pupil or teacher in the country could obtain the book they wanted. In addition to book distribution on a national scale, the Service developed an advisory group of librarians who, at the request of a school, would set up or reorganise a school library and offer expert advice for planned selection and systems of service. This advisory role of the Service produced publications such as manuals on school libraries, recommended collection lists and bibliographies, and a periodical reviewing and recommending current books for young people which was distributed free to all schools, as a guide for the schools' own purchasing. All these services were offered by the twelve district centres, established throughout the country, which corresponded geographically to the education board districts.

Over the years, as the School Library Service has expanded (it now has a collection of approximately three million books), and as more schools developed libraries worth the name, the emphasis of service has changed and in the past few years the long-term exchange loans of books have given way to permanent or repository loans to almost half the individual schools. At the same time, increased emphasis is placed on the information and request services, which now issue approximately one and a half million volumes a year, and on the work of the advisory officers with the schools.

As it will be realised, the School Library Service, since its inception, has played a major role in strengthening, advising and raising standards, and without it school libraries, particularly those in small schools and those outside the main centres, would be more inadequate than they are. However, it was established, and has remained, as a national support service on the fringe, rather than in the centre, of government education planning. Although school library developments must be considered against the background of the School Library Service, it has not and cannot supersede the need for improvement in school libraries themselves.

After the early success of the School Library Service, there was slow but steady improvement in the conditions of school libraries during the 1950s. Primary school libraries remained at the mercy of individual teacher and parent support, the Education Department subsidising any money raised by local effort; and schools acquired their library through converting unused classrooms, bicycle sheds or cloakrooms. There was no provision for a library room in the building code for primary schools, with the exception of intermediate schools; and finance for stock remained meagre, ranging from the equivalent of a few cents to approximately one dollar per pupil.

Secondary schools, on the other hand, saw some significant improvements. Provision for stock and buildings and equipment remained low, but the need for staffing the school library was recognised by the Department of Education. The position of 'Teacher librarian' was created, and as a consideration of the amount of time involved in running the school library, the teacher so designated was freed from classroom teaching commitment for a number of hours each week. The time allocated was geared to the size of the school roll and ranged from as little as one hour to approximately ten hours per week. In return for this time allowance, teacher librarians were expected to play the professional role of school librarians, were responsible for the administering and professional management of school libraries, and were to do so with no opportunity of training in librarianship. It is a measure of the devotion and hard work of so many teacher librarians since then that much of the improvement of secondary school libraries is due to them. This move on the part of the Department was an advance at the time, but as it will be seen, its establishment has proved to be one of the major obstacles in achieving recommended staffing standards in school libraries. By providing a little, the Department has been able to avoid, for the past twenty years, providing any more.

The 1960s saw further efforts to ensure that school library standards improved. The New Zealand Library Association (NZLA), a critic of the situation since the 1930s, had maintained its recommendations to government for significant development and in the early 1960s renewed its submissions on the subject. In 1962, it made formal submissions to the Commission on New Zealand Education, basing its case on the current state of school libraries and on a report, commissioned by the NZLA from Dr A. D. Osborn, entitled *New Zealand Library Resources*. In the Osborn Report of 1960, school libraries were weighed and, as in the Munn-Barr Report, found wanting. The forceful comments listed the familiar catalogue of inadequate buildings, a dearth of funding for stock, and no real staffing. The staffing situation had in fact worsened since 1959 as the Education Department, concerned at teacher shortages, had revoked the allowance of 'free' hours for teacher librarians and ordered their resumption of full classroom teaching duties. To offset this, and to provide some minimum assistance in the running of school libraries, a scheme of ancillary staffing had been introduced. This meant that secondary schools could employ a school library assistant for a number of hours per week, the hours being dependent on the size of the school roll. Most schools availed themselves of this help, and what was said then to be an 'interim' solution to staffing needs has remained as standard practice in New Zealand. Almost without exception, secondary school libraries and some primary ones are staffed by library assistants who, while often devoted to their work, are usually untrained and very poorly paid. The slow resumption of an allowance of library hours for teacher librarians through the 1970s has not significantly improved the situation.

The NZLA sought to capitalise on the findings of the Osborn Report and particularly on its recommendations, which were that 'school libraries must be fully organised, staffed and developed. The NZLA will have to grapple with the problem of training school librarians in considerable numbers through either the Library School or teacher-training institutions. Bookstocks should be built up with insight and design to serve educational, vocational and general cultural processes.' The stress was now placed on the need for trained staff in school libraries and through the decade intermittent discussions were held with the Education Department, government and the teaching organisations. No real progress eventuated, however, beyond proposals for a course in school librarianship, which was presented as a training scheme to Cabinet by the Department several times and each time deferred because of cost. In 1969 the NZLA again made submissions to the Minister of Education, pointing out that new curriculum developments, increased emphasis on individual research, and new teaching approaches made the need for full-time professional school librarians imperative. In this they were supported by the two teaching associations in New Zealand, particularly the Post-Primary Teachers' Association which had recommended 'that provision should be made in post-primary staffing for the appointment of professional librarians on a full-time basis, salaries and conditions to be equivalent to those of teachers'.

No immediate action followed these submissions and the NZLA, now at the beginning of the 1970s, became even more concerned over the poor state of school libraries. It was felt that the lack of commitment, and indeed established policy, on the part of the Department would mean that school library development, if left entirely to the Department, would remain slow and uneven, widening still further the gap between the advances overseas and the situation in New Zealand.

During this period the new Minister of Education launched a national Education Development Conference (EDC), intended as a major reappraisal of New Zealand's educational system. Amongst the specialist committees set up by the Working Party of Improving Learning and Teaching of the EDC was one on libraries. This study group was composed of librarians, teachers and departmental representatives and in 1973 presented to the Working Party a report entitled *Libraries in Education*, later published in 1974. This report was the first department-backed review of educational libraries, and it was hardly surprising that the main emphasis of the report was placed on the urgent needs of school libraries. The recommendations were clear in terms of the building and financial provisions considered desirable, and those on staffing were for the appointment of teacher librarians to primary schools with libraries, and of professional librarians on a full-time basis in secondary schools. Considerable enthusiasm was expressed for the report, but in the final deliberations of the Working Party on Improving Learning and Teaching, little space was afforded the report's major recommendations and the much hoped-for development appeared to be bogged down in general departmental considerations.

It thus became increasingly clear that the NZLA needed to act decisively and, as a non-governmental and professionally involved organisation, act as a spur to the state and provide a blue-print for the development that was sorely needed. This awareness crystallised into a decision to undertake a national survey of library services to children and young people, and to use this survey as an informational base for a full report by a visiting consultant. It was hoped that this would, for the first time, provide accurate data, particularly on school libraries, and an objective assessment of existing resources and facilities. Equally importantly, it would recommend future lines of development; provide the much-needed stimulation to librarians, teachers and administrators; and through the interest aroused by the visit of a notable overseas librarian, focus attention on the problem and highlight the inadequacies of school libraries.

Such an undertaking was a formidable task and it is greatly to the Association's credit, and that of its members who were directly involved, that it was successfully accomplished. The Association was fortunate in securing the co-operation and expertise of the New Zealand Council for Educational Research, considerable financial assistance from the McKenzie Education Foundation and, above all, as the visiting consultant Professor Sara Fenwick, of the Graduate Library School,

University of Chicago, who was already well-versed in the inadequacies of Australian library services to children. After much preparatory work, the survey began in 1974. Professor Fenwick spent an intensive two months visiting libraries of all kinds throughout the country and speaking formally and informally with large numbers of librarians, teachers and Education Department officers; and in 1975 her report was published. It was followed in 1977 by the companion report of the full statistical survey.

Although there is insufficient space here to discuss the Fenwick Report as fully as it deserves, major aspects must be noted because of their impact and bearing on the progress of the past few years. The report was, and remains, the most authoritative and well-documented assessment of New Zealand's library services to children. Its coverage included the public library service, the School Library Service and its effect on the national scene, what was and should be available as professional preparation of librarians working with children, and an overview of international trends in library development. The main thrust of the report, however, lay in the emphasis placed on primary and secondary school libraries and in the detailed recommendations. Though moderately worded, the report made damning statements on the state of school library facilities and resources, and the attitudes of many of those involved. It observed that in primary schools 'the library was most frequently regarded by the school staff as sometimes a luxury, sometimes a nuisance, but seldom as an essential learning resource for development of discovery skills, individualisation of teaching, improvement of curriculum, extension of textbook experiences, and sharing of humanistic pleasures of reading, viewing and listening by teachers and students.' It noted that 'the range and quality of the physical provision for libraries included, at the best, a few planned and furnished rooms of adequate size', and that 'these were not more than 10 per cent of the primary schools visited by the survey team'.

Describing the library resources held in primary schools, the report remarked on the cases of apparently adequate bookstock figures but added 'these figures should not be a cause for complacency . . . Ten books per child, or twenty books, are of marginal value in a school library if a high percentage of those books are out-dated in information or concepts, if they are mediocre sets of cheap fiction or shallow, over-generalised non-fiction.' The financial provision for resources was recognised as being too low, but 'the most serious aspect of the financial problem, however, is the mismanagement of the available funds. Not intentionally, of course, but through inattention and lack of knowledge, library grants for books are spent without the critical appraisal of professional experts or critical reviews, without considering the balance of present collections, and without comparing titles with other materials of like subject or format.'

In considering secondary school libraries, the report noted that facilities and stock were substantially better than those for primary school children, but while 'it is recognised that these new libraries represent a substantial financial investment on the part of the Department of Education . . . it is the unrealised potential of the improved facilities that underscores the lack of appropriate stock and the absence of trained, full-time staff as especially critical.' Discussing the resources available in secondary school libraries, the general paucity of both print and non-print material was emphasised: 'a few schools visited by the survey team had good to excellent school library collections' but 'in fiction collections, there is frequently a polarisation at both ends of the quality scale . . . [these] are often more representative than the non-fiction where large gaps appear in mathematics, science and the social sciences'. In addition, 'few libraries included audio-visual resources or facilities for using them in the library'. The most serious defect of all school libraries, however, was considered by Professor Fenwick to be the absence of professional full-time school librarians. She reported that 'of the 29 [primary] schools visited eight had no teacher librarian. Of the 21 who had a designated teacher librarian all but two were classroom teachers and 18 had no time scheduled during the week for the library. One had half an hour a day, at lunch time, one had one and a half hours during the week, one had two hours and two had three hours, statistics that should be of major concern'. The secondary schools presented a similar, but slightly improved, picture: '. . . of the 57 teacher librarians in the schools [responding to the survey] only 2 had training in librarianship leading to a qualification. Twenty-two of these librarians indicated they were not interested in qualifying as school librarians, although 31 indicated that they would be interested. Only 3 per cent of the responding teacher librarians have as much as 14 hours [per week] timetabled for library work, 29 per cent have under one hour, and this was frequently described as "none".'

As Professor Fenwick observed, 'obviously where there is no full-time or part-time professional staff the library cannot become the media centre that present-day teaching assumes and modern technology makes possible. This evolution of book-centred library to multi-media centre is happening in the majority of modern schools in all countries where education is advancing.'

It was hardly surprising, then, that the recommendations of the report focused on the appointment of full-time professionally trained [school] librarians in all secondary schools, in all intermediate schools and, within six years, to all primary schools with enrolments of 300 or more, as its first priority. While a phased-in program for staffing was envisaged, it was firmly stated that this should not be the final goal, but should be the basic platform for a satisfactory school library program, such as that outlined in the equally firm recommendations for increased and improved resources and facilities. Furthermore, the recommendations stressed that the development of programs for the professional preparation of school librarians was an immediate necessity if any plans for improvement of stock and services were to be implemented, and gave priority to the recommendations for the setting up of a one-year course in school librarianship, open both to qualified, experienced teachers and to librarians with suitable qualifications.

The impact of the Fenwick Report was considerable. It stated unequivocally that New Zealand school libraries were, in the main, highly inadequate and it drew together and emphasised all the needs described in past comments and reports that had been ignored. Its importance also lay in the fact that the recommendations, while moderate in the face of the situation, went beyond anything previously published on New Zealand school libraries. Most significantly of all, it made clear that the greatest gap was lack of school librarians, and it took the authoritative stand that school librarians must be full-time professionals with, what was in effect, dual qualifications, in both teaching and specialised librarianship. This was the very point on which librarians and teachers had traditionally failed to agree, and that disagreement had separated and negated much of the previous activity of both professions aimed at improving school libraries. After publication of the Fenwick Report in 1975 and the discussions that followed, the disagreement was finally laid to rest.

During Professor Fenwick's tour of New Zealand, the librarians involved had been planning the course of action that would follow the report's publication. They recognized that the NZLA was a small group in the educational world and that one of the major problems in the past had been the lack of discussion and agreement and concerted effort between the professions and organisations most concerned with school libraries. It was clear that little short of a revolution in thinking and consequent pressure from large numbers of involved people would force the

Department of Education into decisive action. The NZLA therefore invited the New Zealand Educational Institute (NZEI) (which represents primary teachers), and the Post-Primary Teachers Association (NZPPTA) to join them in forming a tripartite committee. This joint committee, which is still in existence, was to orchestrate the publicity following the Fenwick Report, and to formulate a common policy on school libraries that the three associations would support and give priority to, and present to government on a united front. To reach this point, however, was not particularly easy.

During the first public discussion on the Fenwick Report and the demands to government that immediate improvements be forthcoming, the then Minister of Education, the Hon. P. Amos, made it clear that as the report had been commissioned by the NZLA and not by the Education Department, the NZLA must consider the report first and then inform the Minister of the extent to which it would adopt the report's recommendations as policy. And in the first informal meeting between the Joint Committee and the Director-General of Education, Mr W. Renwick, the same view was expressed. The Department of Education, perhaps surprised and certainly a little dismayed at the strong criticisms of the report and the amount of public support received, had adopted a stance of defensive pique. The report was declared 'unofficial' in Departmental eyes, on the grounds they had had no hand in it. But at the same time the Minister and Departmental officials firmly declared that they saw the development of school libraries as a matter of high priority. In order to combat this, the NZLA formally adopted the recommendations of the Fenwick Report as official Association policy in 1976 and accorded them top priority. It remained for the NZPPTA and NZEI to follow suit, and this they did in the same year. However, there were still areas where agreement between the three organisations was not complete, and it must be remembered that while many primary and secondary teachers wholeheartedly endorsed the Fenwick Report the policies of their associations lagged somewhat, particularly on the staffing question. Furthermore, when the NZPPTA and NZEI did adopt policies in keeping with the Fenwick Report, they were divided over the priority their demands for school libraries and improved school libraries should have; and while attaching considerable importance to their policies, neither gave this the highest possible priority. Nevertheless, sufficient pressure had been built up through discussions, regional seminars and the publicly expressed views of many groups and individuals, for the Education Department to adopt a more positive attitude. When further approaches on the school library issue were made by the two teachers' associations, the Minister of Education, the Hon. L. W. Gandar, indicated that the Department was keen to investigate the problems and agreed to the setting up of a Working Party on School Libraries. As the report of the Working Party wryly noted at a later date, this would be the third major report on the needs of school libraries in as many years. Considerable disappointment and a certain resignation was felt by those involved in the previous work, but it was clearly recognised that if the only way government would come to the party was through setting up its own investigative group, then this chance must be seized.

Early in 1977, representatives were called for, from NZPPTA, the NZEI, the NZLA, the Teachers' College Association and the School Library Service, and, together with officers of the Department, the Working Party of ten was formed. Its terms of reference were astonishingly wide and are worth noting here. They were:

1. to review existing policies for the accommodation, equipment, setting up, staffing and funding of libraries and library rooms in primary, intermediate, area and secondary schools;
2. to review the recommendations of the Lawrence Working Party and the final report of the Educational Development Conference, and to take note of the recommendations of the Fenwick Report, commissioned by the New Zealand Library Association;
3. to consider building codes, standards of equipment, levels of funding and staffing (including technician and ancillary staffing) that could be recommended to the Minister for his consideration; and in doing so, to have regard to:
   changing conceptions of the role of school libraries in relation to audio-visual and other non-book materials, and to supporting services, such as the School Library Service, and the National Film Library;
   possibilities of developing school libraries for community use;
   the priority to be given to the provision of suitable trained librarians or teacher librarians.

After a rather slow start, the Working Party completed its report and presented it to the Minister of Education in June 1978. The Minister agreed to publication and it became available late in 1978. It was distributed widely, and all schools, interested organisations, members of parliament and the media received copies, just as they had with the Fenwick report and *Libraries in Education*.

The Foley Report, as the report of the Working Party on School Libraries is known, is, in many ways, the most comprehensive. It states what it considers should be the objectives of the school library in New Zealand and then in five short chapters outlines concisely its case and subsequent recommendations on staffing, buildings, resources, support services (which include School Publications, the Visual Production Unit, the National Film Library as part of the Education Department, and the School Library Service as part of the National Library) and the community use of school libraries. In a series of appendices to the report there are detailed proposals for staffing and for the establishment of courses in school librarianship. One appendix lists the submissions received by the working party from individuals, institutions and organisations and gives a good picture of how widespread was the concern and interest in the report's conclusions.

It seems almost unnecessary at this stage to comment on where the Foley Report's emphasis lay. Predictably, the first and largest number of recommendations made clear the report's unequivocal stand on the great need, that of full-time school librarians in all but the smallest schools. It was a reaffirmation of the Fenwick Report, which it followed closely on many points, and it left no doubt in the mind of anyone reading it of exactly how the development of school libraries was to be achieved. Furthermore, it stated in considerable detail the total number of school librarians needed and proposed an immediate implementation of a one-year course in school librarianship for trained teachers. The emphasis on who was to be trained, and how and where, was to a certain extent made easier by the fact that a major change in library education in New Zealand had been announced in early 1978. One of the problems that had faced both the EDC libraries' study group and Professor Fenwick was where courses in school librarianship could be established. Education for librarianship in New Zealand was available from only one institution, the New Zealand Library School, a division of the National Library. Teacher education was available only from the teachers' colleges and was split into different courses for primary and secondary teacher training. There was no one institution, as a consequence, that appeared to offer a suitable basis for courses involving both professions. However, since discussions in 1975, a planned change for library education recommended that the post-graduate course of the New Zealand Library School be the responsibility of a new Department of Librarianship at Victoria University of Wellington and that the intermediate Certificate in Librarianship be offered by a new School of Library Studies at

Wellington Teachers' College. The discussions of 1975 had, significantly, planned the consequent establishment of a school librarianship course at Wellington Teachers' College, and in conjunction with the change in library education. This was to take effect in 1980, and with the publication of the Foley Report, all seemed set for the long-awaited government decision to establish full-time positions for school librarians and develop courses through which the necessary qualifications could be gained. During 1979 the NZPPTA, the NZEI and the NZLA had individual meetings with the new Minister of Education, Mr M. L. Wellington. Though assuring them of the Government's commitment to the recommendations of the Foley Report, the Minister would give no date for their implementation. Fiscal reasons, it was explained, prevented a definite beginning. So far, the associations' answer has been to work towards increasing public pressure for action on what is now a clear issue.

In summing up the past forty or so years in the struggle to achieve satisfactory school library provision and development in New Zealand, it is very easy to take a despondent view. It is true that the endeavours by so many in the past decade have not brought about the desired results, but it is equally true that a great change has been made in the thinking of the way in which school libraries should develop. Six years ago there was no departmental policy, and very little agreement on how development should proceed. School libraries were treated, far more then than now, as unnecessary, time-consuming and expensive extras with no serious relevance to education. But if the thinking has changed, the situation, though constantly improving in minor ways, has not. We still do not have adequate school libraries throughout the country. One can only hope that the 1980s, despite the financial problems and the lack of decision, will see some action on all those reports. It remains, however, a remarkable illustration of the 'mills of God grind slowly . . .'

Bibliography
FENWICK, SARA INNIS. *Library Services for Children in New Zealand Schools and Public Libraries: A Report to the New Zealand Library Association.* (Studies in Education, no. 24) New Zealand Council for Educational Research and New Zealand Library Association, Wellington, 1975.
Libraries in Education: A Report Prepared for the Working Party on Improving Learning and Teaching of the Educational Development Conference. Educational Development Conference, Wellington, 1974.
Library Services for Children in New Zealand Schools and Public Libraries: A Statistical Appendix to the Report by Sara Innis Fenwick. (Studies in Education, no. 24, part 2) New Zealand Council for Educational Research and New Zealand Library Association, Wellington, 1977.

MUNN, RALPH and BARR, JOHN, *New Zealand Libraries: A Survey of Conditions and Suggestions for their Improvement*. Libraries Association of New Zealand, Christchurch, 1934.

NEW ZEALAND. Working Party on School Libraries. *Report of the Working Party on School Libraries* (The Foley Report). Department of Education, Wellington, 1978.

OSBORN, ANDREW D. *New Zealand Library Resources: Report of a Survey made for the New Zealand Library Association* . . . New Zealand Library Association, Wellington, 1960.

CHAPTER 3

The Educational Role
of the School Library

Joan Brewer

In recent years school libraries have assumed a more important role in education and large sums of money have been spent to improve their facilities in many countries of the world. In Australia, for example, a federal government program to develop secondary school libraries began in 1969, to be followed in 1974 by assistance to libraries in primary schools. This development was influenced strongly by what had happened in American school libraries.

Why has there been such an emphasis on the important role of the library in the educational program of the school? Certainly the present situation is in direct contrast to the situation that pertained thirty years ago when libraries in most schools consisted of either inadequate classroom collections, changing little from year to year or, at best, a book collection in a room remote from the teaching areas. Students visited the library occasionally for recreational reading, or classes were taken there for fairly formal, rigidly timetabled library lessons. Even in the best of schools, the library was usually considered to be a desirable extra rather than an essential element in the serious business of teaching and learning.

But now school libraries are referred to as instructional materials centres or media centres or resource centres. Many people still prefer the word 'libraries' but the use of the words 'instructional', 'media' and 'centre' is, as we shall see, indicative of a great change in attitude. Let us look at libraries in schools, noting that they have changed, and let us ask ourselves why the changes have taken place.

Reasons for the changes in school libraries

Emphasis on the learner
Emphasis is now very much on learning rather than on teaching, on students discovering ideas or information for themselves. They are encouraged to be curious rather than to be passive recipients of the teacher's words: this change in emphasis from teacher to learner has been forced on teachers in any case, because of the knowledge explosion. There is a diagram in Davies' book that illustrates graphically the alarming rate at which knowledge has been increasing, so that now it doubles every eight to ten years.[1] Obviously a fixed body of knowledge cannot be taught. Rather, students have to be educated in such a way that they are able to continue discovering and learning for themselves. They also have to be encouraged to be flexible, to have the confidence to tackle new tasks. This is very pertinent in the present situation when job obsolescence is one of the problems facing our technological society. It has been suggested that present-day school leavers will have to change their employment several times in their working lives. Thus they must be equipped so that they can learn new tasks easily. And it is not only change but the accelerated pace of change that is one of the challenging and frightening features of our era.

We have a shift from the teacher to the student, from the almost exclusive use of chalk and talk to the use of many different kinds of resources, and these resources are found in the school library. The emphasis is on problem–solving rather than on rote learning, as in the teaching of mathematics. In art and language there is free expression and encouragement of creativity rather than of copying. An interesting article by Taylor which appeared some years ago was concerned with the nature of creative enquiry and the role of the school library in its development.[2]

Individual differences
For many years educators have talked about individual differences. Now schools are doing more to meet the needs of individual students, with individual progression in subject areas and with the recognition that each student learns in his or her own way. Some learn easily by reading, some by listening, some by talking, some by doing something with their hands, some by looking, and often by a combination of two or more of these. We must remember that it often depends on what the student is trying to learn and on the student's background and skills as to which of the above methods of learning will be used. The facilities and resources available in the school library assist in individualised instruction.

Technological change

Another important factor in the changes in schools and particularly in libraries is the technological revolution. Now we have film and tape to give us audio and visual materials or a combination of the two. These materials are important as a means of learning, both inside and outside the school. Can today's child imagine a world without television? There have been numerous studies made to assess the amount of time that children spend in front of a television set. Often it is greater than the numbers of hours spent in the school.

But we cannot ignore these materials and we must realise that new forms of media are being developed all the time. They are becoming easier to use, cheaper and available to more people. Consider, for example, the difference between the cassette tape recorder and the reel-to-reel machine. Some teachers are still reluctant to use these media. Students are not; many of them have tape recorders and sophisticated camera equipment and movie projectors at home. The format of the medium can be matched to the needs of an individual and can be an important factor in learning. An article by Langrehr discussed research in the United States, in which attempts have been made to match curriculum materials to learners.[3]

Changes in curriculum

There have also been important changes in curriculum content and design. Rigid divisions between subjects have been disregarded; teachers have been encouraged to design courses to suit the students in their own school, using a variety of materials and, increasingly, making their own materials or adapting commercially prepared materials. In this situation we can see the changing role of the school librarian who works with teachers to prepare suitable materials.

Changes in methods of instruction

There have been changes in methods of instruction too. There is still some large-group instruction, but there is also emphasis on small groups working together, as well as on individuals working alone at their own pace. All three methods will be used by most teachers at various times. Again there are implications for the library which must provide facilities in terms of space, materials and staffing, for individuals, for small groups, for large groups and for all these combinations to be accommodated at the one time.

Education for leisure

In most countries we accept the fact that education, in particular secondary education, should be available for all, not just for a small elite. This affects courses and methods and the choice of materials to be used. Students stay longer at school. In some places at eighteen they are legally adults, with the right to vote. This affects the library and the choice of materials. There is talk about educating people to use their leisure time because it seems likely that there will be more free time available to individuals in the future in the western world. Yet again this affects the library which must provide a wide variety of recreational materials, from fiction to hobbies, and provide them in different formats. The library staff must be concerned about reading and listening and viewing for pleasure.

Need for information

The emphasis is increasingly being placed on the need for information. The ordinary citizen needs a wide variety of information, such as how to contact the various government agencies, how to improve skills, how to provide finance for a home, how to be a responsible voter, how to cope with the mass media and to be more selective and critical— the list could be a long one. School librarians have to provide students with the opportunities to learn skills that will enable them to find the sources of the information they need.

The library as an instructional materials centre

The library is central

The use of the word 'centre' is significant because it implies that the library is central to the school's educational program. Ideally it is situated in a central position so that it is more readily accessible. This question of accessibility is something that librarians must be very aware of, because it involves much more than having a central location. It includes hours of opening, loan rules, provision of bulk loans to teaching areas, facilities for teachers and, above all, the librarian's attitude to the users. The library should be central in the school's educational planning. Here it is important to remember that a library is more than a building. It must involve an area or space but more than that it should include materials, staff and services to users. All these parts are necessary if there is to be an effective school library. For example, some schools have provided magnificent buildings with all the designated areas but have not provided enough materials. Others have acquired the building and the materials but have not been prepared to provide adequate staffing, and this of course is essential if the facilities and materials are to be fully used.

Variety of materials
The modern school library contains all kinds of material that aid instruction. Ellsworth refers to these as 'carriers of knowledge'.[4] There is now an acknowledgement that no one type of material is necessarily superior. The needs of the student at a particular time may best be served by a model or by a recording or by a book or by a map or by a periodical. It is the content and the presentation that is important. Consequently there is a need not only for a wide variety of materials but also for instruction in how to use the various forms of media. This must involve both classroom teachers and librarians.

The librarian a member of the teaching team
The centre can be viewed as a laboratory where individuals or small groups or large groups are discovering answers to problems. In this context the librarian is one of a teaching team, involved in what is to be studied and in the method of approach being used by the grade or subject teacher. Such school libraries are used well by students when teachers are closely involved in planning the library program with the librarian. One of the greatest inhibitors of good library usage is lack of knowledge on the part of teachers of how best to use libraries.

Differences in the new school library
There are four obvious differences between the old traditional library and this new library resources centre.
Design   The first change is in the design of the building. The school library is no longer one room, with shelving along the walls and large tables set out in neat rows with several chairs at each table. Instead there are several clearly defined areas designed to cater for different activities. There are individual study carrels, some wired for the use of audio-visual materials. There are group study rooms, both small and large, where students, with or without a teacher, can work as a group. There is usually a relaxed reading area or a story-telling corner, as well as an area for quiet study and research. Of course, there is a librarian's office and a workroom and a storeroom. Increasingly in libraries the divisions between areas are created by furniture and moveable screens so that the arrangement is flexible and can be changed to suit the needs of the school. Occasionally these areas may be provided in different parts of the school

building rather than in one centralised location, if that suits the school's program. There must be centralised organisation and control but not necessarily centralised storage of materials. However, decentralisation requires staff if materials are to be used well.

Materials   A second obvious change which has already been mentioned is in the materials available in school libraries. There is not only a greater number of books and printed materials but a wide range of non-print media and all the hardware that goes with them.

Staffing   A third change is in staffing. This varies from country to country and from region to region within any one country. But whereas in years gone by some hard-working teacher looked after the library in spare teaching periods, it is now generally accepted that it is a full-time position requiring a person with a special education. Some schools have more than one school librarian, depending on the school enrolment. Some may have specialists attached to the library, such as experts in educational technology or subject specialists. In addition there is usually some kind of support staff, doing clerical, typing and technical duties.

Use   The fourth and most important change is in the use that is made of the library. It is now considered in most schools to be an essential element in the learning program. In this context the librarian has a very definite teaching role. In the past, librarians in schools seemed to be primarily concerned with their role as custodians, but today's librarians are more concerned with teaching and learning. This concern has priority over library organisation and over the concentration on technical processes.

The librarian's teaching role

Curriculum
School librarians, often called teacher librarians to emphasise their educational role, work with other teachers in designing situations in which learning takes place. This requires that they are closely involved in the planning of courses, which is particularly relevant in schools that design curricula to suit the needs of their students. Materials must be chosen carefully to meet curricula needs. Librarians must be able to offer advice on materials, to know the strengths and to recognise the limitations of the various media. They must provide facilities and staff assistance, so that teachers and students can make materials or can adapt commercially produced materials to suit the school's particular programs.

If real co-operation is to occur, librarians must spend time at staff and curriculum meetings as well as in working closely with teachers and students in the library. In some schools there is evidence of very close co-operation from planning the curriculum, including course content and methodology to be used, to the implementation of the program, both in teaching areas and in the library, and finally to the evaluation of the success of the program. One secondary school in South Australia, which has consistently attempted to put these ideas into practice, was the subject of an interesting article.[5]

This important role of the librarian in curriculum has been emphasised by librarians, as is illustrated by the titles of at least two conferences held in Australia in recent years: the Australian School Library Association conference in Sydney in 1974 had as its theme the role of the librarian as a curriculum consultant.[6] Four years later, in Melbourne, the International Association of School Librarianship discussed the librarian and school-based curriculum.[7] Yet educational administrators and teachers have not always accepted the fact that librarians have a role in this area, as Broadbent points out in a recently published article based on some research into this question.[8] But if materials are important in learning, then those who select these materials, organise them for easy use, and assist students and teachers to use them effectively, must have a place in curriculum planning, if resources are to be adequate to the task.

Effective school librarians do not wait to be asked and then respond to requests from teachers and from students. They sometimes initiate programs, suggest ideas to teachers, and create further needs.

Study skills

School librarians are not only experts at retrieving information and in showing others how to do the same, but they are also at least partly responsible for helping students to interpret information, as in note-taking or in using bibliographies. Helping the library user to decide which of the materials best suits the task in hand is a major responsibility. This varies from knowing that a ready reference book is what is needed to find out a particular fact, to realising that a visual presentation is required to understand a concept.

This question of the teaching of study and research skills is another important area for close co-operation between teachers and school librarians. It is essential that students become independent learners, but if this is to happen they must learn the techniques of finding information, of selecting what is relevant to their needs, and of recording it in an appropriate form. Librarians in tertiary institutions have been increasingly concerned with user education programs, which suggests that more needs to be done in primary and secondary schools to improve students' skills in this regard. This does not mean a stereotyped library lesson, in which students are instructed on dictionaries, to be followed by a lesson on encyclopaedias and so on ad nauseam. Such lessons, if divorced from the studies taking place in various subject areas, can be a waste of time. Instruction in the techniques of finding information quickly and easily is more likely to be effective if there is a need for a particular skill arising directly from classroom demands or from personal interests. There may be a need for some group instruction, while at other times individual tuition is required. It seems advisable to avoid long instructional sessions in favour of succinct, frequent and informal assistance. School librarians and teachers must co-operate in this important area of learning. Some skills, such as alphabetical order or dictionary use, are more likely to be discussed and practised in the classroom. Others, such as the ability to use a catalogue or to search through indexes and abstracting journals, are probably implemented in the library. The important factor is the co-operative planning between classroom or subject teachers and school librarians. An overall plan needs to be drawn up, decisions should be made as to who teaches the various skills and as to where the instruction should take place. Librarians may go to classrooms, teachers may work with students in the library. The overall objective is that each student should develop into a competent and confident user of library materials.

Various attempts have been made to list the skills that need to be acquired, with some distinction being made between library skills and research skills. In the first grades, emphasis is placed on how to handle a book, and later on the various parts of the book, such as the imprint and the contents and the index. Students are shown how to read for information, how to take notes, how to follow up cross-references and bibliographies, how to interpret maps, charts, graphs and diagrams. Students also need to develop skills in listening and viewing. Various vocabulary skills, especially the special vocabulary associated with a particular subject area, are significant in learning too, as outlined by J. S. Simmons.[9] Lists of skills that should be mastered at various levels have been published in many books. Articles on the teaching of a particular skill appear regularly in the literature. One of the most comprehensive and carefully planned programs was that designed for Montgomery County Public Schools, in the United States.[10] This chart suggested the scope of the instruction and the sequence in which various techniques should be taught. Kits have been produced by educational establishments or by commercial firms. Many librarians have created self-instructional devices, ranging from the use of a tape/slide presentation to the use of booklets or a videotape. Great assistance can be given to users by adequate notices, clear instructions and various types of printed library guides. Displays are another effective means of assisting students and staff to use the library's resources more effectively. Of course, the most significant factor will be the attitude of the librarian and the atmosphere of the library. Library staff should be visible and readily available to offer unobtrusive assistance to readers. Much valuable instruction is given incidentally, as the need arises, to particular individuals. In an address given in England in 1975, Maurice B. Line stated, 'The importance of information handling skills is fundamental. We cannot have a democratic society without wide availability of knowledge, and widespread ability to obtain access to it and handle it critically.'[11]

Reading program

The school librarian obviously has a role to play in the school's reading program. For many children, unfortunately, the school library may be their only contact with literature and with a library. Some will not visit public libraries nor will they have books available to them in their homes. The materials available in the school library and the way in which these materials are introduced to students will be of great significance. This question is being discussed in detail in another chapter, but reading guidance is really everything that brings together children and books. School librarians should encourage students to enjoy reading, to choose it as a pleasurable pastime and to grow and mature in their reading tastes. This guidance takes place both inside and outside the library. The librarian should aim to help the reader but should allow the reader to make the final choice. Enthusiasm for books and reading on the part of the librarian is essential. Allied to this is wise selection of materials that will meet the varied needs of all types of readers, keeping standards of excellence in mind, while recognising the reading abilities and interests of the prospective readers. Consequently a wide diversity of materials on many subjects and at various levels of difficulty is required. It is important to start where the child is and to lead him on gently. The librarian's approach to a reader may make a lasting impression.

Having selected wisely to meet the needs of the readers in that school, the librarian must become acquainted with the collection and be able to speak from personal experience. The other essential element is to study the readers, to talk with them, to talk about them to their parents and teachers, to find out what their current as well as their long-term interests are. The librarian can facilitate reading by making certain that readers have the necessary knowledge and skills and, above all, the confidence to use the library and to use the books. The library itself must be attractive and welcoming and relaxed. Publicity of all kinds, from bibliographies on certain topics to accession lists and handouts of various types is necessary. Exhibitions, displays and posters are very important too, not to mention story-telling and reading aloud. In other words, methods of reading guidance will vary as widely as do libraries, librarians and clients, and the effective school librarian is always looking for ideas in this area.

Evaluation
In recent years, educational institutions at all levels have been subjected to close scrutiny, not only by those responsible for the administration and funding of education but also by the community at large. Increasing costs, inflation, and the general economic problems of some of the developed countries, such as the United States, Great Britain and Australia, have resulted in various attempts to measure the effectiveness of educational programs, particularly in relation to the needs of society. Accountability, measurement and evaluation are frequently the subjects of discussions and conferences. School libraries have inevitably been involved in such deliberations, particularly where special programs of providing extra funds to school libraries have been inititated. Consequently, attempts have been made to measure the success of school library programs. A special research program, funded by the Australian Government, and implemented first at the University of Queensland and later at Monash University, set out to assess the impact of the special federal library program.[12] Sullivan's report on the Knapp School Library Project is another example.[13] An overview of various evaluation instruments and of research in this area appeared in *School Media Quarterly;* the writer pointed out that 'Continued emphasis should be placed on research studies and evaluative techniques that can produce measurable output as expansion of services in the future may well depend on an indication, backed by research findings, that the change will produce a favourable result.'[14] At school level the librarian, as an educator, must be concerned to discover how well the library program serves the total educational program of that school. Evaluation of this kind is a necessary part of planning for the future. Questions will be asked to find out whether the library is improving the students' learning and whether the library is really meeting the needs of the students and of the

teachers and, perhaps, of the wider community which may have access to the school.

Evaluation is time-consuming, it involves careful planning. Decisions have to be made in the beginning as to who the evaluation is intended for and how it is to be used. It is unlikely that the total school library program can be examined in detail, so selection must be made of those aspects which will be subject to close scrutiny. An assessment of materials, considering not only quantities but quality and how effectively they are organised is one aspect that may be measured. Accommodation and facilities, administrative practices and routines, and services to readers may be the subject of investigation.

Staffing needs and staff performance could be considered. Articles by Phillips[15] and Fast[16] may be of use to librarians who are trying to evaluate staff performance. But the most important area, and the most difficult to measure, is the use of the library by students and teachers and the degree to which the library improves the educational program of the school. This is a very important part of the school librarian's role as an educator. Liesener's book will help librarians who are planning and evaluating school library programs.[17]

The community
School libraries are more involved with the community outside the school than used to be the case. Of course, parents are usually concerned with the library through their membership of school governing bodies or of committees. In some cases certain members of the general community may be granted access to the facilities of the school, including the library. In other cases, and it is occurring more frequently in certain parts of Australia, the school library becomes a school/community library, receiving financial support not only from the educational authority but also from local and State government authorities, which have responsibility for the provision of public libraries. This has an impact on the role of the school library and of the librarian. The needs of the wider community have to be considered when materials, facilities and services are being provided.

The school librarian, as an educator, must be aware of the other educational institutions in the neighbourhood so that useful links can be established. This is particularly important as far as the local public library is concerned, where co-operative planning can avoid unnecessary duplication of materials and services and can ensure a better service to the students in the area.

The school librarian will receive support and advice and access to supplementary materials and services from the regional or district educational centre. These centres augment the school collection and enable the librarian to provide a better service to students and staff of the school. Increasingly, too, school libraries are becoming part of wider library networks, some of which offer computerised services, giving access to data bases of various kinds. It may be a centralised cataloguing system that is provided or it may be a more sophisticated reference service. But the effective librarian makes certain that the school has access to any outside support that will improve the library's services to its users.

The librarian's administrative role

To provide the services described above requires administrative skills of a high order. The role of the librarian as an administrator is discussed in detail elsewhere, but it must be mentioned briefly here because the educational and administrative roles are obviously closely interrelated. Setting objectives for the library program, planning the implementation of this program, evaluating its success and preparing reports for administrators and school boards or councils are part of this task. Deciding on administrative systems that must be set up in the library and making a case for the staffing necessary to maintain such systems are also important. School librarians are involved in drawing up budgets, in selecting, training and supervising support staff, in discussing plans for modification of existing facilities or for the design of a completely new building. They are responsible for the selection, acquisition and organisation of all the materials in the library resource centre. In particular, they are concerned with the way in which materials are used to support the educational goals of the school. Administrative decisions and practices will be designed to facilitate effective use of all the library's materials and services.

Conclusion

It has been shown that school libraries have changed not only because of developments in education that place an increasing emphasis on the learner but also because of changes in curriculum content and design and in methods of instruction. Rapid technological change which has provided libraries with different materials and with access to various networks has also been an important factor. The emphasis on the need for information and on the necessity of preparing students to make use of their increased leisure time are significant. Now the library is central in the school's educational program and the librarian is seen as an important member of the teaching team. Change is evident in the design of library facilities, in the materials available to users, in the staffing of the library and particularly in the use of the resources provided. School librarians, as teachers, are involved in curriculum planning, in study skills and reading programs, and in liaison with the community. They are continually assessing what they are doing and are ready to introduce changes in administrative practices or in the kinds of services provided, if this promotes the educational objectives of the school.

Programs of media services are designed to assist learners to grow in their ability to find, generate, evaluate and apply information that helps them to function effectively as individuals and to participate fully in society.[18]

References

1. R. A. Davies, *The School Library Media Center: A Force for Educational Excellence* (2nd edn, Bowker, New York, 1974), p. 20.
2. K. I. Taylor, 'The instructional materials center: a theory underlying its development', *Wilson Library Bulletin* 43, 2 (1968), 165–8. *
3. J. Langrehr, 'Match the materials and the learners', *Audiovisual Instruction* 23, 6 (1978), 19–22.
4. R. E. Ellsworth and H. D. Wagener, *The School Library: Facilities for Independent Study in the Secondary School* (Educational Facilities Laboratories, New York, 1963), p. 15.
5. L. Thachuk and R. Owen, 'Media specialists and teacher librarians: chalk, cheese or how we tried to minimize the differences and maximise the service', *Review* 5, 1 (1977), 24–7.
6. *The Teacher-Librarian: Curator or Innovator,* Proceedings of the Fourth National Conference of School Librarians, held in Sydney, 13–17 May 1974 (Australian School Library Association, Sydney, 1974).
7. *The Democratization of Education: Implications for School Libraries,* Conference Papers, International Association of School Librarianship Conference, Melbourne, 26 July–1 August 1978 (Melbourne, 1978).
8. M. Broadbent and R. Broadbent, 'Overworked but underused: school librarians and curriculum planning', *Orana* 15, 4 (1979), 147–58.
9. J. S. Simmons, 'Word study skills', in H. L. Herber (ed.), *Developing Study Skills in Secondary Schools* (International Reading Association, Newark, N.J., 1965).
10. *Instructional Objectives for Media Research and Communication Skills: Suggested Scope and Sequence Chart,* Work copy 7 (Montgomery County Public Schools, 1975).
11. M. Line, 'The prospect before us', *School Librarian* 24, 1 (1976), 12.
12. *Secondary School Libraries in Australia: A Report on the Evaluation of the Commonwealth Secondary Schools Libraries Program* (Department of Education, University of Queensland, Brisbane, 1972).
13. P. Sullivan, *Realization: The Final Report of the Knapp School Libraries Project* (American Library Association, Chicago, 1968).

14. J. Stroud, 'Current research', *School Media Quarterly* 7, 4 (Summer 1979), 277–81.
15. L. V. Phillips, 'A quick but not easy test to help you determine how you're doing as a school librarian or media specialist', *Wilson Library Bulletin* 50, 5 (1976), 399–401.
16. E. T. Fast, 'In-service staff development as a logical part of performance evaluation', *School Media Quarterly* 3, 1 (Fall 1974), 35–41.
17. J. W. Liesener, *A Systematic Process for Planning Media Programs* (American Library Association, Chicago, 1976).
18. American Association of School Librarians and Association for Educational Communications and Technology, *Media Programs: District and School* (Chicago, 1975) p. 4.

CHAPTER 4

Selection and Acquisition of Print and Non-print Materials for School Libraries

John Cook

Building a school library's collection of books and other information-carrying materials is one of the school librarian's most important responsibilities. The school library collection is the basis of school library service. To a great extent, the quality of the collection will determine the quality of the service provided. This means that the materials selected for inclusion in the school library should be suited to the needs of the particular school community and the individuals who are part of it.

No school library can include everything that is published, and so every item included should be carefully selected so that it will contribute in a positive way to the educational and recreational aims of the school. Clearly, however, not all needs can be foreseen in advance, and it is unrealistic for a school librarian to aim to make the school library self-sufficient in answering all requests. While it is important for the school library to encourage students by being able to go at least some way to providing suitable materials for their needs, the school library should also act as a referral point to other information resources in the community. Part of the selection process for a school librarian is having an awareness of information sources. This aspect of the school librarian's role is discussed more fully in Chapter 8, 'The School Library's Place in the Community's Information Network'.

People sometimes forget the importance of a good basic collection in the provision of library services in schools. They may become overly concerned with other aspects of school librarianship, such as publicising the library service throughout the school by means of displays and classroom activities, or building up contacts with teachers and students. Important as these activities are, they are pointless if the expectations that they arouse cannot be satisfied. It is necessary to remember that a well-selected collection adequate in size for the school enrolment is basic to school library service. This is particularly so in newer schools, where the techniques of teaching are often based on learning through individual study and use of resources. It is also true that these newer schools are often inadequately provided with books and other library materials, precisely because they are new and have not had time to build up their collections. School librarians and school administrators should be conscious of the need to give high priority to building library collections, and to educational resources generally, particularly in recently established schools.

There are various publications that give guidelines for the size of school library collections according to enrolments. The most appropriate guidelines for Australian and New Zealand conditions are contained in *Books and Beyond: Guidelines for Library Resource Facilities and Services*[1], published by the Australian Schools Commission. Overseas publications such as the American *Media Programs: District and School*[2] and the *Standards of Library Service for Canadian Schools*[3] give figures that are interesting and useful for comparison.

The process of selection

The basic process in collection building is selection, or choice. Selection is a big responsibility for a school librarian. Selection means choice, and choice means the preferment of one item to another. No matter how much the selection process is formalised, and how many safeguards and precautions are followed—these are discussed later in the chapter—in the end a subjective decision has to be made to select an item and reject others. Thus not only should the school librarian have reasons for and be able to justify the selection of the items included in the collection, but also by implication should be able to justify the exclusion of all materials that have not been chosen. In effect, the school librarian is censoring this material by denying the school community access to it. Clearly this is an impossible task—no school librarian can see and evaluate every book or other item of library material. Nevertheless a conscientious school librarian aims to see as much as possible, and to use the various aids that are available to appraise the materials that cannot be inspected at first hand. Aids to selection will be described later in this chapter.

Selection is a continuous process. A school librarian continually evaluates everything as being potentially useful for the school library. It may lead to the development of a rather calculating outlook, but nevertheless it is worth cultivating as it is amazing how many useful items one can pick up.

Selection is a continuous process because the needs of the school are constantly changing. The school librarian must know what these needs are—these are discussed later in this chapter—but even when they are known, the collection cannot be matched exactly to those needs. It is an ideal to be aimed at, but never achieved. The population of the school will change, new teachers will be appointed, new courses introduced, and so on.

The school librarian must know the various media, and criteria for evaluating them. As one of the media experts in the school (or perhaps the only one), the school librarian knows the strengths and weaknesses of each medium. For example, the school librarian may be able to suggest a film or set of slides for arousing interest and introducing a particular topic. Reference works and non-fiction books may provide factual material for intensive study of the topic, periodical articles may cater for specialised interests within the topic, and works of fiction may broaden awareness of the topic in a pleasurable way. So the school librarian, in consultation with the teacher, must understand what are the aims of a particular program or course of study (indeed, may help formulate these aims), and then provide suitable materials to achieve these aims.

To know materials the school librarian must read widely, or more than that, must be an aware person. Some people are naturally good at this, while others must cultivate their skills. The day of the legendary shy and retiring librarian has passed—school librarians are now aware of the informational and educational materials that are available, and are also aware of changes in society and in people's ways of thinking. School libraries and resource centres should be leading educational excellence and innovation, and in many places they are.

The breadth of interests and awareness required is unlikely to be contained in one person. The staff and students of any school will make up an important resource for information gathering on many diverse topics. However, the school librarian must become known and trusted for teachers and students to volunteer this information. So the school librarian is a visible person, moving around the school talking to people and taking part in school activities. This is an important part of a school librarian's job generally: to be, and to be recognised as, a full member of the school's teaching team, albeit with a specialist role in the provision and management of educational resources. But it is particularly important to be involved in the whole life of the school community when it comes to the selection of materials.

In formal terms the school librarian should advise and be consulted through the school's normal procedures of curriculum planning. This will usually involve attendance at curriculum meetings and subject planning meetings. The involvement is important for two reasons: the school librarian can advise on curriculum through a knowledge of what educational resources are available; and secondly, when courses are decided upon, the school librarian can make sure that the necessary resources are available in the school library or from other sources.

Before the actual procedure of selection and acquisition is commenced, the school librarian should become aware of the extent of the existing collection. There are several ways of doing this. The first is to glance through the shelf list, which is a file of the library's collection, one card for each item arranged in the same order as the items on the shelves. These are, of course, usually arranged according to their subject. (This is more fully explained in Chapter 7, 'Bibliographic Organisation of Print and Non-print materials for School Libraries'.) By looking through the shelf list, one can note any imbalances or omissions. There may be reasons for these—for example, there is little point having many books on a particular subject that is not covered by the school's curriculum. The second step is to look carefully through the materials on the shelves, noting once again any obvious deficiences or imbalances and also taking note of the age of the stock, its condition and appearance. This comes second after examining the shelf list, because all the materials may not actually be present in the library—indeed one would hope that they are not, that they are out around the school being used. The shelf list, on the other hand, is a permanent and comprehensive record of the library's collection.

An awareness of the school library's existing collection, particularly if it is of any size, cannot be gained quickly. Nevertheless, scanning the shelf list and the actual materials on the shelves will give initial impressions of the extent, age and perhaps even the quality of the collection.

A greater awareness of the strengths and weaknesses of the existing collection, and hence where attention must be paid in future selections, will be gained through using the collection. Answering requests for information is the best way to find out where weaknesses are, and where additional materials need to be purchased. On the other hand, a few long stints on the loans desk or shelving books and other materials will show what items and subject areas are in demand, and will also help the school librarian to become familiar with the collection.

The selection file

A practical suggestion to commence selecting materials is to keep a selection file. This involves providing some sort of suggestion card which people—teachers or students—can fill in with as much information as they know about the item they want; this information can then be checked by library staff, and any blanks filled in. The school librarian can also use these suggestion cards—an interesting item may be discovered in another library or in a shop, or there may be a review or advertisement in a journal, so before the details are forgotten or mislaid, they can be entered on a card. A standard-sized catalogue card will do, and has the advantage that it can be adapted for later use in an 'on order' file, or even as a shelf list card if required. A larger file card will of course give more room for details.

Selection File/On Order Card

Author:	No. of copies:
Title:	School Order No.:
Publisher:	Price:
Date:	Date Ordered:
Place:	Date Received:
Bookseller:	Invoice No.:
Suggested by:	

The most important reason for having such a selection file is to enable priorities to be decided. Not everything can be bought, and those items which are to be bought cannot all be bought at once. So the file can be arranged alphabetically by author, and then in groups according to the priority of need to purchase: first priority, second priority, and so on. This means that the continuous process of selection can continue even when the money has run out for the year, and the next year's allocation is eagerly awaited. Such a file can also provide part of the justification for budget submissions for future allocations. Alternatively, a selection file enables the school librarian to cope with grants of funds that arrive unexpectedly and must be spent quickly before the end of the year or budgetary period. If the school librarian has priorities organised and a bunch of suggestions ready at hand, the money can be spent rationally and not rashly.

Background considerations for selection and collection building

The school librarian must consider very carefully several factors when selecting materials and building the library collection. These are the school, the students and the teaching staff.

Firstly, *the school*. The school librarian of course is immediately aware of the type of school—junior primary/infant, primary/elementary, or secondary/high school. Likewise the size of the school's enrolment is also easily discovered, though whether the enrolment is growing, static or declining may be less obvious. All these facts will have a bearing on the type and number of materials selected.

The school librarian should have a clear idea of the school's educational objectives. Quite often in the past these have been implicit and assumed, rather than clearly defined and stated, so it may be necessary to find out what these objectives are by talking to the school administrators, teachers and students. However, many schools now have published policy statements, which are available to teachers and parents, and which have been decided upon by the whole school community—teachers, parents and students. If such a document does exist, then it is easier for the school librarian to align the library's objectives with those of the school.

The development of clearly stated and agreed-upon school policies is one aspect of a general move towards greater autonomy in decision-making in schools, and greater parental and community involvement. The school librarian should become aware of the role of such bodies as school councils, parents' and citizens' associations and central education departments, and be quite clear as to where the legal responsibility rests for the conduct of the school, and in particular the library and its collection.

The school librarian must consider the total school program; the school library exists to serve the school, so the library's objectives are the same as those of the school. (There is a full discussion of this in Chapter 3, 'The Educational Role of the School Library'.) For the same reason, because different schools have different objectives, no two library collections will be the same. The school's objectives have an important influence on selection. The library exists to enrich the curriculum and to serve the individual reading and information needs of the students. Any item chosen must either support the curriculum or serve individual students, or both, and through these aims support the school's objectives.

The school library serves the curriculum, so the school librarian must be aware of what is taught and the teaching methods used. The librarian should be familiar with the textbooks, if any, that are set for study and make sure the library holds or can gain access to the materials listed in their bibliographies. As mentioned earlier in this chapter, the school librarian should serve on committees that meet to plan and implement courses. This may be difficult in some schools where the status of the position of school librarian is low, but the situation is improving in many places. More school librarians are being promoted to senior positions in schools, and even where they are not, it is being recognised that there is educational value in including them in curriculum development.

The school librarian should be familiar with the social environment of the school, its locality and the community of which it is a part. The school librarian should be aware of the occupations of parents, and the opportunities that are likely to be available for students when they leave school. Parent nights at the school can be a first step towards meeting people and getting involved. If there is a local newspaper, it is often a useful source of local information—it is very important for the library to receive it. The school librarian should also build up a working relationship with other librarians in the district; these could include public librarians or librarians in tertiary educational institutions.

If there are any special groups within the school, their activities should be served and assisted by the library. These could include special classes or programs for ethnic children, remedial reading or numeracy groups, a speech and hearing centre, and so on.

The second basic consideration in building the collection is *the needs of the students*.

The school librarian should become aware of the age distribution of students in the school. This may link with a knowledge of community changes, which may be causing changes in enrolment patterns. For instance, the school may have more older students than younger ones. There may be significant ethnic groups within the school, with their own particular needs. Even if there are only individual representatives of particular cultures, they should be helped as much as possible. As few as one or two items in their native language will help non-English speakers feel much more relaxed and comfortable in the library, and more willing to try other less-familiar learning materials.

It goes without saying, of course, that the school librarian should get to know individual students and their individual needs. Many school librarians, dealing with the whole population of the school and without the intensive contact with their 'own' class that other teachers have, find this the most difficult part of their job. Nevertheless it is very important to get to know students personally through activities both within and outside the library.

Knowledge of students' reading abilities will have an important bearing on the types of material selected, and in particular their degree of reading difficulty. Some indication of reading levels can be found by talking to teachers, examining school records, talking to the reading teacher, if there is one, and by personal observation. Reading interests are also important here, as quite often students who are very interested in a particular topic will read well above their notional reading ability. The school librarian's knowledge of the school and students will help here. The school librarian's knowledge of the students' recreational interests is also important—these activities which students undertake outside school time will, of course, influence their choices and preferences of material in the library.

The third basic consideration in building the collection is *the needs of teaching staff*.

The school librarian should know personally all the teachers; and for this reason it is important that school librarians regard themselves and are regarded as full members of staff, specialist members of the teaching team, taking as active a part as possible in all school and staff activities.

The library needs of teachers can be divided into four areas, and these are more fully discussed in a later section in this chapter under the heading 'Selection for teachers'. Briefly, they are:

(a) professional reading—materials on the theory and practice of education;

(b) materials to support the curriculum in greater depth than may be required by students;

(c) materials to provide a breadth of information not necessarily related to the curriculum to enable teachers to teach in an increasingly complex world;

(d) recreational reading—this is particularly important in isolated communities where other sources of recent literature and informational material are not available.

In building the school library collection, the school library should aim for balance, variety and currency. To achieve this aim, the collection should be reassessed continuously as it grows, to keep in step with the policies of the library and the school.

A wide variety of materials in different formats, at different levels and covering different topics should be acquired. The value of fiction should not be overlooked in the constant demands for more non-fiction material (see Chapter 5, 'Children's Literature and the School Reading Program'). Important new publications should always be considered, but quality should come before novelty as a reason for acquisition.

The needs of staff and students should always be paramount in selecting materials. However, the school librarian can create demands and develop tastes among the users of the library, as well as catering for existing needs. The school librarian should also plan ahead for the future, both in a general sense by selecting materials that will help prepare students for a world of uncertainty and change, and also specifically in building areas of study that are to be introduced or further developed. When all these background considerations are taken into account, the school librarian should set down, after full consultation within the school community, a written selection policy giving specific guidelines as to which types of material shall be selected for the school library, and which rejected.

Selection policy

Selection is a difficult and piecemeal process, so it is important that the school librarian and the whole school community consult on the issues involved, and agree on the criteria to be used in selection. The building of a library collection is made up of thousands of individual decisions; unless there is an agreed policy setting out the school's aims and the school library's aims, the collection will soon reflect only the librarian's interests and prejudices, and not support the school's teaching and learning programs.

The development of a selection policy will clarify the aims of the school library. Leaving aside its value as a working document in assisting selection, its writing is a very valuable experience for all involved. It forces the whole school to decide what the role of the school library is.

A secondary reason for writing a selection policy is so that the school librarian is able to justify the selection of particular books or other items. This justification can be on the general grounds of intellectual freedom and can refer to, or quote in full, such documents as the Library Association of Australia's 'Statement on Freedom to Read', the Australian School Library Association's 'Australian School Library Bill of Rights' and the New Zealand Library Association's 'Statement of Policy on Censorship of Books and other Printed Material for Library Use'.

Statement on Freedom to Read
The Library Association of Australia, believing that freedom can be protected in a democratic society only if its citizens have access to information and ideas through books and other sources of information, affirms the following principles as basic and distinctive of the obligations and responsibilities of a librarian:

1. A primary purpose of a library service is to provide information through books and other media on all matters which are appropriate to the library concerned.

2. A librarian must protect the essential confidential relationship which exists between a library user and the library.

3. The functions of the librarian include: to promote the use of materials in his care; to ensure that the resources of his library are adequate to its purpose; to obtain additional information from outside sources to meet the needs of readers; to cater for interest in all relevant facets of knowledge, literature and contemporary issues, including those of a controversial nature; but neither to promote nor suppress particular ideas and beliefs.

4. A librarian, while recognizing that powers of censorship exist and are legally vested in State and Federal governments, should resist attempts by individuals or organized groups within the community to determine what library materials are to be, or are not to be, available to the users of the library.

5. A librarian should not exercise censorship in the selection of materials by rejecting on moral, political, racial or religious grounds alone material which is otherwise relevant to the purpose of the library and meets the standards, such as historical importance, intellectual integrity, effectiveness of expression or accuracy of information which are required by the library concerned. Material should not be rejected on the grounds that its content is controversial or likely to offend some sections of the library's community.

6. A librarian should uphold the right of all Australians to have access to library services and materials and should not discriminate against users on the grounds of age, sex, race, religion, national origin, disability, economic condition, individual lifestyle or political or social views.

7. A librarian must obey the laws relating to books and libraries, but if the laws or their administration conflict with the principles put forward in this statement, he should be free to move for the amendment of these laws.

(Reprinted by permission of the Library Association of Australia)

Australian School Library Bill of Rights
School libraries are concerned with generating understanding of freedom and with the preservation of this freedom through the development of informed

and responsible citizens. The responsibility of the school library is:

To provide materials that will enrich and support the curriculum, taking into consideration the varied interests, abilities, and maturity levels of the pupils served.

To provide materials that will stimulate growth in factual knowledge, literary appreciation, aesthetic values and ethical standards.

To provide a background of information which will enable pupils to make intelligent judgements in their daily life.

To provide materials on opposing sides of controversial issues so that young citizens may develop under guidance the practice of critical reading and thinking.

To provide materials representative of the many religious, ethnic, and cultural groups and their contributions to our heritage.

To place principle above personal opinion and reason above prejudice in the selection of materials of the highest quality in order to assure a comprehensive collection appropriate to the users of the library.

(Reprinted by permission of the Australian School Library Association)

Statement of Policy on Censorship of Books
and Other Printed Material for Library Use

1. This statement sets out the general policy of the New Zealand Library Association, Inc. in the matter of censorship of books and other materials for libraries.

2. The Association takes the view that in adopting a policy on this matter, it shall have as its basic premises, first, that the law of the land will be observed at all times; second, that the aims and objectives of the Association, as an incorporated society, will be furthered; third, that librarianship will be seen as an academic discipline, with all the rights and responsibilities appropriate to that description.

3. From these premises, the Association concludes and holds as its policy, that the interests of the individual and of society as a whole, and the advancement of librarianship as a branch of scholarship, are best served by there being no censorship of books and other materials for libraries. The Association believes that such control of the acquisition, lending or other use of books and other library materials as may be thought necessary for the personal, sectional or general good, would result in any case from the proper application of adequate standards of librarianship. This being the case, it is the view of the Association that given effective and informed librarianship, censorship, as commonly understood, is unnecessary and, therefore, undesirable.

(Reprinted by permission of the New Zealand Library Association)

Selection of particular items may also be justified by reference to the specific criteria set out in a selection policy. It may also be possible that while the librarian or others involved in the selection of a particular item are aware of defects or possible controversial sections, they believe that the good qualities of the item justify its inclusion.

A selection policy should also outline a procedure for reconsideration of particular items. Because there is such a mass of material published, and because it is impossible for the school librarian to inspect every page or frame of every item, and often has to rely on the opinions of others (reviews, subject experts, etc.), it is possible for mistakes to be made. Parents, teachers, students and interested members of the community do have a legitimate interest in their school's activities, and their opinions on the items selected should be welcomed. It is important, however, for a person raising an objection to state clearly, preferably in writing, just what the objection is. If this is not done, then verbal discussions of particular books can wander dangerously from the point at issue. Of course, the school librarian should exercise judgement here; if there is an obvious misunderstanding, then it can perhaps be cleared up in discussion.

A suggested format for a 'Request for Reconsideration of a Library Item' is given below.

Request for Reconsideration of a Library Item
Author:
Title:
Format: (book, film, tape etc.)
Publisher:
Request initiated by:
  Address:
  Telephone:
  Representing: (name of organisation, if applicable)

1. To what in the item do you object?
  (Please give examples, page numbers, etc.)
2. Is the item suitable for a different age group?
3. Is there anything good about the item?
4. Did you examine the entire item? Which parts?
5. What do you believe is the theme of this item?
6. What would you like the school to do about this item?
  ☐ do not assign it to my child.
  ☐ withdraw it from the library.
  ☐ other.
                      Signed:

Adapted from *Books, Young People and Reading Guidance*, by G. H. Pilgrim and M. K. McAllister, 2nd edn, 1968, p. 147.

Suggested format for a school library selection policy

1. *Aims of the library*
This should be an introductory statement clarifying the school library's role in supporting the curriculum and in providing informational and recreational materials to students, teachers and in some cases to the wider community. It should refer to and be compatible with any statement of school aims or policies, if such exists. If not, it may be necessary to incorporate a brief statement of the school's philosophy.

2. *Responsibility for selection*
Where the final responsibility lies for the selection of materials will vary in different institutions. Often it will rest with the school librarian acting on authority delegated by the principal, school council or education department administration. The advisory roles of library committees and parent or community groups should be clearly defined. If there is disagreement about selection, it is important that everyone is aware who has to take the final decision, and what procedures are open to appeal against it.

3. *Criteria for selection*
A general statement should be made that applies to all library materials. Obviously different media have different characteristics which will need consideration, and these will be discussed later in this chapter, under the heading 'Selection of particular types of materials'. It may be thought desirable to include some of these specific criteria in the selection policy, but usually it is sufficient to keep the policy general and applicable to all media.

A useful list of selection criteria that can be applied to books and other materials is found in *Book Selection for School Libraries* by Azile Wofford[4], and is adapted and summarised here. If an item satisfies these criteria for selection, then it deserves a place in the school library.
Authority   The author of the item should be qualified and preferably be recognised as an authority in the field covered. Any indication of sources used in writing the book or compiling the set of audio-visual materials should be noted and, if possible, cross checked for their reliability. The reputation of the publisher, particularly in the subject area concerned, may give an indication of the item's authority.
Scope   The table of contents, or identification of major theme or subject matter, will give an indication of an item's suitability for selection and use in a particular library.

Reliability   Items selected should be both accurate and up-to-date. Recency can be checked by the copyright date, and dates of items cited in bibliographies and most recent dates in charts and tables. Information should be checked for both recency and accuracy against other authorities in the field, and by consulting experts such as subject teachers.

Treatment   The librarian should be aware of how the material is treated, and this can only be discovered by study of the contents. Some sampling may be necessary in large items, but possibly controversial items should be carefully examined. Any bias or prejudice displayed by the author should be noted, and if it is judged sufficiently serious to damage the reliability of the work, it should be rejected. The books' purpose should also be considered—for reference, factual information, recreation or persuasion—and a judgement should be made as to how well the author achieves this purpose.

Suitability for appropriate age levels   Print should be large enough, pictures should illustrate the text and vocabulary should be suitable, including familiar words together with some unfamiliar words to develop learning.

Subject interest   The subject matter dealt with by the item should appeal to some or all students in the school. In selecting materials, the school librarian will apply a knowledge of the students in the school and their interests.

Format   All items selected should be attractive in appearance, well-produced and strongly produced. The high cost of books, in particular, has forced many school librarians to buy paperbacks. (Paperbacks, however, may also be more attractive than hardcover editions to some students.) This may be a false economy, as heavily used items in flimsy covers soon deteriorate. Several library supply firms provide paperbacks strengthened or rebound to stand heavy usage.

Special features   The value of an item may be greatly increased in the school library if it has such items as an index, bibliographies or further reading lists, questions for discussion, a glossary of unusual or specialist terms, charts and diagrams, maps and other helpful material of an appendix nature.

Potential use   Every item added to the school library should contribute to the school's educational program. Some uses to which library material could be put are:

for reference;

to provide factual information;

to help students adjust to and understand their world;

for teachers or librarians to use in reading aloud or story telling;
to help students understand their own and other people's culture and
history;
to furnish information for thematic study of topics;
to provide information about current events;
to provide material for hobbies and other interests;
to enable students to experience good writing, art and music;
for recreation.

4. *Positive approach to selection*
A school library selection policy should make it clear that the purpose of
the school library is to provide information and not to deny it. For this
reason, items selected are always included in the collection because of
their good and useful qualities—but may be included even if they have
some deficiencies, if it is thought that these are outweighed by their
positive attributes.

The policy should refer to or include the Australian School Library Bill
of Rights, the Statement on Freedom to Read (LAA) or the Statement of
Policy on Censorship of Books and other Printed Material for Library Use
(NZLA).

The whole school should reaffirm, through its library's selection
policy, a commitment of the right of every citizen and every child in a
democratic society to have free access to information.

Materials dealing with pornography, violence or hatred, or of an
inaccurate, biased or misleading nature have no place in the school
library, and this should also be stated. Controversial materials can be
included, however, if it is thought that their positive qualities justify it,
and as long as a genuine effort is made to include as many different points
of view as possible.

Selection aids

There are many sources of assistance in selection available to school
librarians. These vary widely from place to place, so the following list is
not intended to be prescriptive but to give an indication of what may be
available. Many of the education department services listed are also
available to independent schools.

School library central services
Chapter 11, 'Centralised Services for School Libraries', discusses the
role of the school libraries branches of government departments of

education; however, their role in aiding selection of school library materials can be noted here. They provide some or all of the following services:

a model library where materials can be examined without commercial pressures;

a range of expensive materials—for example, encyclopaedias and atlases—which can be compared directly, and compared without commercial pressures;

selection advice, in the form of published evaluations and reviews, and booklists and bibliographies on particular topics;

advice by school library advisers on particular matters in selection and on other areas of school librarianship;

in-service courses in all aspects of school librarianship.

Educational technology centres
or audio-visual education centres

These centres provide evaluation services for audio-visual materials through demonstration collections, published reviews, personal help and advice, and in-service courses.

Reading centres

Reading centres provide information on the teaching of reading, and, of particular interest to school librarians, give assistance in recommending materials through publications, a specialist library collection, personal advice and in-service courses.

Teachers centres

Teachers centres usually have a library or resource centre from which materials may be borrowed for use in schools and where materials can be examined, plus facilities for making materials for use in schools, in-service courses, and opportunities for teachers to meet and share ideas and knowledge.

Service branches

Such specialist areas as music, physical education, religious education and consumer education may have their own branches of education departments, with libraries, reviewing services and advisory personnel.

In-service education

In-service courses in librarianship and in media, and in curriculum subject areas, often provide information about new and recommended materials.

National, State and public libraries
These bodies are often important publishers in their own right, and their annual reports will list their publications. They often publish bibliographies and lists of recommended materials in particular subject areas, drawn from their own collections. They may put out helpful guides for teachers and parents, such as lists for Christmas buying. Very often their collections are carefully selected by specialist staff, so they may provide an indication of value; the staff are usually willing to discuss their reasons for selection of particular items.

Government departments, associations and firms
Education departments produce very important material for school libraries in the form of courses and reading lists, the reports of projects and task forces, and official directives and communications from the administration to schools and teachers. Every school library should have a comprehensive collection of these materials. Other departments, associations and firms put out vast quantities of material, much of it useful, though some may have biased or misleading information and should be treated with caution. (This is discussed later in this chapter under the heading 'Selection of free and sponsored materials'.) Two helpful publications that give names and addresses of sources of useful material are:
> *Where Do You Get It?*, by Ron Mercier, PO Box H145, Australia Square Post Office, Sydney, NSW, 2000. (1979)
> *How and Where Directory*, School Library Association of New South Wales, PO Box 80, Balmain, NSW, 2041. (5th edn, 1980)

Government publications and government bookshops
The Australian Government Publishing Service has bookshops in each capital city which carry a comprehensive range of legislative papers, reports to Parliament and other government publications. It also publishes a monthly newsletter of new publications, and has a mail order service.

There are New Zealand Government Bookshops in Auckland, Hamilton, Wellington, Christchurch and Dunedin.

The Australian States also have government bookshops and information centres dealing with State government publications in the State capitals.

Professional associations

The professional associations in the field of librarianship provide valuable opportunities for assistance in selection. The Library Association of Australia, the New Zealand Library Association and the Australian School Library Association (through its State member associations) all provide advice and guidance on selection, as on many other topics, through their meetings, conferences, and publications. All school librarians should belong to their professional association as the benefits are great, and become greater if the association is strong.

School librarians, as teachers, should also maintain an interest in their teaching field through specialist teacher associations, such as history (or mathematics, etc.) teacher associations. Publications issued by such groups will probably have news and reviews of new materials, and are useful aids to selection.

Journals

Australia and New Zealand are small English-language markets dominated by the United States and the United Kingdom publishing giants, and this gives both advantages and disadvantages. The main disadvantage is that many of their publications may not be appropriate for use in Australia and New Zealand; but, on the other hand, there is a huge range of materials available. Basic selection aids used in school libraries overseas may not be suitable for use here (an example is the definitive United States publication *The Elementary School Library Collection*[5], now in its 12th edition). However, overseas reviewing journals are essential for promoting awareness of new publications, but they should always be read critically and with the needs of the particular school in mind.

The following is a list of journals that are helpful in selection, through their reviews and general articles. There may also be journals of a local nature that are useful, or even essential, for schools in particular areas. It will not be possible for individual school libraries to subscribe to all these journals; however, after perusing several issues of each, the school librarian can judge which are the most useful for the school and should be purchased. Budgetary restraints will be crucial here. Those journals not purchased should be regularly scanned in other, larger libraries. Or it may be possible for several schools to form a co-operative group, whereby each school purchases different journals and then circulates them to the other schools after use. It should be noted that not all publications of central school library services are available outside their own State.

Australian Audio Visual News (4 issues p.a.), D. W. Thorpe Pty Ltd, 384 Spencer St, Melbourne, Vic., 3003, Australia.

Australian Book Review (11 issues p.a.), National Book Council, Peter Isaacson Publications Pty Ltd, 46–49 Porter St, Prahran, Vic., 3181, Australia.

Australian Bookseller and Publisher (11 issues p.a.), D. W. Thorpe Pty Ltd, 384 Spencer St, Melbourne, Vic., 3003, Australia.

Australian Library Journal (4 issues p.a.), Library Association of Australia, Science Centre, 35 Clarence St, Sydney, NSW, 2000, Australia.

Australian Library News (10 issues p.a.), Australian Library Promotion Council, 328 Swanston St, Melbourne, Vic., 3000, Australia.

Australian School Librarian (4 issues p.a.), School Library Association of Victoria, PO Box 280, East Melbourne, Vic., 3002, Australia.

Bookbird (4 issues p.a.), International Board on Books for Young People (IBBY) and the International Institute for Children's Literature and Reading Research, Herman Schaffstein Verlag, Deggingstr. 93, 4600 Dortmund 1, Federal Republic of Germany.

Booklist (23 issues p.a.), American Library Association, 50 East Huron St, Chicago, Ill., 60611, USA.

Books for Keeps (formerly *School Bookshop News*) (6 issues p.a.), School Bookshop Association, 7 Albemarle St, London, WIX 4BB, UK.

Books for Your Children (4 issues p.a.), Slate House Farm, Parwich, Ashbourne, Derbyshire, UK.

British Book News (12 issues p.a.), British Council, 65 Davies St, London, WIY 2AA, UK.

Bulletin of the Center for Children's Books (11 issues p.a.), Graduate Library School, University of Chicago, 5801 Ellis Ave, Chicago, Ill., 60637, USA.

Central Cataloguing Bulletin (12 issues p.a.), Library Services, NSW Department of Education, PO Box 439, North Sydney, NSW, 2060, Australia.

Children's Book List (Annual), Library Services, NSW Department of Education, PO Box 439, North Sydney, NSW, 2060, Australia.

Choice (11 issues p.a.), Association of College and Research Libraries, American Library Association, 100 Riverview Center, Middletown, Conn., 06457, USA.

Edlib: bulletin of the Library Services Branch of the Education Department of Tasmania (5 issues p.a.), C/- State Library of Tasmania, 91 Murray St, Hobart, Tas., 7000, Australia.

Education Library Services Bulletin (5 issues p.a.), Library Services Branch, Education Department of Western Australia, 664A Murray St, West Perth, 6005, WA, Australia.

Growing Point (6 issues p.a.), Margery Fisher, Ashton Manor, Northampton, NN7 2JL, UK.

Horn Book Magazine (6 issues p.a.), Park Square Building, 31 St James Ave, Boston, Mass., 02116, USA.

Incite (20 issues p.a.), Newsletter of the Library Association of Australia, Science Centre, 35 Clarence St, Sydney, NSW, 2000, Australia.

Instructional Innovator (9 issues p.a.), Association for Educational Communications and Technology, 1126 Sixteenth St, NW, Washington DC, 20036, USA. (Formerly *Audiovisual Instruction*.)

Journal of the School Library Association of Queensland (4 issues p.a.), PO Box 429, Redcliffe, Qld, 4020, Australia.

Junior Bookshelf (6 issues p.a.), Marsh Hall, Thurstonland, Huddersfield, HD4 6XB, UK.

Library Journal (22 issues p.a.), R. R. Bowker Co., 1180 Avenue of the Americas, New York, 10036, USA.

Media Information Australia (4 issues p.a.), Australian Film and Television School, PO Box 305, North Ryde, NSW, 2113, Australia.

Media Memorandum (3 issues p.a.), Resource Services, Queensland Department of Education, PO Box 33, North Quay, Qld, 4000, Australia.

Media Outlook Review Supplement (irregular), Media Services, Department of Education, PMB 25, Winnellie, NT, 5789, Australia.

New Zealand Libraries (4 issues p.a.), New Zealand Library Association, PO Box 12 212, Wellington North, New Zealand.

Orana: Journal of School and Children's Librarianship (4 issues p.a.), Library Association of Australia, School and Children's Libraries Sections, Science Centre, 35 Clarence St, Sydney, NSW, 2000, Australia.

Previews: Audiovisual Software Reviews (9 issues p.a.), R. R. Bowker Co., 1180 Avenue of the Americas, New York, 10036, USA.

Reading Time (4 issues p.a.), Children's Book Council of Australia, PO Box 159, Curtin, ACT, 2695, Australia.

Review (4 issues p.a.), School Libraries Branch, Education Department of South Australia, GPO Box 1152, Adelaide, SA, 5001, Australia.

Review Bulletin (4 issues p.a.), Library Branch, Education Department of Victoria, 449 Swanston St, Melbourne, Vic., 3000, Australia.

Reviewpoint (irregular), Library and Resource Services, Queensland Department of Education, PO Box 33, North Quay, Qld, 4000, Australia.

SARA Journal (4 issues p.a.), South Australian Reading Association, C/- Reading Development Centre, 91 Gilles St, Adelaide, SA, 5000, Australia.

School Librarian (4 issues p.a.), School Library Association, Victoria House, 29–31 George St, Oxford, OX1 2AY, UK.

School Library Journal (9 issues p.a.), R. R. Bowker Co., 1180 Avenue of the Americas, New York, 10036, USA.

School Library Review (formerly *Children's Books to Buy*) (4 issues p.a.), New Zealand School Library Service, 125–7 Thorndon Quay, Wellington, New Zealand.

School Media Quarterly (4 issues p.a.), American Association of School Librarians, 50 East Huron St, Chicago, Ill., 60611, USA.

SMMART Journal (4 issues p.a.), Society for Mass Media and Resource Technology, PO Box 187, Elizabeth, SA, 5112, Australia.

Teacher Librarian (4 issues p.a.), School Library Association of New South Wales, PO Box 80, Balmain, NSW, 2041, Australia.

Times Literary Supplement (weekly), Times Newspapers Ltd, New Printing House Square, Gray's Inn Rd, London, WC1X 8EZ, UK.

Top of the News (4 issues p.a.), Association for Library Service to Children and Young Adult Services Division of American Library Association, 50 East Huron St, Chicago, Ill., 60611, USA.

Wilson Library Bulletin (10 issues p.a.), H. W. Wilson Co., 950 University Ave, Bronx, New York, 10452, USA.

Rather than subscribing to each journal separately, it may be more convenient to subscribe through a subscription agent. School Libraries Branch advisers will supply the names of reliable agents.

Bibliographies

The various national bibliographies published by the national libraries of Australia and New Zealand[6], and other countries, are basic and comprehensive selection tools for all librarians. Their scope may be too wide for smaller school libraries, however, and their cost may be beyond the means of such libraries. Where possible, they should be scanned in neighbouring larger public or academic libraries.

The national libraries, aware of the needs and small budgets of small libraries, publish various lists of basic materials about their own country. Examples are *Australian Books: A Select List of New Publications and Standard Works in Print*[7] and the 'Select Bibliography: New Zealand Books' compiled in the Alexander Turnbull Library, National Library, Wellington, and published in the *New Zealand Official Year Book*[8].

Other useful bibliographies are the annual publications *Australian Books in Print*[9] and *New Zealand Books in Print*[10] and *Australian Audio Visual Reference Book 1979* or subsequent editions.[11] All are published by D. W. Thorpe Pty Ltd, 384 Spencer St, Melbourne, Victoria, 3003, Australia.

Book awards

There are many awards made to authors and illustrators for excellence in books. While school librarians regard such honours as a point in a book's favour when considering it for selection, it does not necessarily make it an automatic selection. The past reputation of the particular award, the method of deciding upon it, the body sponsoring it and the criteria for judgement should all be taken into account. Where possible, as in all selection, the item should be individually examined.

There are various lists of awards made for children's books. *The New Classics*[12] is one list, which also includes a brief statement on the criteria for selecting books for each award. Current awards are publicised in the children's literature journals listed above, notably in *Reading Time, Horn Book Magazine* and *Junior Bookshelf*.

School librarians should be aware of the following awards:
The Book of the Year Award and the Picture Book of the Year

Award—Children's Book Council of Australia;
The Carnegie Medal and the Kate Greenaway Medal (for illustration)—
Library Association (of the United Kingdom);
The Newbery Medal and the Caldecott Medal (for illustration)—the
American Library Association;
The Hans Christian Andersen Medal awarded to authors and illustrators
for their complete works—International Board on Books for Young
People (IBBY).

As well as these specifically children's literature awards, there are many
awards made by literary and library associations, publishers and
booksellers groups, and newspapers and national literary foundations.
School librarians should be aware of all these through regular reading of
selection journals and review pages of newspapers and general
magazines.

Publishers' catalogues

Publishers' catalogues are very useful listings of what is available and
forthcoming. They are uncritical, of course, in their description of items.
Nevertheless they are often the first step in selection, by signalling the
existence of particular items. The school librarian should make sure that
as many catalogues as possible are regularly received by the library, and
if necessary should write to publishers asking to be put on their mailing
lists. On receipt of the latest catalogue, the old one should be discarded,
the new catalogue circulated to interested teaching and library staff, and
then on its return to the library work room it should be shelved
alphabetically by publisher's name for easy reference.

Bookshops

Bookshops are show places of current materials, and as such are valuable
resources for school librarians. A good bookshop affords the opportunity
to handle, examine and compare particular items; and the skills and
knowledge of a good bookseller are invaluable in locating materials,
ordering books not in stock, and generally disseminating information and
advice about books and publishing. In return for these services, and for
the convenience of holding large stocks immediately available,
booksellers are justified in adding a reasonable profit margin to the price
they pay to the publisher or distributor.

On the other hand, some school librarians are finding that they are not
receiving good service from local booksellers, and have decided to
purchase books directly from overseas. There is no advantage, of course,

in buying locally published books from overseas; but for overseas publications, significant monetary savings (often 30 per cent of the local price) can sometimes be made. Against this should be considered the disadvantages of not being able to examine materials and of lengthy delays in delivery. [Note: Under Section 37 of the Copyright Act 1968, only the owner of copyright can import books for resale. Thus an agent importing books for resale to a library could be acting to an extent that is prejudicial to the owner of copyright.] The British Council provides useful information and advice about purchasing books from Britain in its publication *Aids in the Selection of British Books*[13] and notes compiled by the Export Booksellers Group of the Booksellers Association of Great Britain and Ireland entitled *How to Buy British Books*[14]; both publications are available from the British Council Representative in Australia, 203 New South Head Road, Edgecliff, Sydney (postal address PO Box 88, Edgecliff, NSW, 2027). *British Book News*, a monthly publication of the British Council and listed earlier in this chapter under the heading 'Journals', is also a useful source of information about new British books. Some school librarians buy books direct from American suppliers, but this is less usual than purchasing from Britain, due probably to our traditional links with Britain in the fields of purchasing and bookselling. The purchase of books in foreign languages direct from overseas is discussed in a later section of this chapter, 'Selection for special needs: ethnic children'.

Despite some overseas purchasing, school librarians will continue to acquire most of their materials from local suppliers. With co-operation from both sides, a fruitful partnership can be built up. The school librarian should become familiar with the strengths and specialisations of particular booksellers, and should use a selection file (discussed earlier) to make informed requests of the bookseller. Librarians should make a point of regularly visiting bookshops to acquaint themselves with new publications. Some enlightened school administrations are now recognising this essential part of the librarian's job, by allowing time in school hours for visits to bookshops; this is particularly necessary in isolated schools, where travel is required to cities or regional centres.

Selection of particular types of material

Fiction
The selection of fiction for school libraries involves a study of the whole field of children's literature. Critical judgements made on books written

for children should be no less rigorous than those intended for adults. They should include evaluations of the style, plot, characterisation, subject interest and point of view. In material selected, any descriptions of violence, sexual acts or crude language should be necessary to the plot and should not be included to provide gratuitous thrills. While children should not be sheltered from the harshness of life, the age of children for whom a book is intended should be a prime consideration if sensitive topics are covered.

A beginner in the field of children's literature should make a start by reading Chapter 5, 'Children's Literature and the School Reading Program'. Useful general books are *Written for Children* by John Rowe Townsend[15], *Children's Literature in the Elementary School* by Charlotte S. Huck[16] and *A Critical Handbook of Children's Literature* by Rebecca J. Lukens[17]. There are numerous books of readings on children's literature. Three of the best are *Only Connect: Readings on Children's Literature*[18], *Children and Literature: Views and Reviews*[19], and *Issues in Children's Book Selection*[20]. The standard work on Australian children's literature is Maurice Saxby's *History of Australian Children's Literature*[21].

Fiction provides a pleasurable reading experience, as well as giving much wider information than is covered by the curriculum. It also provides a background for studying our own country and other countries, in history and as a means of helping children understand themselves, their friends and their world.

Reference books
Reference books are those designed to be consulted for particular items, and not to be read right through. They include those that give information directly (encyclopaedias, dictionaries, year books, manuals, directories, biographical sources, geographical sources) and those that are keys to sources of information (indexes, abstracts, bibliographies). A full discussion on each of these types of reference book is included in Chapter 6, 'Reference Work in the School Library'.

General non-fiction
Works of non-fiction are very important in supporting the school's curriculum, particularly with the greater emphasis now placed on student-centred learning. Beyond the curriculum, the library's non-fiction collection can balance the curriculum's emphases, and can cater to the specialised interests of individuals. Non-fiction covers a tremendous

range of subjects, and is often a worthwhile source of leisure reading for many students.

The criteria for selection should be carefully applied in respect of non-fiction materials. Mediocre books with inaccurate facts and outdated material have no place in the non-fiction collection.

Periodicals

Periodicals provide current information about recent events in curriculum areas and wider fields. They complement the library's general collection and are widely used for leisure reading.

Periodicals are often a neglected area of the school library, because of their expense, the difficulty of managing them and finding the information they carry, and the bewildering and changing array that is available. There are various overseas published guides to periodicals, but these are of limited use in Australia and New Zealand because their annotations are not applicable to our conditions. One publication that is useful, if now somewhat dated, is *Periodicals for School Libraries: A Select Annotated List*[22], published by the Library Association of Australia.

Indexes to periodicals, such as *APAIS (Australian Public Affairs Information Service)*[23], *Guidelines*[24] and *Pinpointer*[25], add greatly to the value of a periodical collection.

Periodicals should be selected to cover professional reading for teachers and librarians (including selection journals), the major areas of the curriculum, newspapers, and current affairs and recreational material.

As a periodical subscription entails an on-going commitment, usually for a year, and as the value of periodical indexes builds up with a substantial run of each periodical, care should be exercised in selection. Sample copies should be obtained from the publisher or agent, and carefully examined. Expert opinion from the school staff and from outside, and reviews, should be consulted. The cost of a periodical should be weighed against its frequency of publication, its potential use and the standard of its production.

Audio-visual materials

Modern school libraries are designed to provide information in various forms, and are not primarily concerned with the format itself. For this reason, many of the standards and criteria for selection of printed materials, relating to authority, scope, reliability and so on, apply equally to audio-visual materials. However, different media do have different strengths, convey different concepts and can be used in different modes of teaching and learning. The librarian should therefore consider the aims of a particular item when evaluating it, and consider how well those aims have been achieved. For instance, print conveys large amounts of information and closely reasoned arguments; sound recordings are well adapted to convey music or drama and poetry read aloud; pictorial material shows colour, proportion and shape; moving pictures show actions involving motion or development through time. Thus in the selection of all material, and particularly audio-visual material, the librarian is thinking ahead to possible uses of the material.

The various forms of audio-visual materials can be categorised as follows: overhead transparencies, film strips and slides, films, videotapes, flat pictures, graphic materials, multimedia kits, and sound recordings. Where possible, all items should be previewed before purchase so that both content and technical quality can be assessed. To include subject teachers and students in this assessment process, a standard assessment form should be developed, which suits local conditions.

Useful information on selection of audio-visual materials in Australia is contained in *Non-Book Materials* by Paul McNally[27] and *Plugs and Bugs on Audio Visual Resources* by Graeme Foster, Grace Cochrane and Tony Sloane[28].

Free and sponsored materials
There is a great deal of material available to school libraries from commercial, government and voluntary sources. Some of this is worthy of a place in the library but school librarians should always be aware that much of this material aims to convert its readers to a particular point of view. This is often the case in respect of commercial, religious and political material. The selection criteria used in relation to free material should be just as strict as when material is purchased. The two books mentioned previously in this chapter, *Where Do You Get It?* and *The How and Where Directory*, give many sources of free material.

The materials evaluation form (right) is adapted from *Developing Multi-Media Libraries*[26] (with permission of the R. R. Bowker Company, copyright © 1970 by Xerox Corporation).

Materials Evaluation Form

Title:

Type of material:

☐ Film		☐ Videotape	
☐ Filmstrip		☐ Sound tape	
☐ Slides		☐ Disc	
☐ O/H transparencies		☐ Kit	
		☐ Other	

Producer:

Date produced:

Cost:

Content summary:

Check where applicable	Excellent	Good	Poor
Authority/reliability (accurate, impartial, up-to-date):	☐	☐	☐
Scope (contents, concepts):	☐	☐	☐
Treatment (interest, organisation):	☐	☐	☐
Technical quality (tone, clarity, focus, composition, color, synchronisation):	☐	☐	☐
Special features (notes, guides, accompanying material):	☐	☐	☐
Physical characteristics (for ease of use, storage, durability):	☐	☐	☐

Possible library uses:

☐ Individual		☐ Remedial
☐ Group		☐ Ethnic
☐ Introduction		☐ Overview
		☐ Other

Grade range: ☐ K ☐ 1 ☐ 2 ☐ 3 ☐ 4 ☐ 5 ☐ 6 ☐ 7 ☐ 8 ☐ 9
☐ 10 ☐ 11 ☐ 12 ☐ Parent ☐ Teacher

Curriculum areas:
☐ English lang. ☐ Other lang. ☐ Arts ☐ Social Studies ☐ Maths
☐ Science ☐ Art ☐ Music ☐ P.E. ☐ Other

Comments:

Recommended for purchase: ☐ Yes ☐ No ☐ Defer

Evaluator:

Position:

Date:

Selection for special needs

Teachers

One of the functions of the school library is to be a 'special' library for teachers—that is, to provide them with the information required for their job. Thus the school library should provide information about education in general, and also about specific subject areas, both subject information and how to teach it.

The actual process of selection of materials for teachers involves close co-operation with teachers. Suggestions should be solicited from teachers by circulating periodicals, reviewing journals and other selection tools. Selection committees in subject areas should meet regularly to consider materials; such groups can be of great assistance in selecting general materials, as well as materials specifically for teachers. Further information can be found in *The Teachers' Library: How to Organise It and What to Include*[29].

Ethnic children

School libraries can and should reflect the multicultural diversity of our society through the range of materials made available. Nancye Stanelis puts it well in her book *Resources for Schools: Multicultural Education*[30]:

> Even in a school where few ethnic children are present the inclusion of these types of materials [in English and ethnic languages about the children's countries of origin], and their promotion to staff and students, is a valid expectation of the school library, for the students need to be aware of the value of other cultures and particularly those cultures which are represented in Australia. There is little material to date about migrant cultures in Australia, though the situation is improving. Nance Donkin and David Martin, for example, have both written stories about migrant children in Australia but more needs to be written emphasising the contributions of migrants to Australia's economy and culture.
>
> Material in ethnic language does present difficulties for librarians, particularly in selection and organisation, for few librarians are bilingual and even fewer are familiar with the range of languages which may be found in a single school. Recent immigrants from areas such as Lebanon, Vietnam, Thailand and Timor as well as those from Greece, Italy, Turkey, Yugoslavia, Germany, Chile, Poland, the Netherlands or Cyprus may be represented in a school and the librarian should make an effort to cater for as many as possible. Booksellers and other librarians will help with selections of material and it is often possible to involve a member of the local ethnic community or a bilingual teacher in helping to reach a final selection for the school library. Every effort should be made to obtain books of similar standard to those bought in English and here the librarian's own experience and knowledge is

essential. The librarian, too, will know what kinds of books are popular with students and in which area of the curricula books are needed. The efforts of consultants in Education Departments and groups such as the Ethnic Library Resources Project team will be of assistance to school librarians in establishing guidelines for selection and organisation of materials.

Stanelis's *Resources for Schools: Multicultural Education* also has very useful lists of recommended materials; and under the heading 'Resources', a list of names and addresses of bookshops specialising in ethnic language materials, people who may be useful contacts, schools with on-going multi-cultural programs, libraries that have collections where school librarians can see ethnic materials, and some references that are useful for background information[31].

While it appears that there are some cost advantages in buying English-language materials from traditional English-language book-producing countries such as Britain and the United States, similar advantages in buying materials from foreign language countries are outweighed by other problems. Nancye Stanelis put it this way at the 1978 Australian School Library Association Conference:

> Though some savings can be made by buying direct from overseas, I feel that the quantities purchased by most schools do not warrant the trouble and delay involved, compared with the advantages of buying locally. Buying locally means materials can be previewed before purchase, rather than relying on someone else to make a selection or trying to order from publishers' lists of unfamiliar materials. Considerable fluency in the language is required for overseas ordering, alternative titles must be specified for those which are no longer available (a common occurrence with ethnic language materials) and the likely damage in transit must also be considered. Materials produced in Australia are becoming more readily available because of the increasing demand, and most booksellers are anxious to satisfy their customers' requirements when asked for assistance. Finally, of course, the more we use their services and make our wishes known, the more likely the booksellers will be to appreciate our needs and to stock the type of materials which we require.[32]

Australian school libraries should hold accurate and reliable materials about Aborigines, both for Aboriginal students to learn about their own culture and for white students to learn about Aborigines. Much of the information contained in older books about Aborigines has been inaccurate and unreliable, and very much written from a white European point of view. Examples abound of books stressing the negative aspects in European terms of Aboriginal life—'Aborigines do not wear clothes, do not build houses', and so on—which completely disregard the complex lifestyle and culture that enabled them to live in harmony with an often harsh environment. Improvements are occurring, as Aborigines themselves demand that the truth be told about them, and as soundly based Aboriginal studies courses are established in universities and colleges. Help is available to school librarians in the form of lists of recommended materials published by the Aboriginal Studies Library Project as supplements to the South Australian School Libraries Branch's *Review* (Vol. 3 No. 4 and Vol. 4 No. 4); and more widely available, *Black Australia*, a bibliography of resources about Aborigines by Alex Barlow and Marji Hill, published by the Australian Institute of Aboriginal Studies.[33]

Exceptional children

The school library should aim to cater for all types of exceptional children through its selection of materials for their use. 'Exceptional children' in this context means gifted children, physically and intellectually handicapped children and emotionally disturbed children. The school librarian, in becoming familiar with the students, will get to know what their needs are. The librarian should then consult expert opinion within and outside the school as to what items should be selected—specialist teachers, voluntary associations for the welfare of various groups of children, specialist journals, education department consultants, and so on. One useful book is *Books for the Retarded Reader*.[34]

Younger children

The first task of the librarian in the primary school is to instil the love and habit of reading. To this end, a wide range of fiction and non-fiction should be available that will give pleasure to children. Further, primary school children should have access in their library to well-chosen reference and non-fiction which will encourage them to seek information in books, to learn how to look things up. All materials should be chosen bearing in mind the limited life experiences, language abilities and attention spans of younger children. Nevertheless, such books and other materials should be positive forces in expanding young children's knowledge.

Young adults

Secondary schools cover the whole range of growing up from children aged 11 or 12, to, in some cases, mature adults aged 18; in addition, some schools have significant numbers of mature-age students returning to school to improve their qualifications. Thus 'young adults' are not really a specialised group in the secondary school—they are the whole school population. Nevertheless, it is useful in the selection process to consider their special needs as young adults.

At this period in their lives, young adults are widening their interests and activities, trying out and discarding new ideas and lifestyles. These many opportunities for other activities representing a new or increased interest in sport, social life, cars, music and so on, tend to squeeze the time available for reading. Young adults do read, however, and not surprisingly their reading interests tend to reflect their other activities. Thus the library collection should include newspapers, magazines, comics, recorded music, posters, and paperbacks, if young adults are to see it as being of interest to them. Many young adults will read more serious material—it is wrong to think of them as being interested all the time only in what may be judged to be ephemeral or trivial material. Books and other materials, whether specifically aimed at young adults or not (the so-called 'adolescent novel' is a case in point), may open channels of communication for many young adults bewildered by the changes in their own bodies and feelings, and by the pressures put on them by our society. They will learn that other people have the same feelings, hopes, fears, anxieties, and that these can be resolved.

Two very useful books on materials and methods of librarianship for young adults are *Books and the Teen-Age Reader* by G. Robert Carlsen[35] and *Libraries and Literature for Teenagers* by Margaret Marshall.[36]

The community
Many school librarians now see their responsibility as extending beyond the immediate school population, to the wider community. This may include parents of children in the school, or other community members. The extent to which such service is provided will depend on particular circumstances, and various types of 'school/community library' are discussed in Chapter 10. If the school library is aiming to provide a wider service, its selection of materials should reflect this aim.

In order to provide materials that are relevant to the community, the school librarian must become familiar with the community and its needs. Materials provided will normally be in all formats, and will include items suitable for information gathering and for recreation. It should be remembered that the library will need to cater for all ages, from pre-schoolers to senior citizens. Chapter 8 outlines the ways in which a school library can link with the whole information network of the community; the provision of community information is particularly important when the school library is open for the whole community to use.

Ordering and acquisition procedures

Ordering

After the decision has been made to purchase an item, check the catalogue to ensure that the library does not already have it, and also check the 'On Order' File. Remove the card from the Selection File, fill in name of supplier/bookseller and date, and list all items on school letterhead or official order form. Keep a copy of this order, and file individual cards in the On Order File.

Acquisition

When the materials arrive, check the invoice that arrives with the items against the order form and follow up any not supplied. Check the items for binding, printing, correct edition, etc., and return any that are not satisfactory.

Enter number of items in the stock register, where this is required for audit or statistical purposes. The stock register can also be used to assign accession numbers, if these are used. (An accession number is allocated to each item as it is received in the library, starting from No. 1 for the first item received. The accession number of the most recently received item may be higher than the total stock of the library because of losses or withdrawals. Many libraries no longer assign accession numbers as items can be identified through their call numbers—see Chapter 7, 'Bibliographic Organisation'. Likewise, very few libraries now maintain accession registers in which the details of each item are recorded, as information about price or place of purchase can be entered on the shelf list card.)

Write the accession number (if used) in the book, on the back of the title page, and inside the back cover.

Stamp the book with school stamp.

Remove the order card from 'On Order' File. Fill in date received, and the invoice number.

If there is a large cataloguing backlog, the order card can be placed in an 'Awaiting Cataloguing' File. Otherwise it can be used as the basis for a shelf list card or it can be used as a notification to the person who suggested the item (or other interested people) that it has arrived.

Stock Register: Books

Date	Fiction Added	Fiction Withdrawn	Fiction Total	Non-fiction Added	Non-fiction Withdrawn	Non-fiction Total	Book Total	Accession Numbers (optional)
Total								

The item is now ready for cataloguing and classification and further processing that is required: plastic covering, loan cards and pockets, etc.

It is useful to keep a record of expenditure to correlate with the budget; this can be divided into similar groupings as those in the budget. Many schools have a bursar or secretary who is responsible for payment of accounts. However, the school librarian should also keep a separate record of expenditure in a form convenient for the library. A suggested format for such an expenditure record is given below.

Expenditure Record						
Supplier	Date of Cheque	Total	Art	Social Science	Science	etc.
JAMES BENNETT	28/3/8?	$400	$150	$150	$100	
MARY MARTINS						
THE BOOKCASE						
ETC.						
TOTAL, (END OF MONTH, END OF TERM, ETC)						

Acquisition of periodicals

Periodicals need constant attention and checking because of the possibility of changes of title, publisher and frequency, and because of increasing losses and delays in the mails. Many school librarians consolidate their periodicals orders and subscriptions with a periodicals agent, but some periodicals are not obtainable through these sources and, in any case, the operations of the agent need to be checked. School Libraries Branches in Education Departments will give the names of reliable agents.

Library supply companies and stationery firms have various recording systems for periodicals, on cards or visible indexes. In a small library, an adequate record can be kept on standard catalogue cards as shown below.

Periodical Record Card															
Title:									Frequency:						
Address:															
		Jan.	Feb.	Mar.	Apr.	May	June	July	Aug.	Sep.	Oct.	Nov.	Dec.		
	1981	✓✓ ✓✓	✓✓ ✓✓	✓✓ ✓✓	✓✓ ✓✓	✓✓ ✓✓	✓✓ ✓✓	✓✓ ✓✓	✓✓ ✓✓	✓✓ ✓✓	✓✓ ✓✓	✓✓ ✓✓			
	1982														
	1983														
	1984														

Co-operation in acquisition

Many school librarians are looking for ways in which they can build better collections of resources and achieve cost-savings in the face of rising costs and, often, reduced funding. One way in which they are achieving these aims is by setting up co-operative schemes for the purchase of library materials. Some definite advantages have been gained by groups of co-operating schools:

(a) cost-savings in the prices paid for materials, whether brought locally or overseas;

(b) more information about what is available, particularly in specialised subject areas or from overseas suppliers;

(c) the sharing of expensive resources that are not in constant use in any one school;

(d) the prevention of unnecessary duplication of resources by neighbouring schools.

Before beginning a co-operative scheme, all its implications should be carefully considered. A small group may function well informally, but a larger group may need more formal arrangements, even legally binding agreements. The resources required for the scheme to function effectively should be provided for in advance; staffing, costs of communications and transport, time for personnel to meet, plan and implement the scheme, in-service training, physical accommodation, and so on, should all be quantified and arrangements made for their provision. If these words of caution are taken into account, there may be advantages for many schools in entering into co-operative arrangements with other schools for the acquisition of library resources.

Evaluating the collection

Evaluating the collection, surveying its strengths and its weaknesses, and rectifying these weaknesses by withdrawing some materials and selecting others, is part of the continuous process of the selection of materials for the school library. Evaluation of the collection assesses the collection as it exists in the light of the needs of the library's clientele. Once the collection has been assessed, there are three possible results:

1. The collection exactly fits the clientele's needs, so no action is required (this is unlikely).

2. Some materials have become worn out or so out of date as to be erroneous or misleading. New discoveries and publications have made old materials out of date, so they must be discarded.

3. Gaps or weaknesses in the collection are revealed, perhaps where materials did not previously exist, but now do. Selection and acquisition must continue in these areas.

Conclusion

The selection and acquisition of materials are very important parts of the school librarian's professional role. The quality of the library's collection largely determines the quality of library service, and so it follows that great care and skill should be employed in building the collection.

References

1. Schools Commission, *Books and Beyond: Guidelines for Library Resource Facilities and Services* (2nd edn, AGPS, Canberra, 1979), p. 36.
2. American Association of School Librarians and Association for Educational Communications and Technology, *Media Programs: District and School* (Chicago, 1975), ch. 6.
3. Canadian School Library Association, *Standards of Library Service for Canadian Schools* (McGraw-Hill Ryerson, Toronto, 1967), p. 52.
4. Azile Wofford, *Book Selection for School Libraries* (H. W. Wilson, New York, 1962), ch. 3.
5. Bro-Dart Foundation, *The Elementary School Library Collection* (12th edn, Williamsport, Pennsylvania, 1979).
6. National Library of Australia, *Australian National Bibliography* (Canberra—weekly, with monthly and annual cumulations); National Library of New Zealand, *New Zealand National Bibliography* (Wellington—monthly, annual cumulations).
7. National Library of Australia, *Australian Books: A Select List of New Publications and Standard Works in Print* (Canberra, 1979).
8. New Zealand Department of Statistics, *New Zealand Official Year Book* (Wellington, 1978).
9. Joyce Nicholson (ed.), *Australian Books in Print* (D. W. Thorpe, Melbourne, 1979).
10. Joyce Nicholson (ed.), *New Zealand Books in Print* (D. W. Thorpe, Melbourne, 1979).
11. Joyce Nicholson (ed.), *Australian Audio Visual Reference Book* (5th edn, D. W. Thorpe, Melbourne, 1979).
12. Library Association of Australia, *The New Classics: A Selection of Award-winning Children's Books* (Sydney, 1975).
13. British Council, *Aids in the Selection of British Books* (London, 1974).
14. Export Booksellers Group of the Booksellers Association of Great Britain and Ireland, *How to Buy British Books* (mimeograph, London, n.d.).
15. John Rowe Townsend, *Written for Children* (Kestrel, Harmondsworth, 1974).
16. Charlotte S. Huck, *Children's Literature in the Elementary School* (3rd edn, Holt, Rinehart & Winston, New York, 1976).
17. Rebecca J. Lukens, *A Critical Handbook of Children's Literature* (Scott, Foresman, Glenview, Ill., 1976).
18. Sheila Egoff, G. T. Stubbs and L. F. Ashley (eds), *Only Connect: Readings on Children's Literature* (Oxford, Toronto, 1969).
19. Virginia Haviland (ed.), *Children and Literature: Views and Reviews* (Scott, Foresman, Glenview, Ill., 1973).

20. Lillian N. Gerhardt, *Issues in Children's Book Selection: A School Library Journal/Library Journal Anthology* (Bowker, New York, 1973).
21. H. M. Saxby, *A History of Australian Children's Literature 1841–1941* (Wentworth, Sydney, 1969);
    H. M. Saxby, *A History of Australian Children's Literature 1941–1970* (Wentworth, Sydney, 1971).
22. School Libraries Section, NSW Division, Library Association of Australia, *Periodicals for School Libraries: A Select Annotated List,* (Sydney, 1975).
23. National Library of Australia, *Australian Public Affairs Information Service* (Canberra).
24. Bibliographic Services, *Guidelines* (Mt Waverley, Vic.).
25. State Library of South Australia, *Pinpointer* (Adelaide).
26. Warren B. Hicks and Alma M. Tillin, *Developing Multi-Media Libraries* (Bowker, New York, 1970), p. 37.
27. Paul McNally, *Non-Book Materials* (Sun Books, Melbourne, 1973), ch. 4.
28. Graeme Foster, Grace Cochrane and Tony Sloane, *Plugs and Bugs on Audio Visual Resources* (Ashton Scholastic, Sydney, 1975).
29. American Association of School Librarians/National Education Association, *The Teachers' Library: How to Organise It and What to Include* (Washington, D.C., 1968).
30. Nancye K. Stanelis, *Resources for Schools: Multicultural Education* (rev. edn, Australian Schools Commission, Adelaide, 1978), p. 7.
31. Stanelis, p. 41.
32. Nancye K. Stanelis, 'Ethnic resources in schools', in *Being Resourceful: Proceedings of the 6th Biennial Conference of the Australian School Library Association* (ASLA, Goulburn, 1978), p. 159.
33. Alex Barlow and Marji Hill, *Black Australia* (Australian Institute of Aboriginal Studies, Canberra, 1978).
34. J. A. Richardson, F. T. Caust and J. A. Hart, *Books for the Retarded Reader* (6th edn, Australian Council for Educational Research, Melbourne, 1977).
35. G. Robert Carlsen, *Books and the Teen-Age Reader* (rev. edn, Bantam, 1971).
36. Margaret Marshall, *Libraries and Literature for Teenagers,* (Deutsch, London, 1975).

Bibliography of general books on selection

Many of the items listed above as references for specific points will also be useful.

BARTLE, RAY. *The School Library: A Guide to Selection, Purchase and Management of Resources.* Schools Commission, Canberra, 1978.
BROADUS, ROBERT N. *Selecting Materials for Libraries.* Wilson, New York, 1973.
CABECEIRAS, JAMES. *The Multi-Media Library.* Academic Press, New York, 1978.
CARTER, M. D., BONK, W. J. AND MAGRILL, R. M. *Building Library Collections.* 4th edn, Scarecrow, Metuchen, N.J., 1974.
DAVIES, RUTH ANN. *The School Library Media Center: A Force for Educational Excellence.* 2nd edn, Bowker, New York, 1974.
FISHER, MARGERY. *Matters of Fact.* Brockhampton, Leicester, 1972.
GAVER, MARY VIRGINIA. *Background Readings in Building Library Collections.* 2 vols. Scarecrow, Metuchen, N.J., 1969.
HICKS, W. B. AND TILLIN, A. M. *Developing Multi-Media Libraries.* Bowker, New York, 1970.
HICKS, W. B. AND TILLIN, A. M. *Managing Multi-Media Libraries.* Bowker, New York, 1977.
HOLLINDALE, PETER. *Choosing Books for Children.* Elek, London, 1974.

HUCK, CHARLOTTE S. *Children's Literature in the Elementary School.* 3rd edn, Holt, Rinehart & Winston, New York, 1976.

PILGRIM, G. H. AND MCALLISTER, M. K. *Books, Young People and Reading Guidance.* 2nd edn, Harper & Row, New York, 1968.

SCHOOLS COMMISSION. *Books and Beyond: Guidelines for Library Resource Facilities and Services.* 2nd edn, AGPS, Canberra, 1979.

SPILLER, DAVID. *Book Selection: An Introduction to Principles and Practice.* Bingley, London, 1971.

WOFFORD, AZILE. *Book Selection for School Libraries.* Wilson, New York, 1962.

CHAPTER 5

Children's Literature
and the School Reading Program

Beryl Turner

'Can Dan fan man . . .
Nan can fan Dan
Nan can pat a cat
Can Nan fan a fat man?'

and on and on, for ten minutes a day, 'in and out of weeks, and almost over a year', a small boy in his fifth year unlocked the mystery of learning to read from these beginnings, quoted above, all the way to page 430, where he was assured that 'he would never again feel bored and unhappy when he was alone, now that he knew how to read'.[1]

And so, from one large book, by a method of teaching reading that deliberately divorces meaning from form (and succeeds admirably), the boy became literate at an early age. The time was soon to come when his silent reading capacity outstripped his parents' slower pace of reading aloud; but still basking in the shared enjoyment of the story, his experience of books took on deeper satisfactions, literary, artistic and emotional. Day by day, his experience of story conventions and structures was reinforced, his eyes receiving an early training in aesthetic appreciation and, in the close, warm, physical contact with the reading adult, strong bonds of affection were cementing the emotional experience of story, until at length he went to school. After these pre-school years of a shared experience of story with a parent, leaning closely, quivering with excitement, alight with joy, tense with suspense, tearful with sorrow, quiet and reflective with satisfaction, this small boy, every day, in and out of weeks and almost over two years, was to plod through the pages of another graded reading scheme with all his class fellows.

Luckily for him, and for other children from bookish environments, a pre-school experience of being taught to read by formal methods, or of learning to read for themselves as some do, is embedded in a rich and pleasurable experience of children's literature, shared with a parent. The parent in turn enjoys the deep satisfaction of a gratifying interaction with the child, an experience that enhances and reinforces the stories and is richly rewarding to parent and child alike. It is in the nature of a total engagement—an engagement of adult and child on more than one level, one with the other, the child interacting with the story and the parent responding to the child's pleasure. It is a situation of warmth and deep involvement and security—a situation in which a child's spiritual, emotional, imaginative and intellectual growth can flourish—a situation encouraging the burgeoning of self-confidence and self-awareness. And there are other bonuses. In Don Holdaway's words, 'the child develops strongly positive associations with the flow of story, the language and with the physical characteristics of the books'.[2]

In this engagement with books, even if they haven't learned to read, the children have absorbed before they reach school an immense amount of the literary experience of the sound of words, of the nonsense and complex rhythms of nursery rhymes, as well as concepts of the alphabet and number and a huge store of story. Likewise, they have been engaged in a lively interpretation of a wide variety of art forms. That they do not fully understand every word they hear, or even every picture they pore over in all the books they experience, does not matter.

'Growing understanding of story comes from an initial grasp of the central meaning,' Holdaway suggests, and 'just as speech develops in an environment which is immensely richer than the immediate needs of the infant, so the orientation to book language develops in an environment of rich exposure beyond immediate needs'.[3] From the wide range of literature for the very young child, children will select favourites which they will demand again and again. Adults frequently find such demands only tiresome, but they represent an important fundamental experience of literary language forms and ideas and emotions. Children need the repeated experience of reinforcement to extract deeper levels of meaning from their story-books. Meaningful repetition in this way, is an important early learning experience.

Children who are already oriented to books when they come to school, arrive with high expectations, in which they should not be disappointed. There are many class teachers in junior primary schools now fully aware of the value of story in the school reading program; and with the appointment of librarians at this level, the classroom experience is richly subsidised by accessible supplies of good books. In schools where such conditions exist, where teachers and librarians alike are knowledgeable about books, are themselves eager 'explorers' of the huge range of all that is now offering, and are sensitively engaged in children's responses to books, children will be strongly motivated to learn and will be encouraged to extend and strengthen and reinforce earlier experiences with books. Reading research since World War II amply supports the conclusion, obvious enough, that children who come from homes where reading is valued are much more strongly motivated to become committed readers than those from an environment devoid of books and where reading is not a source of pleasure and enrichment.[4]

The implications seem clear. The conditions of the bookish home should be replicated in the school. Two important factors thus emerge: engagement and environment. 'The school has a responsibility not only to teach reading but also to create an environment that will make children want to read and will enable them to discover the excitement of reading', say the writers of *Reading Matters*.[5]

The key people in creating this environment are the class teacher and the school librarian. In the wings stand a number of others in strongly supportive roles: the parents, the school administrators, and the children's librarian of any local public library; the parents acting as important inspirational models and 'reinforcers', the school administrators facilitating the work of the staff, and the public librarian providing that important source of books beyond the school gates. (Children should be introduced to their public library as soon as possible; it is salutary to remember that school library facilities are generally unavailable for up to three months of the year.)

The present scene

Joan Zahnleiter makes a forceful plea for a central place for children's literature in the teaching of reading, and she blames the over-reliance on the graded reader, with its carefully controlled vocabulary and grammatical syntax, for the substantial failure rate in creating readers and even for producing illiterates.[6] The paucity of content of the graded reader, and its thin engagement with any emotional experience, fails to arouse a child's interest in story and, it follows, in reading. Unfortunately, many teachers have lost sight of the purpose of teaching decoding skills beyond the requirements of literacy and have failed to recognise that there is no better way to reinforce these skills than by reading, which in turn is strengthened and enriched from the whole spread of the language arts—creative self-expression in writing, in drama, dance, song, poetry and art activities.

Reading in school has too often become distasteful, disagreeable and difficult 'work' for many children. For teachers, on the other hand, a schematised system of instruction is 'safe', comfortable and easy to work with. (For publishers, the modern reading kit is a bonanza.) But schemes that have clearly discernible accountability ratings built into them introduce a competitive element which only rewards the successful and undermines the failures. That schemes based on phonetic, word recognition, and linguistic methods are successful in the teaching of reading is undeniable. We can support their claims in many instances, not the least of which is the case of the four-year-old quoted above; such children will become able readers, if they are not so baffled and frustrated by the daily drill of the graded reader that they become members of the 'submerged 60 per cent', as Aidan Chambers described those who become technically literate but remain reluctant to read.[7] As for the outright failures, their prospects are frightening. The personal and social and economic cost of failure in a task central to living in our society is immense. The outward and visible signs of a profound inner disruption, springing out of a severely damaged self-image, are often expressed in destructive acts of criminal violence. Moreover, this social resentment is often directed against the institution that helped to produce it—the school. The modern young criminal is, very often, functionally illiterate; and to function in a fully human way in a modern complex society, one must be literate.

So, in the face of our highly visible school failures, the disturbed personality, the social misfit, the juvenile delinquent, it's 'back to basics' the critics cry with a crack of political whips. Yet, if teachers have not been using basic methods to teach the language arts these many years, it is hard to imagine anything more basic than the use of carefully graded reading schemes, laced with comprehension exercises. Since universal literacy has been required by law for the past century in the western world, the teaching of reading has been subjected to more critical evaluation and experimentation than any other in the school curriculum. Obviously, there are no glib solutions to a problem of immense complexity.

This complexity lies in the nature of our clients, a great seething mass of individuals at varying levels of development and achievement. Our lack of success results partly from a failure to recognise the variation in developmental levels, partly from an over-emphasis on cognitive achievement (which is easy to measure) to the neglect of affective responses (which resist measurement), partly because we see the child as a passive recipient of a system, and partly from a failure to set up the child's own 'powerful energy field'.

Both Zahnleiter and Holdaway see the task of learning to read as very largely self-directed—the teacher, the librarian and the parent acting as catalysts between the child and books. They see children's literature as the core of the reading program, and maintain this with energetic argument and, in Holdaway's case, a carefully detailed approach to the teaching of reading in a manner that is demonstrably exciting.

It is certain that were we to succumb to the clamorous cries of getting back to basics, we should undoubtedly find ourselves more and more tightly enmeshed in deadening programs of vocabulary accountability at the rate of ten to twenty words a week, words hardly won, easily lost. 'Without the stimulus of a lively literature program,' Joan Zahnleiter stoutly declares, 'the acquiring of reading skills becomes just meaningless drudgery. To make reading a more enjoyable experience', she suggests 'that we capture the interest of children by a shift of emphasis from "drills of skills" to the real world of reading so that children's literature has the central role in the teaching of reading, a role that has been neglected for too long. By this means, children will come to see real purpose in reading.'[8]

This is no counsel of anarchy. The busy classroom teacher is glad of guidance based on a sound theoretical approach, but the more pressure there is on teachers to teach 'basics', the more tempting it is to rely on elaborately structured packaged schemes to the exclusion of all other reading experiences. They can be voracious consumers of time and energy.

Though there are significant exceptions to the predictable failure of writers in creating interesting stories in the strait-jacket of controlled vocabulary, length and syntax, the vast output of core reading texts and supplementary readers is so vapid and inane, so lacking in sparkle and fun, that it is small wonder so many children have failed to find any joy or personal meaning in learning to read. While acknowledging that the jaunty, cheerful doggerel of Dr Seuss' *Beginner Books* and contributions to like series with controlled vocabulary by writers and artists of real distinction (such as Else Minarik, Maurice Sendak and Arnold Lobel) have leavened the pervading dreariness of books for the child learner, it has taken reading theorists and practitioners of Don Holdaway's calibre to create schemes of teaching reading with children's literature at the core.

That children's literature has been undervalued in the school reading program is due to a number of factors that originate in public attitudes towards reading. One is obvious. With the lack of a dense network of public libraries in many places, books have been inaccessible, except from a distant central source. It takes the determined and committed reader to tackle this formidable barrier. A source of books has to be at hand. Like a heavy piece of kitchen equipment for the home cook, libraries have to be accessible or they will not be used. The direct outcome of this lack is that reading itself will be undervalued in the community, and teachers are blamed. Faced with school entrants to whom books and reading are new experiences, and who have to be motivated to learn what can become a difficult task in decoding print, they have a formidable program in front of them.

Another factor that has prevented the full acceptance of children's literature in the reading program is a lingering attitude towards fiction, a hangover from the nineteenth century, when the reading of novels, especially by young women, was as severely castigated as the modern use of marijuana. Though few would now impute moral rot to the reading of fiction, it is still often seen as frivolous, a waste of time or peripheral to real 'work'.

In the classroom, teachers are often inclined to *reward* able children who finish their 'work' early by allowing them to 'read a book', thus encouraging them to get even better at reading, while the slower and less able, who need the practice, get left further behind. Moreover, fiction is often seen as a frivolous and feminine activity, so that boys find it hard to accept themselves as readers. And because fiction is thus underrated, girls' pleasure in reading, particularly grown-up 'girls', can degenerate into a guilty self-indulgence in best-sellers.

This last group, fortified by popular acclaim and reassured in their indisputable claims to be readers, are quick to defend themselves, particularly if they happen to be teachers. 'They are readers, aren't they?' So, it 'doesn't matter what children read so long as they learn to read. Why make all this fuss about children's literature? What's wrong with Blyton or Biggles, or Dahl? Children enjoy them and everyone knows that children learn to read quicker if they enjoy their stories—and that is our main concern.'

Granted that enjoyment is essential to the task of learning to read, the attitudes expressed in these remarks are shallow. They are about as responsible as saying that it doesn't matter where you go as long as you learn to walk. They are also rather smugly self-justifying. They betray the speakers' own value-systems and spring from an ignorance of the range and variety of children's literature, of its function in children's lives, of the insights it offers to the responsive reader, child and adult alike, of its imaginative stimulus and of the sheer craft of the distinguished writer and artist working for children. In the misunderstanding of the nature of enjoyment, of its levels and its variety, the teacher who insists that it doesn't matter what children read is 'short-changing' the child. The child reared on best-sellers to the *exclusion* of better-quality literature will almost certainly grow up to be a reader of best-sellers, and little else; and there is little in this type of reading to stir the mud of conventional ideas. The most it can offer is the relief of light entertainment and escape from a drab world, and this is a limited view of reading.

In the face of this entrenched opposition to children's literature, by the lay public and many teachers alike, its acceptance and recognition of its value in school reading programs crawls on very slowly, despite its energetic promotion as an art form since the 1920s. Writers, critics, responsible publishers, librarians, and teachers of children's literature have all been forced into defensive positions, being variously accused of preoccupation with trivia (when are you going to write a real book?) or, paradoxically, of elitism (children will not read literary prize-winners).

To counter the common belief that literature is 'difficult' and will fail to engage the interest of the 'average' reader is a challenge for the school librarian—indeed, one of the most important to be countered.

Educational role of the librarian

One of the main roles of the school librarian is that of a reading consultant, working in close collaboration with the classroom teacher and specialist staff. In essence this is an educational role, which extends beyond the professional staff to parents and the wider public and, of course, to children.

To fulfil this role adequately, the school librarian, in common with the rest of the school professional staff, must have a thorough knowledge of literature and other related materials such as films and audio-tapes. Let it be noted here that the work of the school librarian will be seriously undermined without the full support of the class teacher. All should have a professional commitment to reading, not simply to keep themselves informed of new developments in reading research or to keep abreast with children's books (important as these tasks are), but to be seen as models for children to emulate. If children are to see the activity of reading as well worthwhile, then they must be encouraged by the sight of adults reading. They will also be encouraged to read those children's books whose borrowing cards reveal the name of a teacher who has read them. Though the motivation for the children to read them too may be complex, a teacher's silent recommendation is often taken up, particularly of course, if that teacher has won the children's confidence.

In any event, the act of sharing the pleasure of books with children, listening to their opinion of them, arguing about them, discussing them, betokens an engagement, an involvement, of the utmost importance in promoting a love of reading. The school should therefore create the time and the space for recreational reading. The schools that put aside half an hour at least several times a week, if not daily, for this purpose report a marked increase in interest and substantial gains in reading achievement. Many children's home environments do not encourage reading in any sense. They are often noisy, crowded, dominated by the television set, perhaps even quarrelsome and with non-reading parents.

The parents' role

Many parents feel absolved from taking any responsibility for their children's education. The librarian (and the teaching staff) should take action in impressing on parents the importance of their role as educators. The school can perform a very important socialising role in breaking down the isolation of non-English speaking parents, particularly the house-bound women, by involving them in their children's lives at school, by sending home stories in their own language (or, for that matter, in English to help the parent, who may also be learning to read), and inviting them to the school to take part in school activities by telling stories perhaps or contributing in other ways to the enrichment of the story experience.

The librarian should grasp at opportunities to present books to parents and to share the pleasures of stories at parent-teacher gatherings. Likewise an enthusiastic promotion of new books, in the staffroom, will contribute towards the creation of a school environment conducive to reading.

Enrichment activities with books

The school reading program lends itself to many extensions of activities associated with books. These should not be arid comprehension exercises, nor should they be obligatory for every story shared with the children in, say, the story-telling session. Some stories should be left to simmer in the mind as a private experience. The widely read teacher and librarian, working closely with children, knowing their special interests, their social background and their achievement and alert to the qualities inherent in a story, will be able to interpret children's responses.

On the other hand, a story may be enriched for children through the corporate experience of dramatising it; scripting, re-enacting or miming it, or using puppets, masks or costume, can be an extraordinarily satisfying, meaningful and rewarding exercise. Not so long ago in a local country town, a school librarian involved a whole school in a 'hobbit' experience in which, to everyone's keen enjoyment, the parents also participated. Yet another librarian, using hand puppets, won the many reluctant readers in the school over to the enjoyment of story. By removing herself from a direct confrontation with the children and transferring their attention to the puppet figures, free from threat, she gradually built up pleasure in story and increased their span of attention so that in time they were able to listen without always needing 'props'. In this way, she had restored their confidence in an adult figure previously associated with reading failure.

Children brought together in the corporate experience of story, in whatever form it may take—story-telling, story-reading, watching a film or television version of a story, group discussion, creating a mural, or dramatising it—are being socialised in a special way. The common experience of shared pleasure in story can create a strong bonding of individuals within the group. It can also help the reading program to become purposive. A newcomer to a class of ten-year-olds, and a reluctant reader, was warned in an appeal to the teacher by his classmates that he would have to become a reader, 'because we are a reading class'.

Enrichment activities with books recreate stories in a very special way. Children become not simply receptors but creators; and in being remembered, recalled and interpreted, stories become embedded in the mind. 'It is important', say the writers of *Reading Matters*, 'not to *force* [my italics] response upon the children in any way that destroys the inner satisfactions to be gained from the stories.' 'The most important response anyone can make to a story is talking about it, and for many children, this means telling it,' they add (perhaps controversially), but we can agree with them, when they would hold the teacher (and, by implication, the librarian) responsible for developing discrimination and encouraging thoughtful reasoned responses.[9]

The classroom practice of requiring regular formal book reports is to be condemned, as it can cause unproductive anxiety for children; but as a discipline for the librarian and teacher, it has much to recommend it. The act of assessing a book and recording that assessment in a short annotation on cards (or in other flexible manner) reinforces one's impression of it, and is at once a valuable aid to memory and a resource. In due course, it will lead to a solid foundation of knowledge about children's literature. Generally helpful hints for enriching the story experience will be found in references listed at the close of this chapter.[10]

Accessibility of books: Creation of the environment

Just as books and library services need to be freely available in the wider community in order to create readers, so do library services within the school. For the support of the reading program and the curriculum, the environment needs to be saturated with books of all kinds, fiction and non-fiction. In close co-operation with the class teacher, the librarian should arrange a constant interchange of books between classroom and library. One authority would recommend a classroom core collection of ten books per child to cater for the wide range of reading ability to be found in any class.[11] Another mentions a matter of 200 to 300 titles in paperback, with frequently five or six copies of the same title for in-depth discussion.[12] Yet another emphasises the need for genuine choice and estimates that there should be three times as many books as members of the class.[13] Charlotte Huck reports that children in classrooms containing attractive book collections read 50 per cent more books than children in the same school without such collections.[14] 'There should be no argument,' she says, 'as to whether to have a classroom collection of books or a library media center; both are necessary. Children should have immediate access to books wherever, whenever they need them.'

Children also need to know where to find books outside the school, and should be introduced to their nearest public library as soon as possible. It has been pointed out that school facilities, except in the case of school/community libraries, are not available after hours or during vacations. A school bookshop is another way to encourage reading. Ownership of books acknowledges the value of books and allows the child to build up a collection of favourites which can be read and re-read again and again. A point worth making here is that children should be given many opportunities to satisfy cravings for favourite stories, not only because it allows them to absorb the conventions of story but, perhaps more importantly, because the desire to have things repeated enables children to *grasp* and *understand* problems. For these favourite stories frequently represent some problem existing in the children's own minds; by listening to the story over and over again, they come to understand their own problems and are better able to deal with them. So, following the example of the bookish home, the school environment should be saturated with books.

Need for guidance

But young readers left to themselves, even surrounded by books, will not necessarily be inspired to read. They may even lose an affection for books and a desire to read because of unsuitable choices. If books are too hard, or do not catch their interest, they will make only half-hearted attempts to get beyond the first chapter. Soon they lose confidence in their ability to choose books for themselves and are on their way to becoming reluctant readers. Therefore, to match children to books, teachers and librarians will need to promote books and offer guidance, to answer their needs or stimulate their interest. The display of new books or books on various topics or by certain authors, the use of audio-tapes to introduce books, visits from authors and experts in any given field can inspire reading interests and may even set in motion a life-long career.

But valuable and necessary as these techniques of reading guidance are, the prime impulse must come from the teacher and the librarian whose power to generate enthusiasm for reading is vital. And to press home this point, once again, I cannot emphasise strongly enough that everyone concerned about children's reading must read books written for children. Would that there was equal delight in every obligatory task! Every adult coming freshly to children's books will be richly rewarded for the pleasures, the insights into child behaviour, and the concern with universal themes of great importance, not to mention the satisfactions arising from lively responses from children in an atmosphere of mutual enjoyment. This close engagement of teacher, librarian (and parent) with children and their books will only work in an environment saturated with books, in which the adults are to be seen as catalysts between children and their books.

Guidance in reading should not stop with the end of school days. It should be a function of every public library service to bring books serving many needs to the notice of their readers. In areas devoid of this help, adult readers, no matter how rich an experience of literature they have had at school, commonly degenerate to the level of the best-seller whose popular qualities are noisy and highly visible at every sales outlet.

The role of librarian (*and* teacher, for these two professionals must work in tandem) in developing the school reading program is clear: to become committed and enthusiastic readers, to convey this enthusiasm to colleagues and children, and to create an environment conducive to all the enjoyment and intellectual and emotional satisfactions to be found in books.

The role of children's literature

What is the function of literature in the lives of children? How does it work? What value or effect does reading literature have? Why bother to read literature at all with so many new developments of modern media to provide information and entertainment, from a flourishing newspaper and magazine trade to the compulsive attraction of television? What kind of books appeal to children? What are children's needs and interests which may be met in literature and so stimulate a desire to read?

All these questions raise theoretical considerations which, such is the nature of our audience, must remain unproven. There have been many surveys of reading interests which attempt to answer, ultimately, the question of what books will engage the interest of children to their advantage; although these findings are illuminating, we must remember that they tend to be influenced by their time and place of enquiry.

Findings about interests relating to sex roles, for instance, may be different in the future from what they are now, with the spotlight on the role of women in our society. Significant differences emerge from various national surveys from one country to another. Nevertheless trends become visible and broad assumptions relating to the child's development towards maturity may be made. Studies of interests in the first years of school in ten different countries revealed more common interests than differences.[15] Nevertheless, what emerged most significantly from a recent intensive British survey of the voluntary reading of 10 to 15-year-olds was the enormous variety of children's individual choices and preferences.[16]

Reading interests

If we first examine reading interests, the value of children's literature will, I hope, emerge. Let us look first at children in their situation. There they are, small, surrounded by towering adults, some of whom offer them comfort, kindness and security while others may be full of threat and danger and spell insecurity. Jostling with peers at home, in the neighbourhood and at school, the child has some formidable tasks to accomplish. These tasks are both affective and cognitive, and relate to needs and interests, at successive levels. In their drive towards maturity, children need to develop a self-awareness and self-respect; they need to gain confidence in their strengths, while acknowledging weaknesses and accepting just criticism; they need to learn how to act responsibly and to respond sensitively to their fellows; they need to learn to accommodate to a wide range of individual and idiosyncratic personalities, and yet to choose friends who will be both supportive and enriching and loyal. In an advance on a broad front, these achievements, deeply emotional in nature and closely linked to intellectual achievement, can nevertheless receive severe checks and disturbances.

Young children on arrival at school have already been strongly conditioned by pre-school experience, tempered by their unique personalities. Accordingly, they will find the wider school environment sometimes fearful, often exciting. They will be lightly engaged, such is their ego-centricity, in making new relationships which may be very shifting in nature. They will be exposed to the raw experience of the playground where they will encounter aggressive individuals clustering in groups, and ranged against them. How will they survive? Will they join the bullies, or will they suffer the indignities inflicted on them, or will they be forced to compromise?

And within the school walls, what then? Attitudes to authority will be already conditioned in the pre-school experience. Will the child be trusting, apprehensive or looking for reassurance? Will feelings of insecurity in new surroundings be reinforced or lightened? How confident is this child who stares solemnly on a new world? How fearful that one? How ingratiating that other, who has learned that this is the best way to please those threatening adults or giants?

Here then we see our child at the outset of a ten-year journey, at its shortest. How can we satisfy the needs of this child through literature, which all would agree is most effective and powerful when it touches the inner emotional life of the child. Not, it is certain, by pallid stories about Dick and Dora, or Janet and John acting out a puppet-like existence in a totally alien environment. Rather it will be through the strong sprung rhythms of the nursery rhyme, the rugged, devious, knavish or courtly, kindly, courageous human behaviour met within the traditional tale or in those stories which echo a child's own experience and tune in to the inner life of 'a lucky boy'.[17]

Literature, let us remind ourselves, is experience of life, explored, shaped, recreated and dramatised in story. And its functions are manifold, from simple pleasure in story for its own sake to a communication much more deeply therapeutic. Richard Hughes hit on a very important principle here, children's own experience fantasied in story.[18] His experience of storyteller to war-time evacuees in Wales led him to the recognition that the 'ingredients' they asked for, by his invitation, in their stories (a character, an object, a cat, a Prime Minister, a lobster pot) recalled the symbols of play-therapy. He describes his stories as rhetoric rather than literature, reminding us that it is the function of rhetoric to reflect quite as much of the listener's mind as of the speaker's. 'Could this explain', he says, 'the intense concentration and satisfaction, the evident benefit received with which a child may listen to a story, however outdated and unfamiliar its background? Differences of social experience are superficial, affecting at most the stage properties of a story,' he continues, 'its power to hold the child lies deeper, in its empathy with those deep emotional disturbances all childhood is heir to; an empathy only communicable at the fantasy level'.

Taking a cue from Richard Hughes, we might consider that all literature is, in a sense, therapeutic for those in whom it strikes a responsive chord, a notion that is expressed in bibliotherapy. That one of the functions of literature is to offer solace and comfort and reassurance is widely acclaimed, even if it is no more than confirming one's own humanity. Furthermore—as Aidan Chambers would state it—literature clarifies myself to myself; it explores the diversity of human experience; through literature we may find out what it might be like to suffer war or a bush-fire or reach an understanding of many different modes of behaviour; literature may challenge ingrained attitudes or prejudices. Chambers sums up his statement with the remark that literature does not program us like robots. It brings us to self-awareness, and becoming aware, we are in action.[19]

Some suggestions
From the outset, there are two courses to follow as children acquire skills in reading: namely, select a wide variety of stories to read and tell to children; and provide a rich store of accessible supplementary reading for the child's independent reading.

The first, inevitably, will include stories that will surpass the child's active control of language, in vocabulary and complexity of sentence structure. There is no better way to catch the rhythms and structuring of prose than through the spoken voice. Story-telling or reading aloud by the librarian or class teacher should be practised throughout the primary school. Indeed it makes good sense at every educational stage from school beginners to tertiary level. The slower pace of reading aloud, moreover, allows listeners to grasp the story's meaning. Many educators have no doubt that good prose (or poetry) read aloud has a direct effect on the listeners' own written and spoken language. They are also learning the conventions of story and taking the first steps in becoming critical readers.

Literature offers many opportunities for language play which may range from nursery rhymes for the younger child, nonsense verse and riddles for 6 to 8-year-olds, to the witty use of puns by a writer of William Mayne's calibre for older children.

Researchers, too many to mention individually, confirm that fairy tales and fantasies are favourites from an early age. Fairy tales come under fire from time to time, but, as mentioned earlier, they are the stuff of life. They appear singly in lavish picture-book form for the younger child or in anthologies of retellings for the older reader. Tales from the collections of Perrault and Grimm, Hans Andersen's fairy tales, Joseph Jacobs' retellings of English folktales, and many others from the Norse, Celtic, Asian, North American and Pacific story of tradition, are all now available in handsome editions. The peak of interest in the fairy tale is around eight years.[20] Myths, legends and hero tales for older children are likewise available in attractive and well-told versions. The Greek myths, for instance, have been collected and retold in two spectacular books by Edward Blishen and Leon Garfield and illustrated most fittingly by Charles Keeping.[21]

The child deprived of this 'well of story' is deprived indeed. For the newly independent reader of 7 to 10 years, needing much practice in reading, the fairy tale is ideal. It is short and its conventions make for a high degree of predictability that in turn makes for easy reading.

Fantasy, a strongly developed form of children's literature, ranges all the way from Maurice Sendak's celebrated book *Where the Wild Things Are* for 4 to 6-year-olds, to Ursula Le Guin's trilogy based on *The Wizard of Earthsea* for readers of 11 upwards. It is a particularly rich vein of fictional narrative at which British writers excel.

Realistic stories also take their place in the school literature program. For younger children, they are frequently disguised by anthropomorphic treatment—for example, in Beatrix Potter's tales or the many stories about machines, trains, dolls or even houses. As children mature, animal stories take on a greater measure of realism in which the animal is portrayed interacting with its environment or with man. The miniaturisation of people in the form of dolls or animals or 'borrowers' has an important function in at once reducing the complexity and size of adults to a more manageable state for children, and distancing figures of potential threat. Seen through the wrong end of a telescope, so to speak, they are too tiny to be more than amusing.

Writers for young children have responded to the need for consolation children may find in their literature. Obsessive fears are common. Fear of the dark associated with wild animals, monsters and nameless beings, a fear of loud noises and of things that jump out at you have been reduced for children by stories about friendly ghosts, or more dramatically, in a Western Woods film, *Alexander and the Car with the Missing Headlight* in which a loudly barking dog plays a role. Other fears are of a more ordinary nature: fear of school and authoritarian figures—teachers and policemen, for example.

Philippa Pearce has a story about a lion that accompanies a child to school until there is no longer any need for it[22] and Anne Barrett has the same idea for *Midway*, a book for 10 and over. Hospitalisation has its terrors for many people, let alone for the young child, for whom Ludwig Bemelman's *Madeline* may make a hospital episode a dramatic, exciting and even enviable experience.

Children need stories of daring at any age, about adventures and deeds they would like to be capable of themselves. Some writers supply this need by supplying alter egos, as Philippa Pearce has in her leonine companion, but the more common type is the adventure, the thriller or even the detective story, for which *Emil and the Detectives* by Erich Kästner became the prototype in the 1930s.

Independent readers of from 7 or 8 years onward enjoy reading about the adventures of the same groups of children (or animals or little people) and there is ample opportunity for this, without resorting to loudly acclaimed popular writers of inferior quality. Tove Jansson's *Moomin-troll* books, C. S. Lewis' *Narnia Tales*, Alfred Proysen's *Mrs Pepperpot* stories, Norman Juster's *Professor Branestawm*'s adventures are only a few of the many good fictional series in print.

Though much more remains to be said about the kinds of literature available to children, librarians have access to many sources of information from the wide range of critical reviewing periodicals, fictional bibliographies on genres such as historical fiction, and local children's library services.

It is the librarian's special task to keep the classroom teacher informed from such sources; but let it be said once again, each should have a personal commitment to the *reading* of children's literature. There are many skills in librarianship and in the teaching of reading, but, above all, both depend on those human qualities which will never be replaced by a computer.

Appendix: Children's literature periodicals

The following periodicals are deserving of attention for articles on a variety of topics, the work of authors and artists and reviews of current books.

Australian education departments (School Library Branches) publications:
All States produce their own journals containing articles ranging from practical advice to studies of authors' work, extension activities with books and reviews. Examples of these publications are:

> *Review* (4 issues p.a.; 1973–), South Australian Education Department, School Libraries Branch. News of regular and in-service courses, annotated subject bibliographies, practical articles, reviews with full cataloguing, and classification information for books at all levels to school-leaving age, fiction and non-fiction.

> *Review Bulletin* (4 issues p.a., currently reduced to 3 issues p.a.; 1969–), Victorian Education Department. Comprehensive, quality grading symbols including a 'not recommended' category, reviews only.

> *School Library Bulletin* (3 issues p.a.; 1969–), Victorian Education Department. News of local library activities, practical articles, Australian Book of the Year judge's reports, notes on in-service programs and much else.

> *Appraisal* (3 issues p.a.; 1967–), U.S.A. Reviews science books contributed jointly by children's librarians and science specialists, thus providing two reviews for each book. Alphabetical arrangement by author, age and quality gradings.

> *Bookbird* (4 issues p.a.; 1963–), edited from Vienna. International digest of news about authors, prizes, conferences, problems of juvenile reading not easily obtainable elsewhere.

> *Books in School* (2 issues p.a., April and December; 1977–), United Kingdom Reading Association. A useful annotated list of fiction and non-fiction for all school levels. Short lists of books on adult literacy and apparatus, games and kits are an innovation. Indexed by author, title and subject. Publishing difficulties appear to be threatening its existence.

> Librarians should also be aware of reviewing coverage in other reading association publications; for example, *Language Arts* (U.S.A.) and *Australian Journal of Reading*.

> *Bulletin of the Center for Children's Books* (11 issues p.a.; 1945–), Graduate Library School of the University of Chicago. Book reviews only. Quality

assessments by symbol and grades indicated for reading range. Geared to American needs but highly recommended for its sound, critical and perceptive reviewing.

Canadian Children's Literature (usually 3 issues p.a.; 1975–). Principally concerned with own national literature. Articles with local themes. Reviews.

Children's Literature (1 issue p.a.; 1972–), formerly subtitled 'The great excluded', this annual volume of critical papers from the English Department of the University of Connecticut is about to enter the Ivy League; from vol. 8 on, it is to be published by Yale University Press. Lists notable dissertations and including notes on contributors. A useful source of criticism.

Children's Literature Abstracts (4 issues p.a.; 1973–), Children's Libraries Section of the International Federation of Library Associations. Abstracts periodical articles prepared by an international panel.

Children's Literature Association (1972–), year book of the New Zealand association. Contains reports of meetings and conferences, articles, lists of current international awards and reviews of N.Z. publications.

Children's Literature in Education (4 issues p.a.; 1970–), originated from papers delivered by writers, critics, editors and publishers at the annual conference held at Exeter, England, in 1970; the editorship extended to America and Australia now draws on a wider range of critical opinion. Of high standard and among the best in the field.

Growing Point (6 issues p.a.; 1962–), U.K. Only periodical in the field produced by a single editor, Margery Fisher, distinguished critic of children's literature. Notable for the quality of its reviewing. Special review to a single book per issue. Other reviews grouped under topic headings. Useful list of reminders of past publications under topic headings. Reduced from 9 issues p.a., but still excellent value. Warmly recommended.

Horn Book Magazine (6 issues p.a.; 1924–), U.S.A., subtitled 'About books for children and young adults'. Contains articles, reviews, grouped under form headings (for example, poetry, audio-visual) and age levels; current news on forthcoming conferences and other items; and special sections on science books, and adult books of interest to adolescents. Newbery and Caldecott acceptance speeches. Enjoys long-standing prestige.

Junior Bookshelf (6 issues p.a.; 1936–), U.K. Reviews grouped under headings: for librarians; picture books; children under ten; ten to fourteen; intermediate books for adolescents; as well as articles, contributed by specialists. Longest unbroken record in U.K. field. Geared primarily to public library use, but of interest to schools. (Similar in intent to its American counterpart, the *Horn Book*, but not so wide ranging in its scope or comment).

Phaedrus (2 issues p.a.; 1973/1974–), U.S.A. International coverage of research in children's literature and publishing. Each issue generally thematic; for example, periodicals, antiquarian bookselling, television, national literatures.

Reading Time (4 issues p.a.; 1957–), the organ of the Children's Book Council of Australia. Primarily a reviewing journal with special attention to Australian and New Zealand publications. Covers anthologies and non-fiction, and includes articles and judges' reports on awards. Like the *Horn Book* publishes credentials of reviewers on its panel.

School Librarian (4 issues p.a.; 1937–), U.K. Articles, author interviews, and commentary, reviews, grouped by age and topic. Good for all ages, is especially tailored to students advancing to English A levels.

School Library Journal (9 issues p.a.; 1954–), U.S.A. International and home news snippets, discussion forum, sections on professional reading, buyers' guides (local interest), book reviews graded by class from elementary to adolescent level, section on adult books for young adults. Critical reviewing of uneven quality by school librarians.

Signal (3 issues p.a.; 1970–), U.K., subtitled 'Approaches to children's books'. This journal provides articles on and by authors, considers the current trends in both England and America and runs a critical correspondence between editor Nancy Chambers and writer and critic Lance Salway on recent readings. Of interest to researcher, essayist and browser alike. Has recently instituted own poetry award and consequently promises a lively debating ground here.

Society for Mass Media and Resource Technology (SMMART), (4 issues p.a.; 1971–), Adelaide, South Australia. This journal draws on the local scene, but also attracts contributions from other sources on practical matters of interest to school librarians; occasional literary articles and reviews are featured. Indexed every 4 issues.

Teacher Librarian (4 issues p.a.; 1965–), this bulletin of the New South Wales School Library Association is local in its scope and endeavour. Contains practical articles, literary assessments, reviews, and news of meetings and conferences.

Times Literary Supplement: Children's Books Section (special supplement presently issued 3 or 4 times p.a. as part of the *TLS*; 1902–), U.K. Contains long, well-informed articles, as well as reviews of books grouped under subject headings with illuminating introductory comment, o.p. during 1978.

Top of the News (4 issues p.a.; 1946–), a specialist publication of the American Library Association (Children's and Young Adults' Services Divisions). Newsy and stimulating. Reflects ferment of American enquiry into current scene. Newsletter announces dates of conferences, awards functions, lists books considered for awards, reports on current issues, and often runs a series of articles on a given subject of practical concern to the librarian (for example, book reviewing).

Wilson Library Bulletin (10 issues p.a.; 1914–), U.S.A. The October issue is devoted to children's literature, with a guest editor; articles in this special issue are usually on a given theme, by experts (for example, picture books, antiquarian books). Also includes news and reviews.

References
1. Leonard Bloomfield and C. Barnhart, *Let's Read* (Wayne State University Press, Detroit, 1961).
2. Don Holdaway, *The Foundations of Literacy* (Ashton Scholastic, Sydney, 1979), p. 40.
3. Holdaway, p. 40.
4. Frank Whitehead and others, *Children and Their Books* (Macmillan, London, 1977), p. 275.
5. Moira McKenzie and Aidan Warlow, *Reading Matters* (Hodder & Stoughton, in association with Inner London Education Authority, London, 1977), p. 9.
6. Joan Zahnleiter, *Children's Literacy and Children's Literature* (Kelvin Grove College Monograph vol. 4, no. 2) (Kelvin Grove College of Advanced Education, Brisbane, 1979).
7. Aidan Chambers, *The Reluctant Reader* (Pergamon, Oxford, 1969).
8. Zahnleiter, p. 4.
9. McKenzie and Warlow, p. 25.
10. *Happily Ever After: Ideas for Bringing Books and Children Together* (Education Department of Victoria, Guide no. 3, n.d.);
Charlotte Huck, *Children's Literature in the Elementary School* (3rd edn, Holt, Rinehart & Winston, New York, 1976);
Terry D. Johnson, 'Presenting literature to children', *Children's Literature in Education* 10, 1, 32 (1979), 35–43;
Sam Leaton Sebesta and William J. Iverson, *Literature for Thursday's Child* (Science Research Associates, Chicago, 1975).
11. McKenzie and Warlow, p. 27.
12. Huck, p. 594.
13. Whitehead, p. 287.
14. M. Ann Heibreder, 'Research needed in the fields of reading and communications', *Library Trends*, 22 (October 1973), 4; quoted in Huck, p. 594.
15. H. Alan Robinson and others, 'Expressed reading interests of young children: an international study'. Paper presented at the 5th International Reading Association World Congress on Reading held in Vienna, 12–14 August 1974 (ED 096 614).
16. Whitehead, p. 287.
17. Philippa Pearce, 'Lucky boy', in *What the Neighbours Did and Other Stories* (Longman Young Books, London, 1972).
18. Richard Hughes, *Times Literary Supplement*, 15 July 1977, p. 858.
19. Aidan Chambers, *Introducing Books to Children* (Heinemann Educational Books, London, 1973).
20. F. André Favat, *Child and Tale* (National Council of Teachers of English, Urbana, Ill., 1977, Research report 19).
21. Leon Garfield and Edward Blishen, *The God Beneath the Sea* (Longmans, London, 1970); and *The Golden Shadow* (Longman Young Books, 1973).
22. Philippa Pearce, 'Lion at school', in Sara and Stephen Corrin (eds), *Stories for Five Year Olds* (Faber, London, 1973).

CHAPTER 6

Reference Work
in the School Library

Maureen Nimon

Common sense makes evident that within the confines of one small chapter the reader will not find all the knowledge needed to establish and run a reference service in a school library. In seeking to introduce the reader to the topic, this chapter will concentrate on the aspects of reference service applicable to the school environment, specifically at a practical level, rather than a theoretical level. These limitations require that it be read in conjunction with standard works, and not only texts devoted to school resource centres such as Davies[1] but, equally important, works such as those by Cheney[2], Wynar[3] and Katz[4], the scope of which embraces reference services throughout the library profession. This requirement stems not only from the limitations of this chapter, but more importantly, from the role of the school librarian in providing a reference service in a school.

Such a service is in many ways highly specialised, in some instances even unique. Though the education of library users legitimately concerns all librarians, no other group is vested with such direct and full responsibility for the education of their clientele in information retrieval, evaluation and application. To recognise and meet the priorities of their own reference service, school librarians must view those priorities within a broad perspective of reference service in many other types of libraries, particularly other libraries within the community that they may be expected to call upon or co-operate with in meeting the informational needs of their clients.

What is reference work?

In a school library, reference work is inextricably interwoven with every other strand of library service. Nevertheless, its central importance is clear, when one appreciates that reference work is a service in which the librarian comes face to face with clients' requests and is called upon to meet those requests. It is towards the provision of this service that all other professional activities of the school librarian are directed, and it is the point at which one's competence is tested. Should clients be disappointed in the handling of their queries, their reluctance to ask again or even to come back to the library will be increased in a manner proportionate to their dissatisfaction. Only the responsibilities of reader guidance and the fostering of students' reading habits compete with reference work as being significant in these crucial ways.

Reference work is the provision of information both on request and to meet an anticipated need. As school libraries exist to provide the learning materials by which the objectives of school curricula may be met, school librarians will be chiefly judged by how successful they are in satisfying the queries of staff and students stimulated by curricula. In primary schools, the concern of teaching staff to develop children's reading ability may demand that librarians give a substantial or even major part of their time to all aspects of reader guidance. Nevertheless, even in these schools, requests for information will remain significant. In other primary schools and, above all, in secondary schools, curricula-inspired needs will be virtually synonymous with informational needs.

The first importance, then, of an efficient school reference service is that it enables the school community, both staff and students, to attain desired educational goals. The validity of the goals of today's schools cannot be debated here, but in so far as we do value them, so we must value also the provision of a good reference service.

Yet a school reference service implies far more than the simple provision of adequate informational materials—demanding though that may be in itself. Additionally, school librarians have the duty to teach students how to locate information relevant to a given problem, evaluate it once found, then use it appropriately in solving the original problem. This duty is not theirs alone and should be undertaken as a co-operative effort between librarians and classroom teachers. The professional expertise of school librarians in their knowledge of all forms of information sources, and their familiarity with what is currently available, complements the class teacher's role and specialist subject knowledge. Whether working in conjunction with others or not, school librarians must see their reference work essentially as a process whereby they educate students in the use of information materials, as well as meeting their immediate factual needs. Though this teaching responsibility may be concisely expressed, the difficulties in discharging it are not to be lightly regarded. The students who graduate from our schools able to find, assess and use information as they need it are indeed well equipped, both to continue their education and to cope with many facets of life's challenges.

How do you provide a school reference service?

School librarians establish and maintain reference services in school libraries by:
1. acquiring as thorough a knowledge as possible of the present and future needs of staff and students;
2. providing an adequate, well-balanced and accessible reference collection;
3. being alert to the potential reference use of all other parts of the collection; and
4. investigating all community information sources, both formal and informal, both local and further afield, which might be able to contribute to school information needs.

They will recognise that a good reference service is achieved by informed forward planning directed to the attainment of specific objectives and shaped by policies formulated in the light of those objectives.

Acquiring a thorough knowledge of the present and future needs of the clientele demands a familiarity with all aspects of the school and the community it serves. For the newly appointed, gaining sufficient familiarity presents a special challenge; but even for those long in their present positions, such knowledge is not passively gathered by some convenient form of psychic osmosis, but must be actively sought. Despite demands on their time, school librarians should attend staff, faculty and curricula meetings, parents and friends evenings, and all occasions that offer prospects of a better understanding of the requirements of those they hope to serve. Notice-board requests and requests on distribution lists for minutes of meetings can also be rewarding. Tact, courtesy and a clear explanation of one's purposes must accompany such requests.

Students' needs, other than those dictated by curricula, may be more diverse and unpredictable than those of staff. Additionally, they may not be tapped by such ploys as attendance at meetings, except where interest clubs of various kinds meet at the school. Therefore, some thought should be given to ways of exploring student interests. Direct approaches by students to the librarian will make some needs clear, but those that are felt but not freely communicated are also legitimately part of our concern.

Providing an adequate, well-balanced and accessible reference collection is a true test of professional competence. It requires a thorough knowledge of all forms of reference works and their functions.

What are reference works?

The *ALA Glossary of Library Terms* defines a reference book as one 'designed by its arrangement and treatment to be consulted for definite items of information, rather than to be read consecutively'.[5]

Imaginative librarians, well grounded in the resources of the library collections available to them, will draw on a wide range of materials in answering reference questions. But in doing so, they will be supplementing the reference resources available by the application of professional expertise. Generally speaking, reference questions should be able to be answered quickly and correctly from reference books initially (other library resources being used to add further detail), because the arrangement of material within a reference book and the manner in which it has been treated have been chosen for that very purpose.

Published reference works may be divided into two categories:
1. those that give information directly (encyclopaedias, dictionaries, year books, manuals, directories, biographical sources, geographical sources); and
2. those that are keys to sources of information (indexes, abstracts, bibliographies).

Encyclopaedias

Katz defines encyclopaedias as 'works containing informational articles on subjects in every field of knowledge, usually arranged in alphabetical order' and declares that they are 'the most used single source'[6] of the reference works that give information directly.

Katz's observation regarding the use of encyclopaedias is readily applicable in many school libraries, where the reference collections consist very largely of sets of these works. For small collections, the value of their extensive yet compact coverage is acknowledged, especially where the library is isolated from other supporting facilities, as those in country towns often are.

Nevertheless the conveniences of general encyclopaedias have to be balanced against their indisputable limitations. The aim of providing information in every field of knowledge is one that leads readily to shallow generalisations and makes keeping facts up to date hazardous. Even at their best, general encyclopaedias can only introduce a reader to a topic, providing an overview of the relevant subject area. And not even the most recent edition should be expected to provide the latest facts of a statistical kind. School librarians who buy general encyclopaedias must firstly be rigorous in their selection and secondly be alert to prevent misunderstandings and misuse of encyclopaedias by students. There are still many adults inclined to view encyclopaedias with undue respect; but children are necessarily more susceptible to misplaced faith in encyclopaedia articles, because their restricted experience does not provide them with a yardstick by which to assess the answers found in the articles.

If, in answering set questions, children have learnt to use the index of an encyclopaedia to locate relevant articles, to find pertinent details, then to incorpate these into written or verbal answers, then they have mastered valuable skills. Nor should such mastery be undervalued, for it is an accomplishment. But once past the early years at school, and above all at secondary school, the students who equate searching for information with looking up sets of encyclopaedias have been badly served by their school librarians.

Purchasing general encyclopaedias includes the responsibilities of making students aware of their proper role and training the students to use more specialised reference tools, where appropriate. Even at primary level, general encyclopaedias should be merely the beginning point in an information search. Indeed, Doreen Goodman, when addressing the 1976 Australian School Library Association Conference, argued that by spending the money normally allocated to general encyclopaedias on more specific reference works and on an extended periodicals collection, a school librarian could provide a better reference service.[7] In the face of this challenge, the school librarians who continue to purchase general encyclopaedias must have strong arguments for doing so.

Not all encyclopaedias, however, are general in scope. Many provide introductions to particular fields and, because they have more restricted goals, they can usually achieve greater accuracy and precision than general encyclopaedias whilst maintaining an overview approach. They can therefore prove very useful in school libraries. Nevertheless, the obligation to teach students when and how to use them still has force.

Dictionaries

A dictionary is 'a book dealing with the words of a language, so as to set forth their orthography, pronunciation, signification and use, their synonyms, derivation and history, or at least some of these.'[8]

Most people feel confident that they know what a dictionary is, but the full value of dictionaries in the school library will not be realised until the librarian is conversant with all the kinds of dictionaries available and their many functions.

Subject dictionaries give the meanings of words used in their selected field of knowledge. Frequently they differ from language dictionaries in that the explanation of a technical term can rarely by given in a phrase or two and often requires a brief article to supply a context within which the implications of the term may be grasped. Consequently, subject dictionaries are on occasions hard to distinguish from subject encyclopaedias. The distinction may be further obscured by the use of the word 'dictionary' in the titles of what are actually encyclopaedias, the entries of which are arranged alphabetically. An instance of this custom is found in the well-known subject encyclopaedia, *Grove's Dictionary of Music and Musicians*.[9] Although such complications might make the classifier's task perplexing, the major concern of the librarian engaged in reference work will be the standard of the work and how well it meets the need in hand.

The existence of a range of subject dictionaries in paperback form, such as those published by Penguin, makes it possible for a school library to have a considerable number of subject dictionaries—though standard hardcover works must not be neglected.

The compilers of language dictionaries set themselves an immense task. If they aim to produce a general dictionary of the English language, then they must first decide how complete their coverage is to be. If the dictionary will be an unabridged edition, listing 250 000 words or more, then they will consider for inclusion every English word from times past or present that they can discover. The authoritative *Oxford English Dictionary* takes the form of 13 large volumes, yet supplements continue to appear, listing not only words that have entered the language since the last volume appeared but also older words previously omitted.[10]

Most general language dictionaries are not so ambitious in scope but are abridged, concise or pocket dictionaries. There is no prescribed length for any of these categories, for the chief feature that governs the choice of words treated is that of the needs of the readers for whom the work is intended. Apart from the unabridged works, each dictionary should be designed with a particular audience in mind, as a clear set of criteria is necessary to achieve consistency of purpose among the many decisions taken during its compilation. The editors have to consider the proportion of space to be allotted to words from the oral and literary language, to technical, archaic and foreign words, to phrases and abbreviations. In an informative article, Burchfield gives examples of the problems for the editor in dealing with words from different English-speaking areas, with proprietary names, with racial and religious terms, and with new, specialised academic words.[11] Thus the lack of a strong guiding principle in the compilation of a dictionary will result in erratic and arbitrary decisions as to what is put in or left out, thus diminishing its value for every potential user. Even where the entries have been chosen with consistency and care, no one dictionary will be able to cover the requirements of a reference collection, no matter how small. Buying more than one general English-language dictionary is not pointless duplication, and a librarian will quite sensibly purchase a number of such dictionaries, seeking a balance of English, American and Australian publications.

General language dictionaries are complemented by specialised language dictionaries. These are devoted to limited aspects of the language, such as synonyms and antonyms, abbreviations and acronyms, usage, slang, proper names and names from mythology. All have a place in the school library, which should also provide a range of bilingual dictionaries. Whereas bilingual dictionaries were once bought simply to support language courses in schools, now they have a new importance in the help they may give the many children in our schools who speak a language other than English.

More and more children's dictionaries are appearing on the market. The authors of these take special care to give meanings of words in terms likely to be understood by the age group for whom the dictionary is designed. More space is given to illustrations, which are often in colour, and type faces are chosen to give maximum clarity to entries. Such features are assets, especially when the librarian is introducing children to dictionaries and their uses, as the crowded pages of other dictionaries, packed close with detail, readily confuse the uninitiated. Yet children's dictionaries, like all reference works, should be chosen with great care. Many are North American in origin and therefore have entries unsuitable for Australian schools on the grounds of both spelling and definition. Others are for very young pupils. The educational value of these latter is questionable. If children in the first and second grades do not know the meaning of simple, everyday words, they are best taught these by being given the opportunity to have experiences that give these words meaning, then by being helped to compose their own home-made dictionaries. Perhaps dictionaries intended by publishers for beginning readers may be most useful to the class teacher, as a guide to ways of compiling students' own individual word lists.

Year books, almanacs and news digest services
Year books, almanacs and news digest services form a category of reference works of which new editions are regularly published, to update their contents (especially those of a statistical nature) and to give reports on the latest trends within the scope of knowledge that the items cover.

Year books, as their name suggests, are published annually. Those issued by encyclopaedia publishers do not succeed in updating the main volumes, as publicity blurbs sometimes suggest, but may be useful in their own right. They often provide long articles on political, social and economic developments of the year and are sources of biographical data on persons briefly in the public eye. Most other year books are published by institutions, learned societies and governments and provide information at once both authoritative and difficult to obtain elsewhere. *Year Book Australia*[12] and the year books of the various Australian States are examples of this form of reference work that should be found in Australian school libraries, both primary and secondary, while *The Statesman's Year Book*[13] demonstrates how year books may give quick access to statistical details.

Almanacs originated as specialised calendars, detailing church feast and fast days. Gradually, to these bare foundations were added strangely assorted facts considered of interest to the population at large. General almanacs, such as *Whitaker's Almanack*, reflect the tradition from which they evolved, by their calendar and astronomical information and the diversity of the scope of the rest of their entries.[14] Like year books, they are published annually and so offer, as *Whitaker's Almanack* does, features such as those on recent events in Third World countries. In addition to general almanacs, subject almanacs are also published.

Though published annually, almanacs and year books necessarily date rapidly as each day brings changes that bear on their contents. News digest services, with their concise résumés of events (drawn from the articles of many newspapers), help bridge the gap between today's situation and the situation at the time of compilation of the year books and almanacs. *Keesing's Contemporary Archives* comes out as a weekly summary, the index to which is systematically accumulated into a final, yearly edition.[15] Unfortunately the cost of this service makes it an item that librarians must ponder before puchasing; but even if not bought, the service remains useful to all schools that have access to the resources of a public library.

The vertical file

The limitations of the sources discussed above, together with the lack of published indexes to Australian newspapers, give extra weight to the value of a current information resource that school librarians need to compile for themselves. This is the vertical file, which often begins as a self-indexing file of newspaper clippings, to which is added pamphlets not worth cataloguing but nevertheless useful, articles of ephemeral interest from magazines, photographs, pictures and small maps separately published or culled from discarded library books, and materials of local interest. Local-interest items have, in the past, been treated rather casually by school librarians—when they have bothered to collect them at all. Now that curricula commonly emphasise local history and current community interests, the school librarian should not only obtain items of local relevance but, having got them, consider whether they are better treated as a separate collection, rather than vertical-file material. Whatever decision is made on this matter, the usefulness of a well-planned, well-ordered and well-maintained vertical file in a school library is hard to stress too forcefully. Equally important, though, is that school librarians prepare themselves adequately before embarking on the creation of what can easily become a muddle of irrelevancies, by reading standard texts for guidance on how to go about the task.

Handbooks and manuals

The distinction between handbooks and manuals is largely one of the customary usage of the individual terms. The difficulty of defining either is revealed by the entries in the *ALA Glossary of Library Terms*, which says that a handbook is a 'small reference book, a manual'[16], and that a manual is 'a compact book that treats concisely the essentials of a subject; a handbook'.[17]

The issue may appear even further confused by the frequent similarity of handbooks and manuals to subject dictionaries—a similarity based on the common purpose of all three to assist readers seeking an introduction to certain fields of knowledge. Some reference works fulfil several functions at once and may be regarded by the reference librarian as being equally handbooks or subject dictionaries or even subject encyclopaedias. The *Oxford Companion to . . .* books are examples of such works. Handbooks and manuals differ from year books, which concentrate on recent advances in their emphasis on established knowledge.

Though they serve as an introduction to a subject (there are few *general* handbooks or manuals), it cannot be assumed that they will be suitable for the use of students in schools. Many have very specific limitations and deal with their topic in depth, assuming on the part of the reader some knowledge of the topic. Handbooks such as these would be purchased only if useful for teacher reference.

Directories

A directory is 'a list of persons or organisations, systematically arranged, usually in alphabetic or classed order, giving address, affiliations, etc., for individuals, and address, officers, functions, and similar data for organisations'.[18]

As with other reference works, the value of a directory lies in its editor's choice of scope and firmness of purpose. A directory of all persons in Australia whose surnames began with 'S' would be a remarkably useless document. A directory of sources of audio-visual materials is quite another matter. Local directories such as telephone, street or business directories, professional directories and government directories may all have a place in a school library.

The school librarian will generally find it necessary to compile a home-made reference aid, perhaps a directory of local speakers willing to come to the school, a directory of local organisations willing to supply the school with materials or permit students to visit their facilities, and of any other resource of potential value in the community. Such information is best recorded centrally in the school and not left to the initiative of individual teachers, to avoid missed opportunities and to avoid giving offence to bodies outside the school; the compilation and regular maintenance of such a directory are logically the responsibilities of library personnel.

Biographical sources

Many reference works contain some biographical information, as it is difficult to discuss any field of human endeavour without mentioning the people responsible for its development. However, there are works devoted entirely to biographical entries, and some of these should be considered for inclusion in a school library.

It is important that the selector recognise the *types* of biographical sources available, for these in turn determine the selection of persons for inclusion. A general biographical dictionary will consider only the importance of an individual, as a basis for choice, and exclude no one because of nationality or occupation. Obviously, though, a national biographical dictionary will select subjects precisely by the criterion of their nationality, just as a subject biographical dictionary will be concerned with persons whose occupations have led to their prominence.

A further restriction on entry will be made if the work is exclusively current or retrospective. A current work, such as *Who's Who*[19], will have entries solely for the living; while retrospective works, such as *Who was Who*[20], consider for inclusion only those deceased. Some works such as *Chambers Biographical Dictionary*[21] are general in nature, have both current and retrospective entries, and include people not only famous for academic or political achievement but also of more popular note.

Biographical materials present some difficulties in the assessment of their accuracy where they venture beyond factual information. The evaluation of the worth of a person's achievement is necessarily a product of the values of those making the judgement and, furthermore, is subject to reassessment as time passes. In teaching their pupils the uses of biographical sources, school librarians should discuss these points.

To provide adequate biographical reference coverage, school librarians usually need to compile home-made files, which may be part of the vertical-file system. In formal reference sources, rarely does one find information on persons of local interest or on persons who have only recently become well known. Articles clipped from magazines or newspapers will often be the only information readily available on such people.

Geographical sources

The maps or atlas sections found in encyclopaedias will never serve as adequate geographical sources in a school library, not even in the smallest library. Separate maps and atlases, globes and gazetteers should be bought and, as curricula extend to include study of the Moon, Mars and other planets, these should not be restricted to representations of the Earth.

The most common form of map represents the physical and political features of countries. Since the latter are subject to unpredictable change, otherwise useful maps may be suddenly outdated. As the publication of maps is a costly process, it may be some time before maps showing recent political changes are available, and these may in turn be rendered obsolete by events subsequent to their publication. Newspaper articles on political changes, clipped by school librarians for the vertical file, may be useful in alerting them to such changes.

Many maps are thematic. They may be designed to show changes in patterns of settlement or the distribution of soils in different regions. An atlas is a collection of maps chosen for their complementary nature and their individual contribution to an overall goal. Enormous variation may be found in atlases purporting to cover similar areas, in the proportion of space given to different geographic and political regions, and the manner in which those regions are treated.

Globes of the Earth are valuable as an aid to overcoming confusion among younger students as they struggle with the conventions of geographic representation. Not every child grasps immediately that travellers between countries at either extreme of a flat map of the world do not need to journey across the areas shown as intervening. Globes also help counteract misunderstanding based on the distortions inherent in every system of projection.

Gazetteers are dictionaries of geographical place names. The most comprehensive and respected gazetteers may be beyond the budgetary limitations of small school libraries, but such libraries should find a place for more limited works, especially locally relevant items.

Unless they themselves have specialist knowledge, school librarians are advised to seek the guidance of those with geographical expertise before puchasing geographical reference works. All the criteria normally used in selection for the reference collection are applicable, but consideration must also be given to such points as the implications of the scale chosen and the projection method employed.

So far only the reference works that give information directly to the reader have been mentioned. Yet those that act as keys to other sources of information can contribute to school reference services, even though few of them may be purchased for the collection.

Indexes and Abstracts

Indexes and abstracts are tools designed to make readily available information that appears in other separate publications, especially information appearing in non-book form. *Granger's Index to Poetry*[22] is an example of an index that offers access to the contents of many anthologies; but periodical indexes that make available the contents of selected periodicals are more common.

Two factors contribute to the importance and proliferation of periodical indexes. Firstly, there is the significance of periodicals themselves. Forming by far the largest part of the world's publications, periodicals are the medium in which most research results first appear and current dilemmas are publicly debated. To remain professionally informed and to keep abreast of advances in their specialist subjects, teachers must have access to a wide range of periodicals (though this does not imply that all periodicals relevant to teachers' professional concerns should be purchased by the school library).

The ephemeral interests of both staff and students are catered for by periodicals. Contemporary enthusiasms, from entertainments and hobbies to sporting activities, receive detailed and regular attention in their pages. Local publications appear mainly as periodicals or pamphlets, since the size of their expected audience rarely justifies publication on a more adventurous scale.

Margaret Marshall reminds us of the potent attraction the magazine format has for teenagers.[23] It is more than likely that magazines are the only reading matter, apart from newspapers, which many children find in their homes. School librarians should therefore capitalise on the appeal and familiarity that periodicals have for many of their pupils.

The second factor that gives weight to the role of periodical indexes is the near impossibility of finding, without their aid, even a moderate number of articles on a topic. The annual indexes to individual periodicals are invaluable in assisting the reader to make full use of their contents. But these indexes not only require the examination of each separate volume; they also restrict the searcher to the resources of the collection in which he or she is presently located. Indexes to groups of periodicals, numbering from tens to hundreds of journals, enable the searcher to trace every article listed, which may be obtained by inter-library loan or by the document services that some index publishers provide. For example, searchers consulting the *Australian Public Affairs Information Service*[24] have the opportunity to obtain a copy of any article of interest in it, as the National Library of Australia (which publishes this index) will supply copies for a small fee under certain conditions. Thus *APAIS* not only notifies the public of what has been published in specified Australian journals and newspapers, but also gives school librarians access to a range of periodical literature far beyond the range they would normally consider for purchase.

School librarians should include in their budgets the subscription price of at least one periodical index. Those who cannot readily consult periodical indexes held in other libraries should consider purchasing more, but it is not likely that now, or in the immediate future, schools will need to purchase abstracts.

By cost alone, abstracting journals are normally precluded from the scope of school resources, while their highly specialised contents are designed principally to serve those engaged in research. In addition to informing the reader of recent research, they also provide a brief résumé, or abstract, of the content of each item listed. School librarians need to be aware of the range of abstracts published and familiar with those relevant to education in order to assist teachers in their continuing professional education.

Bibliographies

The form of bibliography of most concern to teacher librarians is enumerative or systematic bibliography 'a list of books, or sources for a particular topic'.[25]

It is important that users of bibliographies recognise that limits of some kind are forced on all bibliographies. No bibliography has yet appeared listing every item ever published in every language. When using a bibliography, therefore, the reader should be aware of the restrictions within which the bibliography has been framed, by looking for the restrictions that have not been admitted nor intended, as well as those that are stated.

There are many published bibliographies of interest to school librarians, but national, trade and subject bibliographies are especially valuable to them. National bibliographies, which attempt to provide complete coverage of the publications of one country, aid school librarians in building collections that reflect the environment with which children of that country are familiar. A national bibliography is usually best purchased co-operatively by a number of schools or located in a regional office that provides centralised library services to schools.

The major trade bibliographies such as *Books in Print*[26] assist librarians when ordering books and when gathering bibliographic details of books only partly identified in the original reference. They are, however, very expensive and generally can only be made available to schools through the services of central or regional libraries. Publishers and booksellers, however, freely supply schools with catalogues and trade announcements, which, though they require organisation, contain details about series which are hard to find elsewhere, as well as informing the librarian of materials currently available.

By listing materials pertinent to its theme, a subject bibliography alerts school librarians to items overlooked when first published, or to items of previously unsuspected relevance. It may also detail titles not reviewed in the literature regularly scanned by school librarians. Some subject bibliographies are published as monographs and may be traced by procedures common to the process of identifying any other book title. Many appear as articles in periodicals, and school librarians who give sufficient time to reading their professional literature will discover subject bibliographies germane to their interests.

One of the principal reference services of a school library is the compilation of bibliographies on behalf of teachers and students. These bibliographies are based mainly on the school's own resources, but may include items obtainable locally or through inter-library loans. The thoroughness with which the school librarian undertakes this task—the skills and judgement exercised in identifying and evaluating items related to the themes and purpose of the bibliography in hand—measure the effectiveness of the librarian in meeting the fundamental requirement of providing materials to support the school's educational program. A guide to the compilation of subject bibliographies is provided in the appendix on pp.128–30.

The selection of reference works

Providing an adequate, well-balanced and accessible reference collection tests the librarian's competence, in that the selection of reference works carries special responsibility. Not only does the quality of service depend on the selections made, but a substantial portion of the budget will also be committed. With the exception of the cost of purchasing audio-visual hardware, the greatest expense faced by the school librarian is the maintenance of an up-to-date reference collection.

Selection should be directed by the school needs, which in turn determine purchasing priorities. Items are not to be considered in a vacuum, as single entities, but in the light of the strengths and weaknesses of the existing collection and any community resources on which the school may draw. Sometimes the duplication of an expensive dictionary or specialist technical work in two nearby institutions is not wasteful, but necessary, because of the consistent in-house use made of it at both locations. Nevertheless, co-operative buying should be considered whenever practical, as it enables participating libraries to have a range of resources not otherwise obtainable.

Once a decision has been made to buy a particular type of reference work, then all possible examples of that category should be critically evaluated. Bibliographies of suitable works should be scanned, and opinions sought from other professionals who have had experience of working with specific titles. Reviews in the professional literature may offer guidance. There is no substitute, however, for the actual examination of the works themselves, given that the school librarian is thoroughly versed in the appropriate criteria.

What are the appropriate criteria?

The first requirement of information is that it be accurate. To check the accuracy of a work, one establishes the expertise of the author, the authority of the sources he or she has consulted, and the reputation of the publisher. A sample of facts given should be cross-checked, where possible, with those found in other, reputable books. An important aspect of accuracy is how up to date is the information given; and bibliographies, references, statistics and dates contained in the work should be scrutinised to ascertain this, even where the publisher's announcements proclaim the work to be a new edition. Members of the teaching staff with relevant subject expertise may be asked for their judgements.

The contribution of a reference work to a school library is chiefly determined by the scope of the facts in it. Attention to its limitations will repay the selector, as what authors choose to omit is as vital to the potential value of their publications as what they choose to include.

One of the characteristics that Katz attributes to a reference work is that 'it concentrates on facts. It is constructed for the reader who has definite questions, and does not raise questions of its own.'[27] There is, then, the requirement that reference works be objective in their treatment of subject matter, eschewing debate although indicating the range of current opinion. There should be a balanced emphasis in the treatment of different subjects according to the scope specified and the work's intended audience. The needs of the market aimed at by the publisher will inevitably bias the work in some way, but this, when recognised, can be used to advantage. Indeed, the reference works that prove inadequate are generally those designed to please as many as possible and which consequently fail through vagueness and the arbitrary nature of their coverage.

Yet accurate, objective and up-to-date information is not in itself enough. One should also expect that it be presented in a manner suitable for both the topic and the intended audience. School librarians should take a particular interest in the language used and the author's clarity of style. Every point that adds to the readability of the work will enhance its value in a school.

The importance of presentation is not simply one of appeal. It should also function as an aid to understanding. Closely packed pages of dense type, a dearth of headings and paragraph guides, obscure diagrams and irrelevant pictures not only discourage readers but also confuse them. The selector should examine all aspects of the format of a book, as a thoughtfully planned layout is essential for efficient information retrieval.

Reference works must be durable, because, if well chosen, they will be in regular use for a long time. Some may even be kept and consulted although a new edition of the same work has been purchased, as changes in editorship may result in alterations to the scope of successive editions. The quality of the paper and the strength of the binding deserve special attention. Ideally, reference books for young children will be produced in a form they can handle with ease. Where necessary, however, librarians can provide special furniture to house a particularly useful but awkwardly large book, to minimise the need for children to move it about. Not even the best binding lasts long if a book is frequently dropped.

It is the arrangement of a reference work that chiefly distinguishes it from other non-fiction. The overall arrangement of the contents, whether chronological, topical or alphabetical, ought to be appropriate to the subject matter and the depth at which it is treated. The use of centred and subordinate headings, boldface type, italics and all other devices for assisting the reader is desirable, but above all, the value of the work depends on the efficiency of its indexing and cross-referencing system. Difficulties flourish in the number of alternative entry words and spellings encountered by the reader in quite minor searches. To compound these difficulties by inconsistencies in the indexing of a book, the very purpose of which is reference, is an inexcusable flaw; and such a book should not be considered for purchase.

Finally, some reference works offer special features claimed to increase their potential use. These should be examined cautiously. Helpful as they may be to the home user, for whom they are primarily intended, they are generally inadequate in a library context.

In discussing these selection criteria, the term 'book' has been used more than once, and it is evident that the selection criteria are applicable to reference works that are, in fact, books; undoubtedly the reference collection in most school libraries will consist predominantly of books for the foreseeable future, much as it has in the past. Nevertheless, school librarians should be aware of the possibilities created by the increasing availability of microfiche readers in schools. The cheapness of microfiche and their ease of storage hold promise of opportunities to have resources that could not previously have been considered. Already some schools are supplementing the professional reading of teaching staff by the purchase of selected ERIC Documents.[28] Some reference works in microfiche are so regularly revised that subscribing libraries find themselves with numerous outdated editions. Several school libraries in Adelaide have taken advantage of the monthly updating of *British Books in Print*[29] by asking tertiary libraries for editions they no longer require. By obtaining other libraries' discards, they acquire a valuable bibliography, the cost of which prohibits its direct purchase by schools.

Making the reference collection accessible

The responsibility of school librarians to provide a reference service does not cease once they have selected and purchased their reference collections. Those collections must be located, arranged and presented in ways designed to maximise their effective use.

The location of the reference collection should be convenient to both library staff and their clients. A poorly located collection is liable to be ignored, setting at nought the effort and expertise invested in its acquisition. In planning the location of the collection, the librarian should consider not only furniture for housing items when not in use, but also the provision of special stands and tables for weighty or outsized works.

When formulating library policies, librarians should recognise their implications for reference service. Cataloguing and classification decisions may help or inhibit those seeking information, according to how well these decisions reflect an understanding of the library's clientele. In particular, decisions regarding subject headings and analytical entries significantly affect the reader's ability to retrieve information from materials not obviously relevant to the topic in hand. This is especially true when these materials are part of the general collection.

In the past, reference works were sometimes defined as books that were not for loan. Many librarians no longer adhere to the policy of never lending from the reference collection, being prepared to let readers borrow from it for periods when the library is shut. Others permit the loan of superseded editions of a title, while keeping the most recent copy on hand. Yet, however liberal the loan policy may be, most reference works must be consulted *in situ*, and it is therefore helpful if the library can offer photocopying facilities to clients.

The school librarian as reference librarian

So far the discussion has covered work that is largely preparatory in nature—time and effort expended before actual service is possible. It has been emphasised that this preparation should be guided at every turn by the librarian's judgement of the school's present and future needs. Hence the librarian's role is critical in laying the foundations of service.

It is not less important when working directly with clients. The quality of the service will rest on the librarian's knowledge of the collection, of resources existing beyond the school and his or her skills of information retrieval. Additionally, the school librarian's responsibility to impart to students a basic understanding of reference works and search techniques demands proven teaching ability, together with an understanding of how to structure the library experiences of pupils to optimise their learning opportunities. This is best done in co-operation with teachers, so that pupils' assignments in the library are integrated with their normal studies.

Finally, those who would be reference librarians need certain personal attributes which, if not inborn, must be cultivated. The first is a concern to find the best possible answer to every client's request, whether that person be staff or student, pleasant or otherwise. Other attributes are patience, tolerance and flexibility in working with, and for, a spectrum of personalities, from those youthfully gauche to the brusque teacher who has just discovered he must do 'relief' teaching in his non-contact time. A sense of humour is of great benefit, not least to the librarian possessing it.

Appendix: Compiling subject bibliographies for teachers

Obtaining material
 1. Consult the catalogue
    Look under the name of the specific subject to locate materials such as:
    non-fiction books;
    materials from the vertical file (e.g. Jackdaws);
    film strips;
    loop films;
    disc records;
    cassette tapes;

video tapes;
kits, etc.

2. Remember that non-fiction books on the wider subject will often have chapters on the specific subject; e.g.
    books on general science, for chapters on astronomy;
    books on Asia, for information on Japan;
    books on the history of Europe, for chapters on the history of Germany.
3. Consult general encyclopaedia.
4. Consult other reference books, such as year books, special subject encyclopaedias, atlases, biographical dictionaries; e.g.
    historical atlas;
    a gazetteer;
    science encyclopaedias, etc.
5. Consider each of the Dewey classes. There may be books in other classes which could be useful and which would break down the watertight compartments of school subjects; e.g.
    for an historical period such as the Middle Ages, include books on the history of weapons, art, transport, law, science, costume, furniture, music, theatre, architecture, food, recreations, etc.
6. Check whether there is any material in the Biography section which could be useful.
7. Do not neglect fiction; e.g.
    historical fiction;
    fiction set in a particular region;
    fiction involving social issues.
8. Consult an index to periodicals, such as *Guidelines*, to locate up-to-date material in periodicals.
9. Consult the pamphlet collection, and pictorial material.
10. Consult *Keesing's Contemporary Archives* and newspapers for additional information.

Information required
1. You will need to make a note of:

call number;	place of publication;
author;	publisher;
title;	date.

2. You may also need to make brief descriptive notes; e.g.
    number of pages;
    number of frames in a filmstrip;
    black & white/colour (filmstrip)
    length of film (in minutes), etc.

Setting out
1. It is helpful to subject teachers to arrange the bibliography under headings according to the type of material; e.g.
    books;
    periodical articles;
    filmstrips, etc.

2. Under each heading, entries should be arranged either alphabetically (by author, or by title if there is no author); or by call number (classified order).
3. The accepted order for each entry is:
author (surname first);
title;
place of publication;
publisher;
date of publication;
call number (which may be placed first if the arrangement is by call number); any descriptive notes.
4. For periodical articles the accepted order is:
author (of article);
title (of article);
this is followed by the word 'in';
title of magazine;
volume;
number;
date;
page references.
5. All titles should be underlined.
6. When in doubt, follow the order on the catalogue card.

Examples: Books
Fitzgerald, C. P. *The Chinese View of Their Place in the World.* London, Oxford University Press, 1964.
Spear, P. *A History of India.* Harmondsworth, Penguin, 1965.

Periodical Articles
Harcourt, David. 'Aborigines: a year of militancy?', in *The Bulletin,* vol. 94, 8 January 1972, pp. 9–10.
Spencer, Geoff. 'Turn in those aboriginal relics', in *Wildlife*, vol. 8, December 1971, pp. 98–9.

Make duplicate copies.
Date your bibliography, when first drawn up and again when revised.
File at least one copy.
(This guide was originally written by E. Meyer. It has been extended and modified by M. Nimon.)

References

1. R. A. Davies, *The School Library Media Centre* (2nd edn, Bowker, New York, 1974).
2. F. N. Cheney, *Fundamental Reference Sources* (American Library Association, Chicago, 1971).
3. B. S. Wynar, *Introduction to Bibliography and Reference Work* (4th rev. edn, Libraries Unlimited, Rochester, N.Y., 1967).
4. W. A. Katz, *Introduction to Reference Work* (3rd edn, McGraw-Hill, New York, 1978) , 2 vols.
5. *ALA Glossary of Library Terms* (American Library Association, Chicago, 1943), p. 112.

6. Katz, vol. 1, p. 17.
7. D. Goodman, 'Information services: a new role for the school librarian'. Paper delivered at the 5th Biennial Conference of the Australian School Library Association, held in Canberra, 29 August–3 September 1976.
8. *The Shorter Oxford Dictionary on Historical Principles*, prepared by W. Little and others, revised and edited by C. T. Onions (3rd edn, Clarendon Press, Oxford, 1959), p. 505.
9. *Grove's Dictionary of Music and Musicians*, edited by E. Blom (5th edn, Macmillan, London, 1954), 9 vols and supplement 1961.
10. *The Oxford English Dictionary*, edited by J. A. H. Murray and others (Clarendon Press, Oxford, 1933).
11. R. W. Burchfield, 'The Art of the Lexicographer', *British Book News* (April 1975) 230–2.
12. *Year Book Australia* (Australian Bureau of Statistics, Canberra, 1908 to date).
13. *The Statesman's Year Book* (Macmillan, London, 1864–69, 1871 to date).
14. *Whitaker's Almanack* (Whitaker, London, 1873 to date).
15. *Keesing's Contemporary Archives* (Keesing's Publications, Longman Group, Bath, 1931 to date).
16. *ALA Glossary of Library Terms*, p. 68.
17. *ALA Glossary of Library Terms*, p. 85.
18. *ALA Glossary of Library Terms*, p. 47.
19. *Who's Who* (Black, London, 1849 to date).
20. *Who was Who* (Black, London, 1929– , volumes published decennially).
21. *Chambers Biographical Dictionary* (rev. edn, Chambers, Edinburgh, 1974).
22. *Granger's Index to Poetry* (6th edn, edited by W. J. Smith, Columbia University Press, New York, 1973).
23. M. R. Marshall, *Libraries and Literature for Teenagers* (Andre Deutsch, London, 1975), p. 81.
24. *Australian Public Affairs Information Service* (National Library of Australia, Canberra, July 1945 to date).
25. *Heinemann Australian Dictionary* (Heinemann Educational Australia, Melbourne, 1976), p. 94.
26. *Books in Print* (Bowker, New York, 1948 to date), 2 vols.
27. W. A. Katz, *Introduction to Reference Work* (1st edn, McGraw-Hill, New York, 1969), vol. 1, p. 12.
28. The documents abstracted by *Resources in Education* are, in most cases, available for purchase in microfiche from the ERIC Document Reproduction Service. In Australia, these may be obtained under certain conditions from the National Library of Australia.
29. *British Books in Print* (Whitaker, London, 1965 to date).

CHAPTER 7

Bibliographic Organisation of Print and Non-print Materials for School Libraries

Anne Simpson

The rules for descriptive cataloguing are based on the *Anglo-American Cataloguing Rules*, 2nd edition (*AACR2*); subject headings on *Sears List of Subject Headings*, 11th edition; and classification on *Dewey Decimal Classification*, 11th abridged edition.

This chapter gives broad guidelines for cataloguing in a medium-sized secondary school library. Many school librarians have access to some kind of centralised service, but all have to catalogue material at some stage. Most school librarians do not have the time (or inclination) to spend many hours cataloguing their collection; therefore at times I suggest abbreviations, ideas for simplification or short cuts that are not specifically allowed for in the rules. In doing so, I try to keep in mind the needs of the student who requires an easily read, uncluttered card, as well as the needs of the teacher who may want rather more information about an item than author and title. (I am assuming that most school librarians will be dealing with a normal card catalogue—though an 'entry' can relate to any form of catalogue, such as book, microfiche or on-line computer, as well as to a card in a catalogue drawer.)

A practice that many school librarians have followed and found invaluable is the compilation of a loose-leaf cataloguing manual. Many times in the course of this outline I refer to texts which contain details and examples there is not room to reproduce here (for example, the three levels of description set out in *AACR2*). You may find it useful to copy certain key standards, rules, guidelines, glossaries, notes, etc., and index them carefully for your own reference. In the same manual you could include examples of items you have catalogued, alternative rules you have adopted and various practices you have decided to follow. A manual such as this, provided it is well indexed, is an excellent way to gain familiarisation with the rules, ensuring uniformity and consistency as well as providing a quick and easy reference. *Commonsense Cataloguing*, by Piercy, has some very useful checklists you might also consult.

AACR2

A second edition of the *Anglo-American Cataloguing Rules* was published in 1978. It is being adopted by the major cataloguing agencies, including the National Library of Australia and Library of Congress in 1981. Some of the more significant changes incorporated in this edition have already been introduced and are current practice in many libraries. For example, for books that had an editor, compiler or selector named on the title page, the rule was to enter the book under the name of the person; such works of diffuse authorship are now entered under title, and have been done so by major libraries for some time.

The new edition reflects the needs of larger libraries which have computerised, the emphasis changing from 'choice of main entry' to a basic description of the item. Having established this descriptive part, the rules in *AACR2* then go on to consider choice of various 'access points'. There is also an effort to make the rules applicable to all types of material rather than merely books. The first chapter states these general rules, and subsequent chapters go on to deal with the peculiarities of specific kinds of material.

If you cannot buy a copy of the rules (it has been published in paperback), then at least go to a library where there is a copy, read the preface, the general introduction (10 pages in all) and look through the contents. It contains a very useful glossary which you might include in your manual, and a list of standard abbreviations from which you could extract the most common into a separate list, adding any local ones you use.

Apart from its use of International Standard Bibliographic Description (ISBD), another significant feature of the rules is its provision for three levels of description.

Third-level description incorporates all the elements set out in the rules and is most appropriate for large academic/research libraries. Second-level description is only slightly less detailed, and the rules set out the minimum elements required for this level. First-level description is very simple and basic, and requires only that the cataloguer include at least the title; the first statement of responsibility (if it is different from the main entry or if there is no main entry); the edition statement, if there is one; the publisher; the date; the extent of the item (the number of pages); notes; and standard book number. It does not require certain elements that I will discuss, such as general material designation, subtitle, place of publication, series, etc. However, the cataloguer is permitted to include extra information, as long as the basic elements remain.

Parts of a book

Before going into any more detail, it might be useful to summarise the parts of a book and terms that are used to describe it. (For full details, refer to any standard text on books; and perhaps include a summary in your manual.)

A *book* is defined as a publication of 49 pages or more. Anything less is arbitrarily defined as a pamphlet.

The *dust-jacket* is the paper cover wrapped around the bound book. The front inside flap often contains the *blurb*, which is the publisher's interpretation of the book. The back inside flap often contains information about the author. If the library practice is to discard the jacket, it is often worthwhile cutting out this information and sticking it inside the book.

The *half-title* (or *bastard title*) is a title appearing alone on the page preceding the proper title page. The *frontispiece* is an illustration facing the title page.

The *title page* is, for cataloguers, the most important feature of the book. Always catalogue from the title page, never from the cover or the dust jacket. The title page of the book is the chief source of information. (For the chief source of information for non-book materials, refer to the relevant chapter in *AACR2*.) The title page contains the title proper, as well as some or all of the following information: subtitle, author (or persons responsible), edition, publisher, place of publication and date. This latter information, called the imprint, is often found on the *verso* of the title page, and will also indicate when the book was copyrighted and when it has been reprinted.

All *preliminary pages* up to the beginning of the text proper may be numbered in Roman numerals; from the first page of the text, the pages are usually numbered in Arabic numerals. Preliminary pages may contain a *dedication*; a *preface* (written by the author); a *foreword* (contributed by someone else); a *table of contents*, which lists the chapters in the sequence in which they appear in the book; a *list of illustrations* (in the same order); and an *introduction* (written by the author). The introduction usually leads directly into the text; it introduces the text, in contrast to the preface which is usually more explanatory about the author and which acknowledges the help that was received and how the book came to be written.

At the end of the book, there may be *appendices* which contain extra information that would have broken the flow of the book if it had been included in the main text. *Notes* or *references* relate to specific points or books quoted in the text. The *index* is an alphabetical listing (as opposed to the contents, which is a sequential listing) of key words, names, places, etc., mentioned in the text, referring the reader to the page or pages where information on that topic can be found.

Few books will contain all these features, and of course non-fiction books are more likely to contain them than fiction. Different publishing houses have different practices, and some picture books and foreign-language children's books may have imprint information at the back of the book, often on the endpapers.

Elements of the catalogue entry

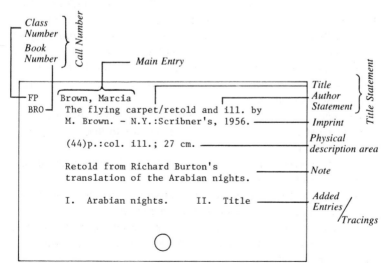

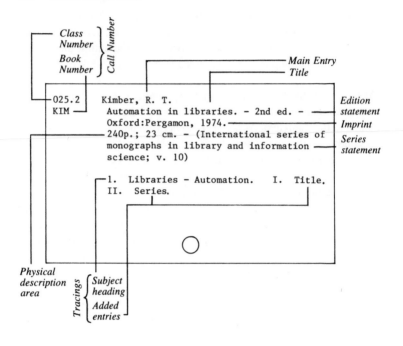

Although the examples above have been set out in the traditional form that appears on most cards, this is largely a matter of convention. Different libraries will have different 'house rules' governing layout; and, again, the use of computers has contributed toward certain changes. Nevertheless, the elements of the entry remain standard. They are formulated in accordance to *AACR2* and the directives set out later in this chapter. Sequentially these are:

Call number, which includes the entire set of symbols allocated to an item. In most cases it will be a number unique to that item within a particular library.

Classification number is the number by which the item has been classed, usually according to its subject or content.

Book number is derived from the main entry of the item itself, whether it be author or title. Most school libraries find the first three letters of the main entry sufficient, though larger libraries need the Cutter-Sanborn tables, which use the first letter of the author's surname along with three numbers; this permits much more accurate filing on the shelf.

Main entry heading is the principal heading under which the item is uniformly identified.

Main entry card is filed under the main entry heading, and contains the most information about the item, including a record of other entries that may have been used for the item.

Title statement includes the *title proper*, the *subtitle* and the *author statement*.

Author statement includes statements regarding editors, illustrators, translators, selectors, etc., as well as joint authorship. An author statement is not always necessary and should not be confused with the main entry heading.

Edition statement indicates second or subsequent editions of an item, or type of edition (for example, rev.ed. or 4th ed.).

Imprint consists of place of publication or distribution, name of publisher or distributor, and date of publication.

Physical description area. For a book this will be what has traditionally been called the collation. It may include number of pages, whether it is illustrated or not, and the size. For other types of material it will include a specific material designation (for example, 1 tape, 3 film-strips, 36 slides, etc.) and such information as running time, r.p.m., number of frames, etc.

Series statement indicates whether the item belongs to a series, usually a publisher's series.

Notes are added by the cataloguer where he or she feels additional information would be useful to the catalogue user.

Tracings are the record of all other entries that have been made for the item in the catalogue. They include a record of the subject headings that have been used, as well as other headings (added entries) under which the item has been filed.

ISBN is the International Standard Book Number which is allocated by the publisher to every title published. It is unique to each title, and can be used for ordering or citing instead of the main entry. Although you may use it for ordering cards, it probably isn't necessary to add it to your own catalogue card.

International Standard Bibliographic Description (ISBD)

This is a system of punctuation that has been incorporated into *AACR2*, and which it is recommended that all libraries follow. Whereas layout and spacing might differ between libraries, the *punctuation* should be standard. Consequently, no matter what the language, each area of the catalogue entry can be recognised, guided by the preceding punctuation. As very few typewriters in schools have square brackets, I will make no distinction here between square brackets and parentheses.

To start with, each main area of the catalogue entry is separated from the next by a period (.), space ( ), dash (–), space ( ) [that is, '. – '] except at the end or beginning of a paragraph. So we have:

    Title statement. – Edition statement. – Imprint. – Physical description. – Series.

    Notes.

    Tracings.

Within each main area, the punctuation can be shown as:

    Title: subtitle/statement of authorship. – Edition statement. – Place of publication: publisher, date. – Extent (pages): other physical details (illustration); extent (size or dimensions) – (Series).

    Notes.

    Tracings.

It is important to remember that ISBD is concerned with *preceding* punctuation, so that in the physical description, for example, the rule is *not* 'pages followed by a colon' but rather 'colon preceding illustration'. Hence if the book is not illustrated, the collation would read '125p. ; 30 cm.

In more detail, the regulations are:

Area	*Preceding Punctuation*	*Element of Entry*
1. Title and statement of responsibility area		Title proper
	( )	General medium designation
	=	Parallel title
	:	Other title and other title information
	/	First statement of responsibility
	;	Second or subsequent statement of responsibility
2. Edition or issue area		Edition or issue statement
	/	Statement of responsibility relating to the edition

3. Publication, distribution, etc., area		First place of publication, distribution, etc.
	:	Name of publisher, distributor, etc.
	,	Date of publication, distribution, etc.
	(	Place of manufacture
	:)	Name of manufacturer
4. Physical description area		Specific medium designation
	()	Extent of item
	:	Other physical details
	;	Dimensions of item
	+	Accompanying material
5. Series area		Series statement
Each set of information relating to a series is enclosed by parentheses (())	:	Standard serial numbering of series
	;	Numbering within series
7. Notes area		Note

Remember, each 'area' is separated by a space, dash, space.

Description of the item

It is obviously impossible to present all the rules governing the description of an item and for all types of material in one short chapter. Consequently my comments must be brief, directed primarily toward books, and provide only basic guidance. For every general rule I quote, *AACR2* gives specific variations, exceptions, etc., especially in the case of non-book materials. In discussing particular rules, I include the general medium designation, subtitle, statement of responsibility, place of publication, series, etc., which, as I mentioned earlier, are not provided for by the first level description of *AACR2*. I think they are useful, optional additions for a large secondary school library. Whether they are included in cataloguing depends on an interpretation of the needs of each library. However, for future uniformity, remember to make a note in your manual of what you decide to include or omit.

Title proper
The title of the item should come from the title page. If the title on the cover or the half-title varies, this variation is described in a note at the bottom of the entry. It is most important that the title be transcribed exactly as it appears on the title page, including order, spelling and wording. Capitalise only the first letter of the first word, unless the title includes proper names. There is provision for the insertion, in square brackets, of a general medium designation directly after the title proper—for example, Africa [slide]. I give a list of general medium designations (GMD) below, in the section on special classes of material; it should not be necessary to use the GMD 'text' for books.

The subtitle
The subtitle, where there is one, is preceded by a colon. Long titles can be abridged, but the first five words are always included. All omissions from the title are indicated by '…'.

Author statement
The author statement includes, in addition to the names of the authors, the names of subsidiary authors, editors, compilers, illustrators, etc. It is not necessary to repeat the author's name in the author statement if it is exactly the same as in the main entry heading, for example,

   Sharrad, Robert
     A book of ticks. — Adel. …

In the case of joint authorship, both authors' names must appear in the author statement; for example,

   Sampson, Julia
     High tide/ by J. Sampson & V. Simpson.

First names may be abbreviated to initials in the author statement.

If there are more than three authors, or more than three subsidiary authors performing the same function in the author statement, all after the first named are omitted. The omission is indicated as '… (*et al.*)'.

The edition statement
The edition statement is recorded as found in the work, except that abbreviations are used (for example, 3rd ed.). Do not confuse the edition with an impression. A new edition implies some contextual change— some new content or variation. A new impression on the other hand is just another printing of the same content.

Imprint, or Publication, distribution, etc., area

If there is more than one place of publication, choose the first, with its corresponding publisher or distributor, unless another is given greater prominence. If there are two places with the same name, or if the place is a suburb or small town, then it should be followed by its state or some similar designation; for example,

Ringwood, Vic.; Harmondsworth, Middx.

If the place of publication is unknown, give the abbreviation 's.l.' (*sine loco*).

The publisher statement is abridged as much as possible without loss of intelligibility or identification; for example,

Penguin *not* Penguin Books

Scribner's *not* Scribner's Sons

Omit 'and company', 'incorporated', 'limited', etc. Also omit the name of a publishing firm if it is used with the name of a branch or division that is adequately identified by its own name; for example,

Kestrel *not* Penguin

If the name of the publisher is unknown, give the abbreviation 's.n.' (*sine nomine*).

In the case of much non-book material, the place and publisher may be replaced by place of distribution, and the distributor, or manufacturer.

The date recorded is that of the first impression of the edition you have in front of you. Dates of later impressions are not recorded. For example, if you have a book that was first published in 1963 and reprinted several times, the last impression being 1978, then the date recorded is 1963. Any other information about the date of publication is best put in the notes.

If there is no date, make an intelligent guess and enclose it in brackets with a query; for example, (197-?).

Physical description area

The first part of this area is the *extent* of the item, including specific material designation for non-book materials; for example, 24 slides, 1 chart, 2 cassettes. Playing time (the extent) is included in brackets immediately after the specific material designation; for example, 1 disc (45 min).

For books the extent is the number of volumes or the number of pages—ignore any Roman numerals and give the last Arabic numbered page. If the pages are not numbered, and there are about 50 or fewer, count them and enclose the figure in brackets: '(36) p.'. If it looks as if there are well over 50 pages, you may write '1v (unpaged)'. If there is more than one volume to an item, record only the number of volumes, not the number of pages; for example, 2v.

Following the extent of the item, and preceded by a colon, come *other physical details*, such as whether the item is illustrated, whether the illustrations are in colour, the nature of the material, etc. For books, 'ill.' or 'col. ill.' should do to cover all types of illustration whether charts, diagrams, maps or whatever. For other material such as slides and film-strips, it will be necessary to put 'b & w' or 'col.'. Examples taken from *AACR2* are:

1 filmstrip (70 fr) : b & w.

321 p. : ill.

1 disc (20 min) : 33⅓rpm

1 model (4 pieces) : polystyrene

The *dimensions* of an item are given in centimetres to the next highest centimetre. For books, only the height need be given unless the width is greater, in which case give both: height x width; for example, 15 x 32 cm.

Records are still described in inches; for example, 1 disc (20 min) : 33⅓ rpm; 12 in. Films are described in millimetres; for example, 1 filmstrip (70 fr) : col.; 35 mm.

Accompanying material can either be added to this area, as '387 p. : ill.; 27 cm + teacher's notes.' Or it may be added as a note; for example,

387 p. : ill.; 27 cm.

Accompanied by teacher's notes

The physical description area may follow straight on from the imprint, or it may start on a new paragraph. Usually the entry is easier for students to read if it is started in a new paragraph.

The series statement

The series statement is given in brackets following straight after the physical description area, separated by space, dash, space. I suggest always giving a series statement in schools, even if the giving of series added entries is restricted, as it can often give important clues as to the format of the item; for example,

. . . –

London : Pan, 1972.

(20) p. : col. ill.; 19 cm – (A Piccolo picture book).

The notes

This area should start on a new paragraph, and each new note thereafter on a new paragraph. They are added by the cataloguer at his or her discretion and include information that might be too cumbersome to put in the body of the entry, or would have been inappropriate. Notes include such statements as:

First publ. Sweden, 1906

Published in U.S. as *A patch of blue*

The order for notes is:

1. Nature, scope or artistic form of the item; for example, 'Documentary'.
2. Other title information.
3. Statements of responsibility; for example, 'Based on Richard Burton's translation of the Arabian Nights'.
4. Edition and history; for example, 'Sequel to . . .'.
5. Accompanying material.
6. Audience; for example, 'For children 4–7'.
7. Other formats available.
8. Summary.
9. Contents.
10. 'With' notes; for example, 'With : New World Symphony/Dvorak'.

Tracings

The subject headings are listed first, numbered consecutively with Arabic numerals, followed by the added entry headings, numbered with Roman numerals.

Special classes of material

AACR2 is designed to be equally applicable to all types of media, so you should follow the principles that have been set out in the previous section. There are special chapters dealing with the peculiarities of particular types of material but the basic principles remain standard, as emphasis is on content rather than form. A few examples are given at the end of this chapter. On the whole, the rules are compatible with those set out in Weiss, Lewis and Macdonald, *Non-book Materials: The Organization of Integrated Collections*, which many libraries have been using.

Main entry will more often be under title in the case of non-book materials, simply because authorship is more often diffuse. Provision has been made for entering records and cassettes, etc., where authorship is diffuse, under the name of the performer when this seems most reasonable—for example, Abba, The Beatles, Shirley Bassey, Joan Sutherland—rather than title.

Except in the case of books (for which most libraries do not feel the need for a general material designation), the GMD follows straight after the title proper. Choose the appropriate term from the list below and use it always in the singular:

art original	machine-readable	music
chart	data file	picture
diorama	manuscript	realia
filmstrip	map	slide
flashcard	microform	sound recording
game	microscope slide	technical drawing
globe	model	text
kit	motion picture	transparency
		videorecording

for example,

Indonesia today (kit)

Bees (slide)

If an item contains more than one medium (for example, tape and slides), then catalogue by the dominant medium and describe the other as accompanying material. If neither seems to predominate, then it should be described as a kit. In the physical description area, give the details that relate to what you have stated as the dominant medium in the GMD; for example,

Bees (slide)/ . . .

40 slides : col. + 1 audio-cassette

Optionally, the accompanying material—that is, the audio-cassette—could be put in the notes area.

If you decide on the other hand, that neither the slides nor the cassette are dominant, then the components of the item are simply listed; for example,

Bees (kit)/ . . .

40 slides, 1 audio-cassette

or   Learning language (kit)/ . . .

20 flash cards, 2 charts, teacher's handbook.

If the parts come in a container, then the dimensions of the container follow; for example,

25 activity cards, 3 filmstrips, 25 study prints,

teacher's handbook, in container; 18 x 24 x 20 cm.

Some items, particularly games, contain too many components to list. In such cases use the term 'various pieces', or, if you can count them,

1 game (38 various pieces), in container; 12 x 2 x 6 cm.

Don't forget to give the scale for maps. The rules indicate that it should be given after the edition area, but you may feel that it is better placed in the notes area.

It is important when describing non-book material that is not as immediately accessible for scanning or examination as a book, to give a summary of the item, when possible. This is given in the notes area, preceded by the word 'summary'; for example,

Oil (filmstrip) / . . .

Summary: Explains how oil has become a powerful political weapon.

or   Form-a-sound (flash card)/ . . .

Summary: Aids children in the identification of vowel, consonant and digraph sounds and in the correction of speech difficulties.

Some libraries like to use coloured cards in the catalogue to indicate the type of material described. However, with the lack of standardised colour-coding, and the fact that centralised systems do not issue coloured cards, it is probably wisest to stick to white cards.

Serials

Most school libraries do not have enough periodicals or newspapers to warrant cataloguing. If, however, you do find it necessary, here are a few condensed rules.

Catalogue under the title. Statements of responsibility are restricted largely to corporate bodies. Do not record as statements of responsibility statements relating to personal editors.

Directly after the title statement give the numbering of the serial, whether by date, number or alphabetical designation; for example,

SMMART journal. – Vol. 1, no. 1 –

Give the number of the serial as the first that *you* have in your library (for example, the first issue you have may be Vol. 3, no. 2).

The entry remains *open* (as above) if you are still receiving issues. A space is left to fill in the final date should you cease subscribing. The entry is *closed* with the last number that you have if you are no longer receiving it; for example,

Australian trail and track. – No. 19 (Apr 1975) – No. 73 (Jan 1978)

The imprint is as given for books, repeating the year even if it is the same as the numbering area; for example,

Review. – Vol. 6. no. 3 (Sept 78) –   Adelaide:
Education Dept. of S.A., School Libraries Branch,
1978 –

v

Quarterly.

The collation can be restricted to the number of volumes—just 'v'—if the entry is still open.

A note is made on the frequency of the serial, as above; for example, Annual, Quarterly, Issued twice a month, or Irregular.

Foreign language material

There are no special rules for cataloguing material in foreign languages, although many school librarians like to add the title in English after the original title. This can certainly help in identifying an item if the librarian doesn't speak the language (as does writing the English translation on the title page). Make added entries for the title in both the English form and foreign language form.

Opinions vary as to the usefulness of transcribing non-Roman alphabets. However, as it is usually the teacher or the librarian who is using the catalogue entry, it is probably worthwhile. Also, not many schools have typewriters with non-Roman characters; and centralised school cataloguing, if it is computerised, is unlikely to be able to justify the expense of acquiring the necessary equipment.

Use the language of the item being catalogued in the description for the title statement, edition, imprint and series.

Parallel titles should not be confused with subtitles. A parallel title is the title proper in another language and/or script; it is separated from the title proper by an equals sign '='. If you supply a parallel title in English, as I recommend, it should be enclosed in brackets; for example,

Lionni, Leo
Il top dalla code verde (=The mouse with the green
tail) – Milano: Emme Edizione, 1973.
(28)p. : col. ill. ; 29 cm.

1. Italian fiction. I. Title II. Title: The
mouse with the green tail.

Choice of access points, or main entry and added entry headings

Items may be entered in the catalogue by personal name, corporate body, or title. The main entry heading is the most important heading and appears on all entries. Added entry headings are additional entries for the item in the catalogue; they are recorded on the bottom of the card (see the example given in the section on 'Elements of the catalogue entry' above).

For *personal authorship* the basic rule is that the main entry heading is under the name of the author. 'Authorship' involves the concept of chief responsibility for the creation of the intellectual or artistic content of a work; so in some instances, it may be the illustrator, the photographer, the musician or the performer. In the case of two or three authors, the main entry is under the first named; all are listed in the author statement, and added entries are given for the other authors; for example,

> Jones, Betty
> Arrival at noon/by B. Jones, F. Brown and H. Aust. –

and added entries are made for Brown and Aust.

If there are more than three authors, the main entry is under title. The most prominently named person on the title page is mentioned in the author statement and given an added entry; for example,

> Sociology/by F. Drew . . . (et al.)–
> added entry for Drew.

> Twelve mediaeval plays/ed. by J. Morrow. –
> added entry for Morrow.

> Poems of today/selected by J. Purdey. –
> added entry for Purdey.

Note that people who select, edit, compile, etc., are usually involved with the works of more than three authors, and the entry is therefore always under the title. When they have edited the work of three or fewer authors, then the main entry is of course under the first-named author. For example, a book entitled *Henry Lawson's World*, which is a selection of his work edited by F. Jones, is entered as

> Lawson, Henry
> Henry Lawson's world/ed. by F. Jones. –

In this case, it should not be necessary in a school library to give an added entry to Jones.

An important rule for school libraries is that applying to adaptations: enter a paraphrase, a rewriting, an adaptation for children, or a version in a different literary form (for example, in verse), under the name of the adapter, with an added entry for the author of the original; for example, for *The Little Glass Slipper*, retold by G. Baines and illustrated by F. Fleur, the main entry is

Baines, G.
The little glass slipper/retold by G. Baines; ill.
by F. Fleur. – . . .

Based on story by Charles Perrault

with an added entry for Perrault.

Translations are not adaptations or retellings, and should be entered under original author or the title, as appropriate. Only rarely would the translator merit an added entry.

Where basic responsibility is shared between an author and an artist, give the main entry to the first named, or the most prominently named, with an added entry for the other.

A *corporate body* is an organisation or a group of persons that is identified by a particular name, and that acts, or may act, as an entity. Typical examples of corporate bodies are associations, institutions, business firms, governments, government agencies, projects, programs, religious bodies, local churches and conferences. The main entry heading is under the name of the corporate body if the work is concerned with the body itself, or records the collective thought or activity of the body (for example, reports or conferences). In general, unless it is very obvious that the main entry should be under the name of the body, enter under the title, with an added entry for the corporate body.

For sacred scriptures (for example, the Bible), for anonymous works and for works where authorship is diffuse or cannot be determined, a *title main entry* is used.

Added entries should be used sparingly in a school library. Many school librarians do not give the second or third joint author an added entry, even though the joint authors must be mentioned in the author statement. In general, try to have at least one entry under the name of a person associated with a work, when the main entry is under the title or a corporate body. In deciding whether to give an added entry, consider the likelihood of anyone attempting to trace the item through that entry. Illustrators of picture books are important here, as are names of series and, most of all, *titles*.

Give all fiction works title added entries. Common practice today is to give title added entries to non-fiction as well. But use your discretion with title added entries for non-fiction; you can reduce the number of cards in the catalogue by *not* giving a title added entry, when the title is almost the same as the subject heading you plan to give, or when the title begins with a common phrase, such as 'Readings in . . .', 'Selections from . . .',

'Introduction to . . .', or 'Journal of . . .' etc.

An important rule is never to give an added entry to a heading that you have not mentioned somewhere on the card. It must be quite clear why you are giving the added entry. For instance, to return to the example of *The Little Glass Slipper*, you must mention in a note that Charles Perrault was the original author before he can be given an added entry.

The headings to which you decide to give added entries appear in the tracings at the bottom of the card, after the subject headings. They are numbered with Roman numerals and appear in the order of persons, corporate bodies, title, series.

All added entries except title and series must be written out *in full* in the form in which they will appear on the added entries cards. The words 'Title' and 'Series' are used instead of writing out the full title or the full series title, keeping in mind that they will appear in the heading exactly as they appear in the body of the entry.

Further practical details are discussed below, in the section on cataloguing routines.

Analytics

'Analytic' entries essentially analyse parts of a book or kit. They may be made, for example, for a collection of plays which are entered in the catalogue under the collective title or the author of the first play.

> Four English comedies of the 17th and 18th
> centuries/ed. by J. Morrell. – Harmondsworth,
> Middx : Penguin, 1950.
>
> 414 p.; 23 cm.
>
> *Contents*: Volpone/by Ben Jonson. – The way of the world/
> by William Congreve. – She stoops to conquer/ by Oliver
> Goldsmith. – School for scandal/by Richard Sheridan.
> I. Morrell, Janet.

Analytics can be made for each play as follows:

> Jonson, Ben
> Volpone
>
> *in*
>
> Four English comedies of the 17th and 18th centuries/ed.
> by Janet Morrell. – Penguin, 1950. – pp. 13–129.

Often an author/title added entry will serve the same purpose, but an analytic entry has the advantage of clarity.

A note can be made on the back of the main entry card to indicate that analytics have been made.

Similar entries can be made for some multi-media kits; for particular articles in periodicals; or for individual volumes in a series that has been catalogued as a set.

Do not confuse analytic entries with added entries for joint authors, etc. Analytics are made only for distinct and separate parts of an item, often distinguished by having a different author or title, or by having been published or cited individually.

Sets

At the other end of the spectrum is the set of materials that may be more usefully and economically catalogued as a whole rather than individually. This is done only when there is a common element under which they can be catalogued (for example, author, or title, or series), and when they can all be given the same class number. Include in the body of the entry only the elements that are common to all the items, and give a contents note or a summary to indicate what the set covers; for example,

> Card 1
> 398.2   Puffin folktales of the world – Harmondsworth,
> PUF   Middx: Puffin, 1976 –
>   4 v : col. ill.; 17cm.
>   For contents see following cards
>   1. Fairy tales   *cont.*

> Card 2
> 398.2   Puffin folktales of the world . . . *cont.*
> PUF   *Contents:*
>   1. Dick Whittington: a story from England.
>   2. The lady of Stavoren: a story from Holland.
>   3. Matt the goosehead: a story from Hungary.
>   4. The mouse king: a story from Tibet.

The call number for Dick Whittington is therefore 398.2/PUF/v1.

Form of heading

The choice of headings having been made, it is not always straightforward as to what should be the *form* of those headings in the catalogue. The general rule is that the heading for a person should be the name by which he or she is commonly known, and this should be determined from the name on the title page. (You do not use the fullest form of the person's name, as has been the practice in the past.)

Mark Twain *not* Samuel Clemens

T. S. Eliot *not* Thomas Stearns Eliot

Jimmy Carter *not* James Earl Carter

If different names are used in different works (as with some pseudonyms), and no one name is better known than any other, enter each work under the name as it appears on the work and cross-reference the entries.

Hyphenated names are entered under the first part of the name; for example, Day-Lewis, Cecil. If there is no hyphen, enter under the element of the surname by which the person prefers to be known; for example, Lloyd George, David. If uncertain, enter under the last part of the name; for example, Doyle, *Sir* Arthur Conan.

Surnames with separate prefixes are entered according to the practice of the language in which the author's works appear. In English, this is by prefix: De La Mare, Walter; Du Maurier, Daphne; Van Buren, Martin; A'Beckett, Thomas. For names in other languages, follow the conventions of the country of the language; some guidance is given in *AACR1* and *AACR2*.

Titles of honour (Sir, Dame, Lord, Lady) are added to the name if the term commonly appears with the name; for example,

Holt, *Dame* Zara

Menzies, *Sir* Robert

but Christie, Agatha (not Christie, *Dame* Agatha)

Russell, Bertrand (not Russell, *Lord* Bertrand)

Other titles such as Mr, Mrs, Dr, etc., are omitted unless required for identification or if the name consists only of a surname; for example,

Seuss, *Dr* (with reference from Dr Seuss).

Corporate bodies

Enter a corporate body directly under the name by which it is predominantly identified. Names are *not* inverted but are entered straight out, as

Museum of . . .

Society for . . .

University of . . .

Bodies identified by initials—for example UNESCO—are entered as such.

AACR2 list five types of corporate bodies that should be entered under a higher or related body, or under the name of a government department; for example, divisions, committees and bureaux. The name of the higher body comes first, followed by the subordinate body; for example,

> British Broadcasting Corporation. *Engineering division*
> Syracuse University. *College of Medicine*
> Telecom Australia. *Technical information library*
> University of Wales. *University Commission*

The same general rule applies to government bodies and agencies. When it is necessary to enter under place, then enter the body or agency under the area in which it exercises a legislative, judicial or executive function; for example,

> Adelaide. City Council.
> Australia. High Court.
> Canada. Army.
> Great Britain. Foreign Office.
> New Zealand. Department of External Affairs.

Try at least to be consistent in your entry of corporate bodies. This can be assisted by the use of an authority file, which I will discuss later, or by entering the heading you have chosen in Sears.

Uniform titles

When different editions or translations, etc., of a work appear under different titles, select a uniform title. This ensures that all the entries for all the editions of the work are filed together in the catalogue. Choose the best-known title, and generally the shortest title, and put it in brackets at the beginning of the title statement, immediately followed by the title that appears on the title page; for example,

> Cervantes, Miguel
> (Don Quixote) The history of the valorous
> and witty knight errant, Don Quixote de la Mancha

> Cervantes, Miguel
> (Don Quixote) Man of la Mancha

> Cervantes, Miguel
> (Don Quixote) The history of the ingenious
> gentleman

The title that appears on the title page can alternatively start on the next line; for example,

Cervantes, Miguel
(Don Quixote)
Man of la Mancha

Shakespeare and Dickens are two authors who often need entries with uniform titles; writers of fairy tales, such as Hans Andersen and the Brothers Grimm, may also need them.

There is usually no need to include a uniform title in an entry under the name of a reteller. Uniform titles are merely *filing titles*.

Anonymous classics, such as the Arabian Nights, Robin Hood, Song of Roland, Beowulf, etc., have the main entry under the uniform title; for example,

(Beowulf) Adventures of Beowulf

Another type of uniform title that may be useful in a larger library is the *collective title*, or form title. It is also used to make the filing sequence more logical, particularly for prolific authors such as Shakespeare, and to bring together collections of work. Examples of collective titles are 'Works', 'Selections', 'Poems', 'Sonnets', 'Short stories'. So, for Shakespeare, individual plays are filed first, (alphabetically by title), followed by collections using the collective title 'Works'; for example,

Shakespeare, William
(Works) Shakespeare's tragedies.

Uniform titles are also used for some legal materials, for treaties and for sacred scriptures such as the Bible. I recommend that librarians in schools with sizeable collections of such material refer to the rules in *AACR2*.

References and authority files

In the previous sections, I have given instances when there should be an entry that refers the catalogue user from one heading to another. A *see* reference directs the user from a heading (name, place, or subject) that is not used to the heading that is. *See* references are placed under headings people might refer to for information. In a school library, they might include:

King Arthur
see
Arthur, *King*

Dr Seuss
see
Seuss, *Dr*

When many title-added entries under a particular title are accumulated—for example 'The ugly duckling'—one *see* reference can be made to reduce the number of cards in the catalogue; for example,

> The ugly duckling
> For editions of this story see under the
> author Andersen, Hans.

A *see also* reference directs the user from a heading that has been used to one that is related; for example,

> Carroll, Lewis
> *See also*
> Dodgson, Charles

This *see also* reference would be necessary only if the library had something catalogued under Carroll's real name: Charles Dodgson.

Sometimes it may make more sense to put in an explanatory reference instead of merely a *see* or *see also* reference. For example, in the case of Lewis Carroll the reference may be:

> Carroll, Lewis
> For works by this author written under his
> real name, see Dodgson, Charles.

There must always be an entry under the heading to which any reference is made. A record must be kept, to ensure that references are withdrawn from the catalogue when the related material is withdrawn, and as a quick check to avoid duplicating particular references. This record is called the *authority file*. It can be conveniently kept on cards, or, in a small library, perhaps written in pencil in the library's copy of *Sears List of Subject Headings*. The record is kept under the heading used. The cards are *not* filed in the main catalogue but are kept in the cataloguing area for reference; only the reference cards themselves are filed in the catalogue. For Dr Seuss, the authority card would read:

> Seuss, *Dr*
> (x) Dr Seuss

The one card therefore keeps the record for both references. 'x' indicates that a reference has been made from the heading next to which the (x) appears, to the heading as it appears on the top of the card.

'xx' indicates that a *see also* reference has been made from the heading next to which (xx) appears to the heading at the top of the card; for example,

> Dodgson, Charles
> (xx) Carroll, Lewis

Because a *see also* reference would also have been made from Dodgson to

Carroll (both headings have been used, for not only do you want to refer users from Carroll to Dodgson but also from Dodgson to Carroll), then you will have another authority card.

Carroll, Lewis
(xx) Dodgson, Charles

The corresponding card in the catalogue will read:

Dodgson, Charles
See also
Carroll, Lewis.

Authority files can also be kept for series and publishers' names. Some central cataloguing services, such as the South Australian Education Resource and Information System (SAERIS), may supply authority lists. If you compile your own, it is probably advisable to ensure that it is consistent with the published authority files. (This also applies to lists of abbreviations; those in *AACR2* could be used as a basis, to which your own preferences can be added.)

Subject headings

All libraries should have copies of *Sears* and *Dewey*, and the principles and structure of these books have not changed significantly in their new editions. (The books by Akers, Piercy and Needham can still be used in this area). The 11th edition of *Sears List of Subject Headings* was published in 1977. *Dewey*'s 19th edition and 11th abridged edition were both published in 1979. Most schools would find the 11th abridged edition of *Dewey* adequate, although many use the unabridged edition.

My advice is to read the introductions to both *Sears* and *Dewey* carefully and follow their directions. When selecting headings that are not in *Sears*, take care to write them in the book and relate them to other headings. Be meticulous about ticking the headings and references you decide to use and making the reference cards.

If you have a divided catalogue—authors and titles in one sequence, and subjects in another—make subject headings independent of your title added entries, and vice versa. If your catalogue is a complete dictionary catalogue (that is, names, titles and subjects are interfiled), do not give title added entries when the subject headings are virtually the same. Conversely, sometimes the title will give better access to the subject than any heading you can find in *Sears*. Do not duplicate headings unnecessarily.

There is a practice in many schools to give subject entries for fiction (hospitals, dogs, the gold rushes, Indians, etc.); for example,

1. Lions – Fiction.

Foreign-language material is given a subject entry under the language—for example, Greek fiction, Greek poetry, Greek drama, etc. Non-fiction material is given the entry 'Greek language', as well as an entry for the particular subject.

Classification

Centralised library services probably classify in more depth than many schools prefer. In deciding to what depth you should classify, keep in mind the size of the library and the school, whether or not it is growing, and what areas are likely to be developed in the curriculum. Try also to be sensitive to areas of local interest or social concern, such as pollution and the environment, for there is likely to be a growing body of material published on such subjects.

You will often have to be satisfied with classifying an item at a point that is not exactly right. It is important to make sure you understand the principles behind the system, and be consistent. Try to work out the author's intention in producing the material; compare it with other, related material and how you classified the latter. Do not put it aside as 'too hard'. As a general rule, consistency is at least as important as accuracy.

Fiction is not usually classified in school libraries but distinguished by the symbol 'F' and then filed alphabetically by author. In primary schools it is probably also useful to have a special sequence and symbol for picture books, as these are usually shelved separately. The same is true for foreign-language material, though many people would argue against separating it from the general collection. (This does not mean that they are not classified according to their subject, but simply that they may be shelved in a separate part of the library.) Biographies are better classed with the subject, where practicable, rather than in 920.

Similarly it is probably wiser to classify textbooks and related material on specific subjects with the subject, where possible, rather than 372; for example, use 513 for a textbook on arithmetic rather than 372.7.

In the end you must base such decisions, including the integration of non-book materials, on the use and expectations of the school staff and students, the size of the collection, and the physical layout of the building.

Shelf list

Whereas the catalogue is usually filed in alphabetical sequence, the shelf list is a record of the library's collection filed in the order in which materials appear on the shelf—that is, by class number. It has obvious usefulness for stocktaking, as well as for checking whether a particular class number has been used, for assessing the strengths and weaknesses of the collection, and for allocating book numbers.

Traditionally the shelf list card contains, in addition to all the information on the main card, the accession number, price, date of purchase, and source. Because it is used mainly by the librarian, it is best kept in the workroom, though some library users find it helpful as a limited classified catalogue, as it brings related material together in a way that the dictionary catalogue (which scatters related subjects about the catalogue according to the alphabet) does not.

Small libraries can reduce duplication of cards by using the 'on order' card or the original handwritten catalogue card for the shelf list card.

Book numbers

To identify particular books, and particular copies of books, and to make shelving and retrieval more efficient, each item in the library should ideally have a unique number. Some libraries use accession numbers, but although this gives a unique number, it does not assist in shelving and retrieval; the more accepted way is to allocate a unique book number.

This number is derived from the main entry heading, whether it be author or title. Cutter-Sanborn tables can be used, but for schools the first three letters of the main entry heading are sufficient. If there is more than one author with the same name, or one with a similar name in the same classification (often the case with fiction) it will be necessary to go on to the next letter, and even the next. If the same author has more than one book in one class number, then different titles are distinguished by a lower case letter taken from the first word of the title; for example,

F   Peyton, K.M.
PEYb   The Beethoven medal

F   Peyton, K.M.
PEYf   Flambards

F   Peyton, K.M.
PEYp   Pennington's heir

F   Peyton, K.M.
PEYpe   Pennington's seventeenth summer

Alternatively, if you do not mind whether items are subfiled alphabetically by title, they can be numbered chronologically as the library
acquires them.

Copy numbers and volume numbers are added below. For example, if
you had two copies of Tolkien's three-volume *Lord of the Rings*, you
would number the six volumes as follows:

F	F	F	F	F	F
TOL	TOL	TOL	TOL	TOL	TOL
v1	v2	v3	v1	v2	v3
copy 1	copy 1	copy 1	copy 2	copy 2	copy 2

Book numbers for biographies classified in the 920s are derived from the
biographee's name rather than that of the author.

Many libraries find it good practice to further distinguish non-book
material (in addition to the general medium designation) by adding a
media code to the call number (for example, FS), but this can become
confusing. However, a location symbol may be necessary if certain
media are shelved away from the general collection.

Basic cataloguing routines

This section deals with the physical process of cataloguing and getting the
cards into the catalogue. Not all libraries follow this routine, but it is a
guide that individual librarians can use and vary to suit their particular
situation.

When an item comes into the resource centre, it is checked off against
the invoice, checked to see that it is complete, and accessioned. (See the
routine in Chapter 4, 'Selection and Acquisition'.) At this time the
accession number, the price and the source is written on the item, it is
stamped with the school stamp, and is then put on the 'to be catalogued'
shelf. The item is catalogued, the shelf list information added to the card,
and a book number allocated after consultation with the shelf list. The call
number is written on the item, which can now be physically processed.

The card is now ready for duplicating; and how this is done will depend
on the resources of your library. If you use the original, handwritten card
for the shelf list, you will need, in addition, a main card and one card for
each subject heading and added entry (indicated by the tracings at the

bottom of the card). Any related references you have written will need to be typed. Any authority cards you have written (and these will probably be few) need not be typed, as they are for your records only.

If you are typing your own cards, you may decide to reduce the amount of information that goes on to subject and added entry cards. If someone else is typing the cards for you, it may be safest to stick to unit entries—that is, have the same basic unit of information on every card, with subject heading or added entry typed at the top of the card above the main entry. Subject headings, which are preceded by Arabic numerals in the tracings, are typed in capitals at the top of the card. Added entries, which are preceded by Roman numerals in the tracings, are typed in lower case at the top of the card. (Although I have not done so in this chapter, it is common practice in many school libraries to capitalise the first word of the main entry.) The cards below show a typical set of cards generated from original cataloguing.

Main Card

```
941.5    Eadie, Peter
EAD      Let's visit Ireland / by P. Eadie and
         C. Duff - Rev. ed. - Lond.:  Burke, 1973.
         92p.:  ill.; 21cm. - (Let's visit series).

         1.  Ireland - Description and travel.
         I.  Duff, Cyril.    II. Series.




                        O
```

Note that there is no need to give this book a title-added entry, as it would file directly in front of the series added entry.

Subject Card

```
           IRELAND - DESCRIPTION AND TRAVEL

941.5    Eadie, Peter
EAD        Let's visit Ireland / by P. Eadie and
           C. Duff - Rev. ed. - Lond.:   Burke, 1973.
           92 p. : ill.; 21 cm - (Let's visit series).

           1.  Ireland - Description and travel.
           I.  Duff, Cyril.    II.  Series.
```

Added Entry Card

```
941.5    Duff, Cyril
EAD      Eadie, Peter
           Let's visit Ireland / by P. Eadie and
           C. Duff. - Rev. ed. - Lond.:   Burke, 1973.
           92p. : ill.; 21 cm. - (Let's visit series).

           1.  Ireland - Description and travel.
           I.  Duff, Cyril.    II.  Series.
```

Shelf List

```
941.5    Eadie, Peter
EAD        Let's visit Ireland/by P. Eadie and C. Duff -
           Rev. ed. - Lond.:   Burke, 1973.
           92p. : ill.; 21 cm - (Let's visit series).

           1.  Ireland - Description and travel.
           I.  Duff, Cyril.    II.  Series

  1035    $5.50    Standards      19/5/74
```

Series Card

When the cards have been typed and checked, the shelf list card and any authority cards are separated out, and the others collected for filing in the catalogue. Even though the main catalogue probably integrates book and non-book materials, you may have separate runs in your shelf list according to the medium—for example, a separate shelf list for filmstrips, records, etc.

If more copies or later editions of a work are acquired at a later stage, it is rarely necessary to re-catalogue. In most cases, after accessioning all that needs to be done is a note added to the shelf list card and the main card; for example,

— — copy 2

or — — 3 copies

There are two ways of generating a series card: firstly, by treating it as another added entry, and making a unit card for it; or secondly, and more economically, by making out a special series card to which is added just the call number, author and title of each item in the series when it is acquired, as in the example above.

Filing

The last routine to be performed is the filing, and here the difficulty may depend on the size of the library and whether you have a dictionary catalogue or a divided catalogue.

Although the practice in many libraries is to file authors, titles and subjects in one alphabetical sequence, I am in favour of divided catalogues. Filing rules, and in particular the interpretation of them, vary so much that it is easy to miss entries in a largish dictionary catalogue. I think students (and staff) are much clearer about the difference between an author and title, and the subject of a book, than they are about the alphabet. And the simpler (and less cumbersome) the filing can be made the better. Guide-cards are particularly helpful, and should be inserted every 2 to 3 cm.

In any case, the rules to follow are those in *ALA Rules for Filing Catalogue Cards*, 2nd abridged edition, 1968. They prescribe word by word filing, disregarding punctuation and initial articles. If possible, always have two people involved in filing so that you have a double check. Something misfiled is virtually lost.

I know it *seems* simple but, like so many things in cataloguing, there are always exceptions. Centralised services should lighten the burden considerably in the future, but unfortunately it is unlikely that they will solve all the cataloguing problems of the school librarian. In fact, you are probably going to end up with the most difficult items to catalogue yourself. I hope this chapter will be of some help to you.

Sample Cards

```
473      Byrne, Robert
BYR        Prehistoric man (transparency). -
           St. Louis : Milliken, 1969.
           12 transparencies : col.; 28x21 cm.

           Includes 4 duplicating masters, teacher's
           guide and student exercises.

           1.  Man, Prehistoric.



                         O
```

```
599     Wakefield, Norman A.
WAK     Australian marsupials (slide) :
        structure and function. - Melbourne :
        Educational Media, (197-?).
        12 slides : col. + 1 cassette and script.

        1.  Marsupials



                         O
```

```
785     Prokoviev, Serge
PRO     Peter and the wolf (sound recording) /
        narrated by Alex McGowen. - Philips,
        1974.
        1 disc (45 min.) : 33 1/3 rpm.; 12 in.
        Concertgebouw Orchestra, Amsterdam
        With:  The young person's guide to the
        orchestra / Benjamin Britten.

        I.  Britten, Benjamin.  The young person's
        guide to the orchestra.     II.  Title.
        III.  Title:  The young person's guide to
        the orchestra.  O
```

(Many libraries just give records and cassettes a running number rather than classifying with *Dewey*)

```
551     Edson, Ann R.
EDS     Geography (filmstrip) / A. R. Edson and
        J. W. Pattyson. - Freeport, N.Y.:
        Educational Activities, 1969.
        2 filmstrips (50 fr. each) : col.;
        35 mm. + 1 disc and script.

        Contents:  1.  What is geography?
        2.  Maps and globes.

          1.  Physical Geography.  I.  Pattyson J.W.



                         O
```

```
843      Saint Exupery, Antoine de
SAI      Le petit prince ( = The little prince) -
         Lond. : Heinemann Educational, 1958.
         105p. : ill. (some in col.); 23 cm.

         Includes notes and vocabulary.

         1.  French fiction.    I.  Title.
         II.  Title:  The little prince.


                         ◯
```

```
994      Australia's yesterdays (sound recording) /
AUS      selected and prepared by M. Print. -
         Perth : Admark, 1976.
         6 cassettes (30 min. each) + teacher's
         guide and work sheets.

         Summary:  A social studies program
         designed around 6 dramatized stories.

         Contents:  1.  First settlement.
         2.  Convicts.  3.  Squatters.  4.  Gold.
         5.  Bush rangers.  6.  Partners of the
         Federation.
                              1.  Australia - History
                         ◯
```

```
591      Zoo animals (picture). - Adelaide :
ZOO      Educational Technology Centre, 1976.
         8 pictures : col.; 29x39 cm. -
         (Pic-a-print; series 1)

         1.  Animals - Pictorial works.  I.  Series




                         ◯
```

614.7　Air pollution (kit). - Lond.:
AIR　　Educational Productions, 1972.
　　　　1 data sheet, 6 study prints, 6 work
　　　　cards + teacher's notes - (EP study kits).

　　　　Produced in collaboration with the Gas
　　　　Council.

　　　　Material from Queensland Air Pollution
　　　　Council and article by B. R. Thiele added
　　　　to kit.

　　　　1. Air-Pollution.　　I. Series

　　　　　　　　　　○

331.7　Cox, Sarah
COX　　People working / by S. Cox and R. Golden -
　　　　Harmondsworth, Middx : Kestrel, 1975-76.
　　　　6 v

　　　　Contents: 1. Dockworker.
　　　　2. Mineworker.　　3. Farmworker.
　　　　4. Car worker.　　5. Textile worker.
　　　　6. Hospital worker.

　　　　1. Occupations.　　I. Golden, R.
　　　　II. Title.

　　　　　　　　　　○

793.7　Dominoes (game). - Sao Paulo :
DOM　　Estrela, n.d.

　　　　1 game (36 pieces): wooden, col.,
　　　　in box; 19x4x6 cm.

　　　　　　　　　　○

Bibliography

AKERS, SUSAN. *Akers' Simple Library Cataloguing*. 6th edn, revised by Curley and Varlejs. Scarecrow Press, Metuchen, N.J., 1977.

ALA Rules for Filing Catalogue Cards. 2nd abr.edn, American Library Association, Chicago, 1968.

Anglo–American Cataloguing Rules. 2nd edn, Library Association, London, 1978.

BOLL, JOHN. *Introduction to Cataloguing*. 3 vols. McGraw-Hill, New York, 1970.

CUTTER, CHARLES. *Alphabetic Order Table*, altered and fitted with three figures by Kate Sanborn. H. R. Huntting, Springfield, Mass.

Dewey Decimal Classification. 11th abr. edn, Forest Press, New York, 1979.

DOWELL, ARLENE. *Cataloguing from Copy*. Libraries Unlimited, Littleton, Colo., 1976.

GOODMAN, DOREEN. *Bibliographic Control of Library Materials*. Canberra CAE, Canberra, 1978.

HUNTER, ERIC. *AACR2*. Bingley, London, 1979.

NEEDHAM, C. D. *Organizing Knowledge in Libraries*. 2nd edn, Deutsch, London, 1971.

PIERCY, ESTHER. *Commonsense Cataloguing*. 2nd edn, revised by Marion Sanner. H. W. Wilson, New York, 1974.

Reader in Classification and Descriptive Cataloguing, edited by Ann Painter. NCR Microcards Editions, Washington, D.C., 1972.

Sears List of Subject Headings. 11th edn, H. W. Wilson, New York, 1977.

WEISS, J. R., LEWIS, S., and MACDONALD, J. *Non-book Materials*. Canadian Library Association, Ottawa, 1973.

CHAPTER 8

The School Library's Place in the Community's Information Network

John Cook

School libraries have undergone a revolution in the past twenty years, changing from passive collections of books to dynamic learning and resource centres. Many of them are now taking a further step, and are gathering, interpreting and making available *information* in all forms. This is a less spectacular development, in that it does not necessarily involve new buildings and audio-visual technology. It does involve a great change of attitude on the part of school librarians, however, who now see their libraries as links in the community's information network.

The first step is to recognise the differing needs of discrete groups within the school, and to provide for them. As well as the needs of students, the school library caters for the information needs of teachers, school administrators and parents. The recognition of these needs, and attempts to serve them, lead to the school library becoming part of the community's, and the nation's, information network. For no school library (nor, for that matter, any library or other information agency) can be self-sufficient. It must refer its clients to other specialised sources of information when necessary; the school librarian should be aware of other information sources that are available, and formal or informal arrangements should exist to make referrals possible.

The school library is a limited and finite resource—as is the largest library in the country—and the school librarian should know where to find information that is not in the school library collection. This requires a wide knowledge of accessible information agencies and sources, both in libraries and in other places. Secondly, the school librarian should be aware of where people do, in fact, acquire information, attitudes and opinions. This vast field includes the mass media, community groups and activities, and informal 'over-the-back-fence' gossip networks.

At first glance it may seem that the school library is moving too far from its proper role in gathering and providing these types of information. However, it should be remembered that children (and teachers) have information needs quite apart from 'straight' school work. There are large numbers of children who, because of their parents' language or literacy problems, are the effective head of the household in finding things out. More importantly perhaps, children and young adults are increasingly expected to make responsible decisions about their own and other people's lives at an early age. If they are to make the right decisions, they should have access to reliable information through their school library. I do not suggest that the school library should supplant the public library, Citizens' Advice Bureau, Environment Information Centre, and so on, but rather act as a link to them, in using their information and in guiding people towards them.

Information not directly related to the school curriculum can be divided into three types:
1. Community information, from public libraries and other public information agencies.
2. Library-based specialist information, from public, special, state and national libraries and library-based computer information networks.
3. Non-specific information, opinions and attitudes, usually formed by peer-group influence and by the pressures of advertising and the mass media.

'Information is power'

It is often said that information is power, which is clearly absurd. Information itself—undisciplined, disorganised, not selective—is of no value. In fact, people who lack guidance and who become lost in a mass of irrelevant details are often extremely powerless. On the other hand, information and the knowledge of how to gain access to it, are necessary precursors to action and power. For example, it is necessary to know the procedures that must be undertaken to alter the traffic flow in a neighbourhood; and it is necessary to know what research in cancer has been undertaken before further advances can be made in the search for a cure.

We live in an information-based society. The problem is that so much of the information an individual receives is irrelevant to his or her needs, and is, in any case, often provided by vested commercial, political or religious interests. One of the most important tasks of the school library of the future will be to help students to be literate, aware, critical and selective in their use of information. Having learnt to use the relatively small information collection of the school library, students should be able to proceed with confidence to the larger storehouses of information outside the school.

School libraries, as a necessary part of education available to all, should help to redress the increasing availability of valuable information only to those able to pay for it. Western societies already deny large numbers of their people access to education and information, by demanding fees for service and tuition. Intelligence does not necessarily correlate with wealth, and so large numbers of intelligent people are being denied the level of participation in society that their abilities would make possible. At one level, they are not learning to read because class sizes are too large and teachers are not sufficiently well educated; at another level, they do not have access to tertiary education because of tuition and service fees, and inadequate student allowances; on yet another level, researchers without adequate support are unable to use machine-readable data banks.

The Library Association of Australia puts its view on access to information clearly and succinctly in its *Statement of Policy on Free Library Service to All*:

1. It is the expressed policy of the Library Association of Australia that each Australian has an equal right to information regardless of the way or for what purpose it is used.
2. Freedom of access to published information is essential to the democratic process and to the social welfare of the community. That freedom can be inhibited as much by poverty as by censorship. Satisfaction of a person's information needs must not be contingent upon his ability to pay.
3. In accordance with its information policy, the Library Association of Australia resolutely opposes any direct charge or fee for information service to users of publicly funded library or information services, whatever the nature or form of the information service and whether or not it entails access to machine readable data bases.

   (Reprinted by permission of the Library Association of Australia)

Community information and the public library

Community information is the information that people need for everyday living. In Jo McIntyre's words, this includes 'information about the services, programs, facilities and activities functioning in a community—more specifically, information about child and old-age care, housing, education, employment, health, welfare and migrant services, environmental issues, social organisations and activities, and so on.'[1]

The public library is an agency well placed to provide such information. It can provide links between (or even co-ordinate) the activities of other agencies in this field, such as social welfare services, Citizens' Advice Bureaux and community development organisations.

The school library, dealing with a defined group of young people in the community, can also provide community information, or it can use the services of the public library and other information agencies for the benefit of students.

This more active role in gathering and supplying information, of both public and school libraries, is at variance with the traditional, passive role of providing recreation, usually in the form of light reading. It is now widely accepted that libraries have a legitimate role in providing information in many published forms. What may not be as acceptable is the view that libraries should gather and provide information for everyday living, whether it has been published or not. Moreover, the provision of such information, as pointed out by Mairéad Browne[2], may involve the librarian's taking an advocacy role, by ensuring that the client receives the service needed from the agency to which he or she is referred. This cuts across the librarian's conventional position of impartiality, of providing as much information as possible and then allowing the user to decide on a course of action. If the librarian presents a point of view, is the role of the social worker being usurped? Are librarians suited, by temperament and training, to adopt such a role? Is it desirable that they do so? The debate continues.

The report of the Committee of Inquiry into Public Libraries (the Horton Report), recommends that public libraries provide access to all types of information:

> The public libraries are part of a system of information services and provide at the local level access points to the total national information resource. This total resource is comprised of existing library and information centres— national, state and municipal or local public libraries; the citizen information centres; school, college and university libraries; government, scientific, industrial and commercial special libraries and information centres and the various data banks available to them—informally linked in a distribution system and holding or having access to the major stores of information in Australia.[3]

However, the report also documents the uneven provision of public libraries across Australia and argues that the deficiencies that exist cannot be remedied from the resources of the existing funding bodies, State and local governments. If libraries are to become a truly national information network, federal funding is required. No such assistance has been forthcoming from the federal government.

Despite the lack of financial resources, public libraries in Australia are developing community information services. In New South Wales the Community Information Sharing Service (CISS) is actively encouraging public libraries to provide community information services. The Library Board of Western Australia has appointed two librarians to provide a community information service through the State Library and local public libraries. Other States are investigating needs and formulating plans for such services. School librarians should be aware of these developments, both to contribute to them and to use them when they begin operations.

School librarians should also be aware of the non-library information centres in the community. Many regions have Citizens' Advice Bureaux, Councils of Social Service, and offices of government departments involved in information and welfare activities. Many of these bodies produce handbooks and directories, which should be available in a school library reference collection. Most major cities have at least one more or less commercially produced directory or handbook of community information. Some Australian examples are *Sydney Inside Info*[4], *Alternative Melbourne*[5], and *City Index: A Resource Guide to Perth*[6]. In addition, many local government authorities produce an information directory of their area as a free service to residents and ratepayers.

School librarians should also collect community information and maintain it in a file. In most situations this will not be a very large-scale operation, as there will be a public library or other information agency within easy reach. If, for some reason (for example, lack of a nearby public library), it is envisaged that the information file will become large, then it is important that expert guidance is used in its planning. A good start can be made by reading the section in *Information and the Community* entitled 'Organisation and Classification: Three Views'[7]. The Library Association of Australia has formed a Community Information Special Interest Group which publishes a newsletter called *Tendril*, giving information and advice about community information.

Special libraries

Special libraries are very similar in their function to school libraries. Both provide information suited to the needs of a defined group of clients. The group served by a special library is usually smaller than that of the school library, but this is not necessarily always so.

Special libraries serve such bodies as research organisations, manufacturing and commercial firms, learned societies, professional associations, government departments and semi-government bodies, public utilities, banks, newspapers, museums, parliaments, and so on. Because they are usually small libraries and are funded and organised to serve the specific needs of their own organisations, they are often unable to respond to 'outside' requests, whether from school libraries or elsewhere. On the other hand, however, precisely because most of them are small and specialised, they depend heavily on networks such as inter-library loans to supplement their own resources.

Special libraries tend to be more *information* oriented and less *materials* oriented than other types of libraries. They build up a continuing relationship or dialogue usually with a small clientele with specific and known interests and needs. These information needs are served through such materials as periodicals, research reports, theses, machine-readable data and specifications of standards and patents. The monograph, still the stock-in-trade of most libraries, is of relative unimportance in most special libraries, although of course one would expect to find a good collection of reference works in the library's subject field, together with some general reference materials.

Many of the services provided by the special library to its clientele can be adapted for use by the school library: for example, the school librarian informs users of current materials as they are received by the library (current awareness services), and uses a knowledge of the needs and interests of particular clients by directing particular items of information to them (selective dissemination of information).

Archives

The term 'archives' can refer to the building or institution, and also to records held in that building or by that institution. The records themselves have been received or created by an organisation in the conduct of its normal affairs and have been selected because of their permanent value. Archives are thus records judged worthy of permanent retention.

If archives are to be preserved permanently, they must be stored in conditions that exclude such damaging agents as dust, airborne pollutants, ultra-violet light, fluctuations in temperature, humidity, theft, fire, insects and other vermin.

It is important for the archivist to identify the records that are worthy of permanent preservation as soon as possible after they have been created. Thus the archivist should build up contacts with the people creating the records, so as to be able to determine which records are worthy of preservation, why they were created and the connections between the records. Such records are no longer always on paper, but include such formats as microform, computer tape, motion picture films, audio tapes, and so on.

An archivist is a custodian of records, whose objective is to preserve those records and to prepare finding aids so that other people can use them. The archivist cannot make assumptions about the uses to which records may be put; for instance, replacing old parchments or bound volumes with the material on microfilm would destroy the evidence for a researcher of record formats. Each archive is unique and irreplaceable, and thus lending of records is not possible, though microform may be used when it is necessary or desirable for the information to be available in more than one place.

Archivists preserve the context in which the records were created and information about where they came from. This is called 'provenance'. It preserves the authenticity and legitimacy of records. The other major principle of archives is *'respect des fonds'*, referring to the preservation of the original order in which records were created or arranged.

School librarians should thus understand that the first priority of archivists is preservation, which may conflict with the librarians' first priority of providing access to information. Once this is understood, the user services of archives, such as facilities for reading and research, publications, communications and exhibitions, may be valuable resources for school libraries.[8, 9]

Library co-operation and networks

Library co-operation, resource sharing and networks of various kinds have great potential for giving more people access to information resources. However, the greatest benefits of such activity occur only when libraries and collections are strong. The sharing of inadequate resources benefits no one.

In Australia, the Australian Advisory Council on Bibliographical Services (AACOBS) provides a forum for representatives of all types of libraries to meet and discuss matters of common interest. Despite an anachronistic and undemocratic membership (all nineteen universities are represented, while there are only two representatives of school libraries[10], AACOBS has initiated many worthwhile activities since its foundation in 1956. These include successful representations to such bodies as the National Library of Australia to develop the National Union Catalogue of Monographs (NUCOM) and the Australian Marc Record Service*, among other advances, and heavy involvement in such schemes as the Australian Government Publishing Service free distribution scheme to major libraries, and the setting up of the Committee of Inquiry into Public Libraries. On the other hand, the efforts of AACOBS in the field of the planning and co-ordination of national library and information resources have been less successful.

Major support for AACOBS throughout its existence has come from the National Library of Australia (NLA). In 1979 the NLA withdrew support from AACOBS Working Parties because of its own financial constraints. Partly because of this, and also because of a perceived need to reform AACOBS, proposals are being considered to replace it with a new body, the Council of Australian Libraries and Information Services.[11]

The best co-ordinated system of libraries in Australia is the group of special libraries and information services that serve the Commonwealth Scientific and Industrial Research Organization (CSIRO). Other groups of libraries have recently begun establishing technical services centres to achieve economics of scale in bibliographic organisation. Examples are CAVAL (Co-operative Action Victorian Academic Libraries) and CLANN (College Libraries Activity Network of New South Wales), serving tertiary education libraries in Victoria and New South Wales, respectively, Technilib serving public libraries in Victoria, and SAERIS/ASCIS (South Australian Education Resources Information System/Australian School Catalogue Information Service) serving school libraries in South Australia and elsewhere in Australia. Most State Library Services and Education Department Libraries Branches have central processing, referral or exchange services of varying degrees of sophistication and development.

The National Library of Australia is beginning to provide computer-based information systems. AUSINET (the Australian Information Network) provides many data bases on-line, including ERIC (the Education Resources Information Centre), Australian Education Index, Australian National Bibliography, and Australian Public Affairs

*Marc = MAchine Readable Cataloguing

Information Service, which, among others, are of interest to schools. From 1979, Australian users were able to gain direct access to American data bases via Midas, a computer telecommunications link of the Overseas Telecommunications Corporation. In addition, the National Library of Australia provides computer-generated current awareness bulletins in many subject areas for people without access to computer terminals.

The culmination of this activity is intended to be the creation of a comprehensive Australian National On-line Bibliographic Network (ANBIBNET) using the Washington Library Network (U.S.) as a prototype[12]. The Washington Library Network includes all types of libraries and is a major example used in a report of the National Commission on Libraries and Information Science (U.S.)[13] as to how school libraries can contribute to, as well as benefit from, multi-type library networks. The Washington Library Network provides a computerised data base, a microfiche printout of all members' listed holdings, cataloguing and processing services, designated resource centres, and a state-supported telephone network to expedite inter-library loans[14]. As school library collections grow, they are becoming major resources in the fields of education, curriculum materials and children's literature. School libraries could contribute to multi-type library networks, just as the school children who are their clients could derive great benefits from their participation in such wider co-operative activities.

Government information and freedom of information

Governments produce vast masses of publications and information. These emanate from national governments, from State or provincial governments, and from local government authorities. Within each tier of government, separate departments and authorities produce an array of materials that can be daunting for the beginner. However, much valuable information for use in school libraries is contained in government publications, and the school librarian should be aware of the range of material. These include parliamentary debates, which in some countries are broadcast on radio or television and are almost always available in verbatim printed form (often called *Hansard* after Thomas C. Hansard, a former publisher of the debates of the British House of Commons). Legislation in the form of bills and Acts is also made available to the public, as are papers and reports considered by legislative bodies and their committees. Governments also publish much material that may not be directly related to law-making; this includes such items as reports and papers of commissions and committees of inquiry. In addition, governments often produce information of a statistical nature; handbooks and manuals on many topics; and tourist and general information about their countries or regions. (Further information about the selection and acquisition of government materials is given in Chapter 4.) A comprehensive treatment of Australian official publications is to be found in the book *Australian Official Publications*, edited by D. H. Borchardt[15]. Another book of the same name, *Australian Official Publications*, by Howard Coxon, is also useful and informative.[16]

Much government information is not generally available to the public, and in some cases this, too, is in the public interest. The confidentiality of cabinet and government papers should be preserved to allow various courses of action to be canvassed; details of defence arrangements should remain secret so that actual or potential enemies cannot prepare to circumvent them; the privacy of individuals should be protected by the non-disclosure of census and other information gathered about them; and so on. However, what government information should remain privy to government, and what should be published, is a matter for debate.

The people who advocate greater freedom of information base their case on the view that for a democracy to function properly, informed public debate must take place. Thus well-informed and perceptive commentators, and private individuals, should have access to information and be able to express their views publicly, through uncensored media, and privately. Several countries have achieved successful freedom of information legislation. Probably the best-known example is the United States of America, where recent legislation has enabled lobby groups and individuals to uncover information from government files about such diverse subjects as nuclear reactor accidents, environmental effects of Concorde, CIA activities, and many more. Canada is considering similar legislation, and Sweden has had successful freedom of government information for many years.

In Australia, a Freedom of Information Bill was introduced in 1978, but had not been made law by 1980. The Bill, together with linked legislation on archives, has been published[17] and would give citizens a legally enforceable right to government documents, give wide discretionary power to public servants to withhold information, allow ministers to stamp documents 'secret' with no right of appeal against this decision, and make many vague categories of documents exempt from disclosure. The legislation has been severely criticised by many community groups concerned with genuine freedom of information. School librarians, who are also concerned with access to information, should follow the progress of this public debate.

The mass media

Most people obtain many of their opinions and attitudes, their information about the world around them, from the mass media. The mass media include newspapers, radio and television and are defined by Mungo MacCallum (at the 1978 Australian School Library Association Conference) as 'that section of communications, whether publicly or privately owned, which is basically concerned with maximising its audience'[18]. Thus a metropolitan daily newspaper is part of the mass media, while a club newsletter is not.

When the mass media are privately owned and gain revenues and profits through advertising, it is particularly important for them to maximise their audience. By being able to demonstrate, through rating and popularity polls and circulation audits, that large numbers of people are receiving their broadcasts or buying their newspapers, organs of the mass media can sell space or time to advertisers at high prices to publicise their products or services. Humphrey McQueen, in his book *Australia's Media Monopolies*[19], puts the view that the mass media are not selling information and entertainment to the public, but are selling the public to the advertisers. The information and entertainment is merely to attract viewers or readers—the advertising is most important because it provides the profits. While this statement may be an oversimplification of McQueen's thesis, it does direct attention to the mass media's need for popularity, popularity that often comes before other considerations such as the public interest or fair and unbiased reporting of events. Thus many people gain an unhealthy and antisocial view of life, particularly in regard to violence in society and attitudes to other people, from such undeniably popular programs as police dramas and the sensational reporting of crime. Children are particularly susceptible to such insidious forces, as they have less experience of the real world and in many developed countries watch many hours each week of television, particularly.

The commercial mass media, dependent as they are on advertising revenues, develop attitudes in the public of the necessity to buy and consume. In a world of increasing population and shrinking resources, these are no longer attitudes beneficial to society as a whole.

The mass media also supply specific information and opinion about the world through their news and current affairs coverage. These reports and commentaries can very easily be slanted to particular viewpoints by journalists, editors, owners and controllers of the media. Such occurrences become more likely as the ownership and control of the media become concentrated in fewer hands. That so much reporting is fair and unbiased says a great deal for the integrity, skill and courage of many journalists and editors.

On the positive side, it is encouraging to note greater awareness of the needs of children, and some attempts to serve them particularly on television, by both commercial and publicly funded media. In addition, there is more recognition of the diversity of society, and a greater range of mass media, such as public and ethnic broadcasting, is coming into existence.

School librarians should be aware of the sources from which the children in their schools do in fact gain information and attitudes. This is not to mean that one should totally debase one's own tastes and interests in search of the lowest common denominator, but neither should one be elitist in attitudes to the interests of the users of one's library.

Information futures

New technologies exist that enable more efficient transfer of information in many forms. Without doubt, these existing technologies will be further developed, and new discoveries will be made. Because of these developments, and whether or not libraries as we now know them continue to exist, information and access to it will become increasingly valuable. The activities of librarians will change, but I believe there will be an increased need for information workers of some kind to organise, provide access to, and interpret information for people. School librarians in the 1980s will need to recognise that more and more they belong to an information profession wider than one that serves only schools. They should work to establish links and networks between libraries and information agencies of all kinds, always with the aim of providing the best possible service to their users.

References

1. Jo McIntyre, 'The library contribution to community information services', in Department of Environment, Housing and Community Development, *Information for the Community: Report of the Short Course Conducted at Kuring-gai CAE, 10–12 May 1978* (AGPS, Canberra, 1978), p. 37.
2. Mairéad Browne, 'Librarians, social workers—and community information: the territorial stake-out', *Australian Library Journal* 25, 16 (November 1976), 383.
3. *Public Libraries in Australia: Report of the Committee of Inquiry into Public Libraries* (The Horton Report) (AGPS, Canberra, 1976), ch. 4, 'The Role of the Public Library', para. 4.4.
4. *Sydney Inside Info*, (Horan, Wall & Walker, Sydney, 1977).
5. *Alternative Melbourne* (Patchwork Press, Melbourne, 1977).
6. *City Index: A Resource Guide to Perth* (Student Guild, W.A. Institute of Technology, Perth, 1979).
7. John Bailey, Peter Allen and Joan Begg, 'Organisation and classification: three views', in *Information for the Community*, p. 61.
8. The author is grateful to Mr Peter Crush, Archivist of the City of Adelaide, for much of the information contained in this section. Any errors of fact or interpretation are of course the author's own.
9. A useful survey of libraries and other information agencies in the South Pacific region can be found in D. H. Borchardt and J. I. Horacek, *Librarianship in Australia, New Zealand and Oceania: A Brief Survey* (Pergamon Press, Sydney, 1975).
10. AACOBS membership: 19 universities, 14 representatives of National and State libraries, 10 representatives of local public libraries, 7 representatives of CAEs, up to 4 laymen, 3 representatives of special libraries, 2 representatives of the LAA, 2 representatives of school libraries, 2 representatives of colleges of technical and further education, 1 archivist, 1 representative of LAA-accredited schools of librarianship, 1 representative of parliamentary libraries, and any conveners of AACOBS working parties not included in any other capacity. Source: Harrison Bryan, 'AACOBS: its purpose, performance and present perils', *Australian Library Journal* 28, 8 (1979), 119.
11. Bryan, p. 124.
12. George Chandler, 'The future pattern of library and information services', in *Alternative Futures: Proceedings of the 20th Biennial Conference of the Library Association of Australia* (LAA, Sydney, 1979), p. 323.
13. Task Force on the Role of the School Library Media Program in the National Program, *The Role of the School Library Media Program in Networking* (National Commission on Libraries and Information Science, Washington, D.C., 1978).
14. *The Role of the School Library Media Program in Networking*, p. 73.
15. D. H. Borchardt (ed.), *Australian Official Publications* (Longman Cheshire, Melbourne, 1979).
16. Howard Coxon, *Australian Official Publications*, Guides to Official Publications, Vol. 5 (Pergamon Press, Oxford, 1980).
17. Parliament of the Commonwealth of Australia, *Freedom of Information: Report by the Senate Standing Committee on Constitutional and Legal Affairs on the Freedom of Information Bill 1978, and Aspects of the Archives Bill 1978* (AGPS, Canberra, 1979).
18. Mungo MacCallum, 'Mass Media in Australia', in *Being Resourceful: Proceedings of the 6th Biennial Conference of the Australian School Library Association* (ASLA, Goulburn, 1978), p. 118.
19. Humphrey McQueen, *Australia's Media Monopolies* (Visa, Melbourne, 1977).

CHAPTER 9

Administrative Aspects
of School Libraries

Joe Hallein

The school library exists to support the aims and objectives of the total school program. The library program should be the centre of the school's learning program and be totally integrated into the learning program. The library does not exist in isolation from the rest of the school, and the library's administrative aims and objectives should ensure that it is administered so that its facilities and instructional resources are adequate to support the school's program and so that the school community will have access to the facilities and materials. School library policies and procedures should be designed to support the educational projects of the school and not for the convenience of the library.

A school library policy

A school needs to develop a written school library policy. This policy should not be written by the library staff alone and, of course, it should never be written without involving the library staff. A committee of school administrators, teachers, school librarians and, if possible, students and parents should develop the general library policy and the policy should be approved by the governing authority of the school. It should state what the aims and objectives of the library are; and these, of course, will be related to the general aims of education in a particular State and the aims and objectives of the individual school. One official document on the aims of education, *Aims of Primary Education in New South Wales*, states that 'the central aim of education which, with home and community groups, the school pursues is to guide individual development in the context of society through recognisable stages of development towards perceptive understanding, mature judgment, responsible self-direction and moral autonomy.'[1] Individual development and achievement are important aims, and school library policies in New South Wales would probably demonstrate that the library is committed to supporting these aims.

In addition to a policy statement of the general aims of the school library, specific policies need to be developed that state the aims and objectives of the functions and activities the library will perform. These would include selection policies, policies on organising the library resources, policies on co-operation with other information agencies, and various administrative policies and procedures. These should all be included in a policy manual, and the procedures for implementing these policies should also be written down. Many schools have high staff turnovers and if new staff are to operate the library effectively they need to have written guidelines about what has been done and why it has been done. Written policies and procedures are also helpful in maintaining good relations with staff and students.

A school library program needs to have certain basic elements if it is able to function effectively. It must have:
(a) adequate financial support;
(b) adequate staff, both professional and non professional;
(c) a wide range of instructional materials that are organised and accessible; and
(d) facilities to house the instructional materials and to enable the materials to be used in a good learning environment.
The administrative policies and procedures of the library should ensure that these basic elements are made available so that the school library can function effectively as a learning centre to support the aims and objectives of the school.

School library personnel

The number and types of staff in a school library vary from school to school depending on the size and educational program of the school. The number of tasks performed by school library staff is immense: in the United States, the School Library Manpower Project has identified 300 different tasks carried out by school library staff.[2] These tasks vary from routine clerical activities to highly professional educational tasks. It is not in the interest of the school to employ professional school librarians to perform tasks that are primarily clerical; and a library that is staffed by individuals who are trained to perform only clerical and technical tasks will never become a real centre for learning and will remain just a store house of books. School libraries usually employ 'differential staffing'—that is, a variety of levels of staff to perform different types of tasks. In most school libraries, staff can be classified into three levels: professional, technical and clerical. Many schools have adult and student volunteers in addition. There is no clear division between professional, technical and clerical tasks, but most can be appropriately assigned to one of these three levels.

School librarians

In Australia, no nationally accepted list of tasks for various school library personnel has yet been developed. Some State Departments of Education have developed lists (see bibliography on p. 214), and the Library Association of Australia and the Australian School Library Association have established a joint working party to prepare a document on the tasks and educational requirements of school library personnel. Although the working party has not prepared a document acceptable to both associations, they did develop in 1977 a list of tasks that are generally accepted as appropriate for professional school librarians[3]—that is, for individuals holding dual qualifications in education and librarianship. Some of these are:

1. To be responsible for the organisation, operation and services of the school library.
2. In consultation with the school library staff, teachers and students, to recommend and implement policies for the development and operation of the library.
3. To ensure that appropriate programs and procedures are developed and that these are continuously evaluated and modified to meet changing needs and to take advantage of new technological developments.
4. To evaluate the collection, bringing to the notice of school staff any deficiencies, idle materials, resource imbalance, extra-curricular needs.
5. To ensure that the school library provides an environment conducive to learning and personal development.
6. In consultation with school library staff and teachers, to determine policies for the selection of materials and equipment; to participate in selection and co-ordinate selection.

7. To recommend and maintain systems for the acquisition, cataloguing, processing and circulation of materials appropriate to the library's needs and to undertake more difficult work in those areas.

8. To supervise and evaluate the performance of school library personnel.

9. To set performance standards for school library equipment, facilities, etc.

10. To submit estimates for the financial requirements of the school library and control expenditure of the budget.

11. To plan, recommend and organise programs appropriate to the needs of school library users and to the educational objectives and programs of the school.

12. To ensure that the resources and facilities of the school library are made known to teachers and students.

13. To act as a resource person in the classroom and to serve on curriculum committees and teaching teams as a resource consultant; to act as a resource consultant to individual teachers.

14. To guide students in their research and other learning activities; to help students to develop information retrieval expertise and acquire skill in the selection of materials and in the techniques of inquiry and evaluation so that they become independent learners.

15. To provide guidance in the use of the library and its resources that is correlated with the curriculum and is educationally sound.

16. To provide advice to teachers, students and technicians in the production of materials for specific learning purposes and to explain to them the uses and operation of equipment.

17. To ensure that school library staff receive adequate in-service training, and assist with in-service training for teachers.

18. To ensure that school library staff and teachers are kept up to date with research and developments in their fields of interest.

19. To participate in the determination of educational goals, policies and programs for the school.

20. To draw to the attention of teachers and students sources of information and materials outside the school and help them to utilise them in appropriate cases.

21. To co-operate with other schools, public libraries, education authorities, etc., to ensure the most beneficial development and economical use of resources and services.

In small school libraries that only employ a single full- or part-time school librarian with no clerical assistance, clerical and technical tasks must also be performed by the school librarian. It is now widely recognised that if maximum educational benefit is to be gained by the school library and the professional expertise of the school librarian, adequate support staff must be employed to free school librarians to carry out their educational functions.

Clerical assistants
Clerical assistants are employed in school libraries all over Australia, and while the types of tasks performed by these individuals vary widely, it is commonly accepted that they should perform the tasks that require no special library or educational training. The New South Wales Department of Education *Clerical Assistant (Library) Handbook* includes a statement of duties for clerical assistants that would be appropriate for most school libraries. This statement says that the clerical assistant is responsible to the principal through the school librarian for the following non-professional duties:

1. Placing and following up orders for new library books as directed.
2. Accessioning, numbering, covering and shelving of books.
3. Filing of catalogue and related cards.
4. General tidiness of the library.
5. Assisting in supervising activities of any library prefects.
6. Charging of books.
7. Following up overdue books and reporting offenders to the school librarian.
8. Interviewing book sellers if directed.
9. Typing and duplicating material for the library.
10. Assisting in arranging book displays.
11. Maintaining material for use on audio-visual aids and such items as maps, pictures, photos, if kept in the library.
12. Repairing books.
13. Assisting with supervision of pupils using the library for exchanging books or general library reading, and with supervision before and after normal school hours when the library is open (supervision is not to include study groups or formal classes).
14. Assisting with library stocktaking.
15. Other related clerical duties as directed by the principal for the proper conduct of the library.[4]

Library technicians
Library technicians—those who have completed a two-year library technicians' course—are being increasingly employed in school libraries

to carry out a wide range of specialised para-professional tasks. In Australia, non-government schools have been the leaders in employing library technicians in school libraries, although some Departments of Education are beginning to create special categories of employment for library technicians. Specialised lists of tasks for library technicians are being developed. In most Australian school libraries, library technician tasks are performed by the professional staff, which means that they have less time to devote to their educational role. Some appropriate tasks for library technicians are:

1. To prepare descriptive cataloguing for library materials; to catalogue duplicates, new editions and fiction and revise printed cards to conform to the library's practice.
2. To classify and assign subject headings for selected materials.
3. To file entries in the catalogue.
4. To search and verify bibliographic data.
5. To maintain circulation systems.
6. To process inter-library loan requests.
7. To maintain loose-leaf reference material.
8. To prepare/file vertical file material.
9. To answer ready reference enquiries and assist the librarian with other reference enquiries.
10. To assist in the planning of library displays; to set up library displays and exhibits.
11. To operate audio-visual equipment; to maintain and make adjustments to audio-visual hardware.
12. To reproduce materials using a wide range of reprographic methods.
13. To make, assemble and assist in the design and planning of multi-media kits.
14. To assist in the production of television programs and motion picture films.
15. To assist in the evaluation and selection of equipment and supplies.
16. To supervise and train non-professional staff and write procedures for tasks supervised.
17. To supervise clerical tasks.[5]

Staffing formulas

The number and variety of staff available in a school library depends on numerous factors. The attitude of the school administration and teachers toward the library, the ability of the library staff to demonstrate the educational value of the library program and official staffing formulas all have an effect on library staffing. While non-government schools are usually free to develop their own staffing patterns, Australian state schools have traditionally been bound to follow official staffing formulas, which means that the total school staff is dependent upon enrolment. Primary school libraries are generally assigned a specific number of professional staff, who are school librarians. In Tasmania and the Australian Capital Territory, each primary school is assigned one school librarian; in other States such as New South Wales, Victoria and South Australia, the number of school librarians assigned to a school depends upon enrolment. The staffing formulas for primary school libraries in two States in 1979 are shown in the table below.

New South Wales		South Australia	
Enrolment	Professional Staff	Enrolment	Professional Staff
76– 175	0.2	150–199	0.2
176– 250	0.4	200–232	0.3
251– 400	0.6	233–265	0.4
401– 600	0.8	266–299	0.5
601– 900	1.0	300–399	0.6
901–1200	1.2	400–499	0.8
1201–1500	1.4	500 +	F/T
1501–1750	1.6		
1751–2000	1.8		
2000 +	2.0		

In 1979, state primary schools in Victoria with an enrolment between 210 and 630 pupils were provided with one school librarian and a second school librarian was provided to the schools with more than 631 pupils. In 1980, however, Victoria proposed to change primary library staffing, so that each school would receive a total staff entitlement and each school would be responsible for nominating the type of staff, including library staff, that it required within this total.

State secondary schools in Victoria and South Australia receive a total staff allocation, and each school decides how to use this staff in all subject fields—including the library. In the Australian Capital Territory, two school librarians are assigned to each secondary school, and schools can opt to increase the number if they wish to use part of their total school staffing allocation. In Tasmania and New South Wales, one school librarian is assigned to high schools, and schools have the option to increase this number if they wish to utilize other staff positions. Most government secondary school libraries in Australia have the option of increasing professional library staff if they can successfully demonstrate to their colleagues that the school will get more educational benefits by assigning an additional staff member to the library rather than to some other area.

In some States, such as Tasmania and South Australia, the number of support staff assigned to the library depends upon the priorities of each school; in other States, such as New South Wales, official staffing formulas exist for school library support staff.

Volunteers

School libraries seldom have enough paid staff members to do all the tasks necessary for a successful library program. Volunteers, both adult and student, are used to perform a wide variety of tasks.

It should be made clear to volunteers that they are expected to conform to the rules and regulations of the library, and they should be under the supervision of one specific staff member. It is not fair to volunteers, or to other staff members, to make the volunteers responsible to a variety of individuals. Each library worker should know to whom they are responsible.

Volunteers are often looked upon as a free source of 'slave' labor and are given only routine jobs to perform, such as pasting labels in books or shelving. However, many adult volunteers have a wide range of talents, such as artistic skills, storytelling skills, educational or library skills, and these should be utilised by the school librarian. Student volunteers can be used to great benefit by the library and at the same time can perform tasks that will contribute to their own satisfaction and profit; it must always be remembered that the students' education and personal development come before library needs. It is a good idea to have a short probation period for student volunteers: many students are keen at first but soon lose interest. Volunteers can be rewarded with minor privileges, such as being the first to borrow new books, having use of the library workroom at lunchtime, and excursions and parties. Students can perform a wide variety of tasks, including telling stories to younger pupils or helping students find material, as well as the usual clerical tasks.

A successful school library program is dependent upon a dedicated staff of professional, para-professional, clerical and volunteer workers who are all clearly aware of the educational role of the library and who know how the library fits into the total school program.

Budgets

All organisations, including school libraries, have budgets. Many school librarians have traditionally had little involvement with developing the school library budget or controlling the expenditure of that budget; however, it is now recognised that he or she must play a major role in both the development and control of the budget. The school library budget is a statement of how the library will use financial resources to achieve its aims and objectives. The school library budget serves three major purposes: to control, to plan and to evaluate the library program. The most important of these has been the control function: making sure that funds are spent in an approved manner on specific items and that only the authorised amount of money is spent. Educators are now recognising that the budget is also closely related to the planning and evaluation of school library programs.

Budgeting for school library programs should not be a once-a-year process; but should be a year-long ongoing activity that is closely linked to the planning of the school's instructional programs and the library programs that will be developed to support them.

Budget planning

School librarians need to have some information available before beginning the planning and budgeting process. They must be aware of the school's budget year, as it makes little sense to submit a budget request after the school budget has been finalised. They must know the extent of the library's collections of print and non-print materials, as well as hardware and other equipment: before demonstrating a need for the purchase of something to meet a specific instructional objective, one needs to know whether there is something already available to meet the objective. A knowledge of the cost of material and equipment is necessary. If one submits budgets with inaccurate cost estimates, the reliability of the total budget process will be suspect. A knowledge of the past performance of the library is also necessary. One should demonstrate that the library/media program is effective in meeting the needs of the school, and proof of past successes is a good indicator that the library really can meet objectives proposed in the new budget. The school librarian must also have knowledge of the priorities established by the school and the various departments of the school. Without this knowledge it is impossible to be able to plan a budget around programs.

It is obvious that the school librarian cannot plan a program budget in isolation from the various faculty members and, indeed, from students of the school. It is the faculty and students who will be setting the instructional objectives for programs, I hope in consultation with the school librarian who should be the school's expert in the use of various instructional materials. There are several ways to learn of the priorities and specific objectives of each department for the coming year; and these can range from informal conversation to statements of behavioural objectives for each unit of study. One useful method for determining priorities in a school is a forced-choice type of instrument such as that developed by James W. Liesener.[6] What is important is that the staff of the school library plan their budget in consultation with other members of the school community so that it is a reflection of what is happening in the school, and everyone in the school community recognises that the budget is being used to buy material not for the librarian but for the whole instructional program.

Line budgets

School media budgets should include provision for three major categories: staff, instructional materials, and supplies. In many schools, staff costs are included in the total school budget and are not allocated to departments such as the library; but often staff trade-offs are possible with the principal's approval, and then staffing would be included in the budget. Most school library budgets in Australia include only instructional materials and supplies. The most common method of presenting a budget report is the line budget: each line of the budget represents a spending category and the amount to be spent in that category. The number of categories will depend on the detail required by the funding authority and also, to some extent, on the ease by which funds can be transferred from one category to another. If transfer of funds from, say, books to periodicals is very difficult or impossible, it would be best to use broad rather than specific categories. The exact form of the budget will vary according to local school practice.

Sample Line Budget

Category	Allotment 1980 $	Projected Increase 1981 $	Recommendation 1981 $
School library books	3000	500	3500
Periodicals & newspapers	500	75	575
Audio-visual material	1500	250	1750
Supplies	700	50	750

Program budgets

Line budgets show expenditures but they do not really help school administrators or funding agencies to become aware of just why these expenditures are required or how the expenditures will be used to help the school achieve its objectives. In order to overcome this problem, school librarians are often adopting program budgeting techniques. The program budget shows not only the funds to be used but also the services and benefits that will result from the expenditures. The budget shows not only dollar relationships but also contains a narrative of program relationship and how expenditures in the library will achieve objectives in language, art or science programs.

The library will develop some programs that are not directly related to specific instructional programs. These should also be included in the budget, with a statement of how the objectives will help to achieve the aims of the school. Just as the form of a line budget will vary according to local practice, so will the format of a program budget.

Sample Program Budget

1. Purchase of instructional materials in a variety of formats on the subject of 'South East Asia'. This material will be used to help students achieve the objective of the Social Science department that 'all Grade 6 children will be able to describe how the geography of a region affects how people live'.

Instructional materials	$500
Supplies	$75

2. Development of a special high-interest low-level reading book collection that will be used to help meet the school's objective that 'all students will develop the attitude that reading is a useful way to spend leisure time'.

Books	$300
Supplies	$35
Promotional posters	$5

Sources of funds

The sources of funds for school libraries vary from State to State in Australia and between non-government and government schools. In some States, such as New South Wales, secondary schools receive no funds specifically for the library, and the library must secure its funds from the general operating budget of the school. Other States, such as Victoria, provide a specific library grant which in 1979 was $6.56 per pupil in Years 7 to 9, and $7.88 per pupil in Years 10 to 12. Other sources of funds for school libraries are Parents and Citizens groups, book sales, and funds from government funding agencies such as the Schools Commission. School libraries have been successful in obtaining funds from the Schools Commission's disadvantaged schools programs, resource sharing grants and the Special Projects (Innovations) Program. A well-designed budget is an important part of the submission for any funds, and school librarians need to develop budget proposals that will allow funding agencies to be aware of the importance of the school library in meeting the school's aims and objectives.

School library records and reports

School librarians need to report to school administrators and to various funding authorities on the effectiveness of the school library. These reports help to demonstrate how funds and other forms of support have been used by the library; and they also serve as a good publicity device, highlighting the major activities of the library. In order to prepare a report, school librarians need to keep a variety of records that will provide data on the library. Some educational authorities will require school librarians to keep specific records in a standard format. In addition to these required records, all school librarians should collect data in the following categories:

1. *The size of the collection*
This information is extracted from a simple record of additions and withdrawals, in which the library staff records the number of volumes added or subtracted. Also the shelf list can be used to estimate the number of volumes in each Dewey Decimal area, by the formula of 100 cards to 2.5 cm. (It is not worth the time and effort to count the items in each Dewey class.) Some libraries maintain an accession book in which the details of each library purchase are recorded; this is required by regulations in some schools, though many librarians have ceased to maintain accession books because they are of no real value to the library. Any details about the price or place of purchase that the librarian feels should be recorded can be written on the shelf list card.

Stocktaking, an inventory of the collection, is done to check whether or not all of the items that are supposed to be in the collection are there. This is a very time-consuming process and, in all but the smallest libraries, it is best to carry out an inventory of only part of the collection each year. In

Record of Additions and Withdrawals
Books

Date	Volumes added	Volumes withdrawn	Collection size
7/80			4375
9/80	20	-10	4386
10/80	5		4391
11/80	15	-5	4401

one year the staff might check the fiction and a few Dewey classes, and in the next year they might check some of the other Dewey classes. The school library should never be closed for stocktaking; it if is, many pupils and staff will feel that the library cannot be really very important in the educational process.

Stocktaking is done by checking the shelf list, which is organized in the same way as the items on the shelf, against the items on the shelf. If a card is in the shelf list for which no item is found on the shelf, a paper clip or similar marker is attached to the card. These cards are then checked against the circulation file to see if the item is out. If the item is not checked out of the library, then the item is missing and the card can be pulled from the shelf list. The number of missing items is then noted on the record of additions and withdrawals. Many librarians keep the cards of missing books for a year and if the item does not turn up in a second inventory, they then pull the card from the shelf list.

2. *The number of library users*

It is not very important to know the exact number of library users, but an estimate of the numbers can be useful in demonstrating the workload of library staff. This can be made by counting the users on one or two days each term, or by counting the users at different hours over a week or two each term. These data can then be used to estimate the number of library users over the year.

3. *Circulation statistics*

Information about the number and types of materials circulated can be a useful indicator of one type of library usage. It is not necessary or worthwhile to keep detailed circulation figures every day. Statistics for circulation can be estimated by collecting data at different times throughout the year.

4. *Record of library program and activities*

The school librarian should keep records of how the library is used to support the instructional programs: for example, information on bulkloans, involvement in curricular development and team teaching. Data should be collected on the number and type of reference questions; and information on questions that could not be answered because of inadequacies in the collection is especially useful for budget submissions. The involvement of the library in any special activities, such as Book

Week or school Open Days, should be noted for inclusion in the school library report.

5. *Financial records*
The school librarian needs to maintain records of library income and expenditure. It is especially useful to be able to show how the library spent its income, and wherever possible this should be done in relation to the school's progress.

6. *School library report*
The school library report should be fairly brief, with any detailed statistics attached as an appendix. Busy administrators will often read and react to a one-page report but will ignore a ten-page report. The report should be in a narrative style, highlighting the library programs and summarising the data collected by the library. Whenever possible, data on the library and its programs should be expressed in terms that relate this material to the school's educational program. The report should highlight the contributions made by the library to the school and should not be just an annual outpouring of grievances. It could be submitted annually or at the end of each term, and should be submitted to the school's chief administrator. Copies of the report should also be circulated to school staff members and interested organisations such as Parents and Citizens groups. It can be a way of reminding the school community of how the library has been used in the school's program and also of the need the library has of continued support to enable it to play an active role in the school.

Circulation of materials

The impression most library users have about a library is formed at the circulation desk. In fact, the only contact that many library users will have with library staff will be when checking out or returning library materials. The actual circulation of materials is a clerical task, performed by library assistants or student volunteers, although some school librarians schedule themselves on the circulation desk because they know that this is an opportunity to come into contact with a variety of library users.

Some circulation control procedures need to be developed, so that library materials can be made available to the maximum number of users and so that a record is kept of what was lent and to whom. Circulation

policies and procedures vary widely from library to library, and it is difficult to state that one system is better than another. All school libraries need to have a written circulation policy, and school librarians should consider several factors when developing their policy, including:
(a) the type of circulation system to be used;
(b) who the borrowers will be;
(c) the length of loans and a renewal procedure;
(d) what types of material will circulate;
(e) procedures for circulating items;
(f) procedures for retrieving overdue items;
(g) overdue fines;
(h) replacement obligations for lost items;
(i) a reserve system;
(j) bulk loans;
(k) interlibrary loans.

The key to developing a circulation policy is to remember that the circulation system exists to meet the needs of library users and should allow for flexibility to satisfy the unique needs of individual borrowers. If possible, the system should be flexible about the number of items that can be borrowed at one time, and about the length of time that materials can be checked out, or by allowing for renewals. Some school librarians feel that because they have a limited stock, limits of one or two books loaned to a user at one time are necessary; but even in these instances, individuals should be allowed to borrow more items if they have a need for them. Users should also be able to exchange materials as often as necessary; students who are finished with an item after one hour or one day should not have to wait for a set period of time before they can exchange the item.

As many items as possible in the library should be made available for loan. Reference books and items in high demand can be lent overnight when the library is closed. Audio-visual software and hardware should be available for loans. Most audio-visual materials are quite sturdy and will not be damaged by home use; and audio-visual software, such as audio cassettes and slide sets, are not more expensive than most books and hence should not be more restricted than other items. Students and teachers should be able to arrange for loans of a large number of items on a given topic to enrich units of study. These 'bulk' loans to classrooms should be made as flexible as possible to meet the needs of the classroom.

Overdue fines and replacement charges for lost or damaged materials can cause problems for school librarians. Small fines are rarely a successful method of getting materials returned on time, and the small amount of revenue generated is rarely worth the trouble in collecting fines and maintaining the necessary records for auditors.

Most overdue items are returned within a week or two of the due date, and an overdue reminder notice will get most borrowers to return items that are a week or more overdue. It is not worthwhile chasing after borrowers who have materials only a few days overdue. With the few students who do not respond to overdue reminders, it is often necessary to withdraw borrowing privileges until the student returns the item. Replacement costs can be charged for items that are lost or wilfully damaged; and if replacement costs are to be charged, they should apply equally to all users of the library—staff, students and outside borrowers.

Overdue Notice
Borrower Date Class   The following materials are overdue at the library. Please return them as soon as possible.
Librarian

There are many circulation systems in use in school libraries, and a school must choose a system that best meets its needs, providing the necessary information of what material is on loan, to whom it is lent and when it is to be returned.

One widely used circulation system that is simple for both user and library staff is the one-item card system, with a one-item card, an item pocket and a date due slip. The borrower writes his or her name and classroom on the item card, which is in a pocket attached to the item to be borrowed. The circulation assistant stamps the date due on the item card

Book Pocket and Card

597		
Jam	James, Henry	
	Australian Fish	

Date due	Borrower	Class

597   James, Henry
Jam   Australian Fish

Date Due			

and on the date due slip. The item card is then filed in the circulation tray by the assistant. The item cards can be filed by the user's classroom, by the date checked out, in a single file by classification number, or by date due. Many school libraries find that filing the cards in Dewey Decimal order for non-fiction and alphabetical order for fiction behind the date due is the most effective method because overdues can be easily identified and particular items located by call number or author's name.

Charging Tray

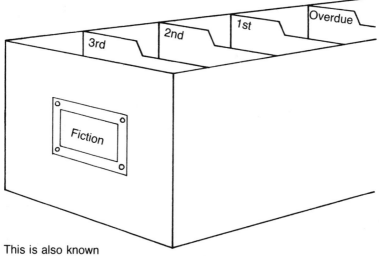

This is also known
as a circulation tray.
The item cards are here filed
according to the date when the item
is due for return.

Item cards can be used for most audio-visual software items, such as slide sets, kits and films, as well as for vertical file items, if the whole file on a subject is circulated. For items that cannot accommodate the one-item card, a reusable software circulation card can be used. For bound copies of periodicals to be circulated, the one-item card system is fine; however, for unbound copies, a reusable circulation card is more satisfactory. These reusable cards can be kept in a separate file.

Some school libraries use a two-card circulation system, which is like the item card system but with an additional borrower's card. The item

Circulation card for Software Slides			
Call No.	Title	Borrower	Date
918	SOUTH AMERICA	LOWIG, Evan	5/6/80
635	CARROTS	OWEN, Tony	10/7/80

Circulation Card for Periodicals The Bulletin		
Date of periodical	Borrower	Date
2/4/80	GOLINO, Sue	16/4/80
10/6/80	RYAN, Anita	24/6/80

borrowed is recorded on the borrower's card at the same time that the borrower's name is recorded on the item card. The borrower's card is usually filed in a circulation tray, behind guide cards indicating the various classes in the school. This system is useful for schools with high student turnover because the librarian can check if students who are leaving the school have any overdue items. The system also provides an individual student's reading record. For most schools the extra work involved in maintaining two separate file systems, one for items loaned and one for borrowers, outweighs any advantages of the two-card system.

Circulation procedures should be written down in the school library policy manual and should also be displayed in the library on a large chart, so that users will become familiar with them. The circulation system and circulation procedures adopted by a library should be convenient for both library staff and users, and should be designed to encourage the use of library materials.

School library facilities

Adequate physical facilities are needed for effective school library programs. These should include sufficient storage space for the school library collection, sufficient seating and work space for school library users, and areas for the wide variety of activities that take place in school libraries. School librarians are usually appointed to a school that already has a school library facility, and they are therefore limited in the design changes they can make to this facility. School libraries should be designed with 'bulk space'—that is, the facility should be free of fixed partitions—and this flexibility should allow for changes in the interior design of the library, to accommodate changes in the school's program or population.

Planning library facilities

Before a new school library facility is constructed, or an existing facility remodelled, questions need to be asked about the school and its library program, because the library should be designed to reflect the school's aims and objectives rather than be planned so that the design will dictate the school library programs. A planning committee that has representatives of the school library, school administration, teaching staff and, if possible, students and community residents, should be formed to determine just what facilities are needed for the school library program. The committee should answer the following questions before it can

determine the nature of the school library facilities:
What are the educational aims and objectives of the school?
What is the nature of the instructional program of the school?
What is the size and nature of the student population to be served?
Will the facility be used by community groups?
Does the design of the school have an effect on the location and nature of the school library facilities?
What media production services will be offered by the school library?

Architect's brief

After the committee has determined the answers to the basic planning questions, it should prepare an architect's brief. If the library is being remodelled without the aid of an architect, the committee would still find it useful to develop a brief that states just what the library hopes to accomplish and what physical facilities are needed to ensure that the library can carry out its programs. The architect's brief should be in narrative form and should be a statement of what facilities are needed to accomplish the aims and objectives of the school and its library program. (The brief should include a statement of the school's aims and objectives and the various instructional programs and organisational patterns of the school.) The size and relationship of resource service areas need to be stated in the brief. It should also state the need for comfortable and useful working areas for library staff members, as well as adequate seating and browsing areas for library users. Any special requests for the storage of library resources should be included, and the concept of flexible 'bulk space' should be stressed. Aesthetic considerations should be outlined, and the architect should be made aware of the type of library atmosphere that is desired. Statements about the amount and kind of lighting need to be included, as well as requirements for acoustical control; the library should be away from noisy areas of the school and noisy areas within the library should not be located near reading and study areas. Provision for adequate power outlets needs to be mentioned so that the architect is aware of the requirements. The library's need for the adequate climate control and adequate visual control should also be included in the brief. The architect would need to know about the amount and type of furnishings required for an effective library program.

The library planning committee should not attempt to design the library; this is the architect's job. However, the committee should ensure that the architect's design does reflect the statements made in the architect's brief.

Planning functional areas

Several resource service areas are needed in every library facility, to enable all the activities of a school library program to be undertaken. Each of these areas has special requirements, which must be taken into consideration by library planners. The planners must be aware of the relationships between the areas, so that library users and workers are able to use the various areas of the library efficiently. The functional areas and the requirements for each area include:

Circulation and display areas   These should be located near the main entrance to the library but also near the office and work space. Space needs to be provided for displays, the card catalogue and the circulation desk.

Reading, browsing, listening and viewing areas   These areas provide accommodation for shelving the main collection of print and non-print resources and should include a browsing area for new and special-interest materials. Provision needs to be made for seating and should include tables and chairs, individual carrels including some that are 'wet' (that is, wired for the individual use of audio-visual equipment), and some informal comfortable seating. Care should be taken to ensure that the natural traffic patterns do not interfere with the activities of the library users, and there should be easy access from the seating areas to the shelving areas.

Large group area   If formal classes are to be held in the library or if large groups are to use video equipment in the library, then a large group area is needed. This should be away from the main reading area of the library. There should be provision to darken the room for films and other video equipment. The area should include screens and chalkboards and have appropriate seating and work spaces.

Small group, activity and seminar areas   These should be located so as to provide easy access to the collections of library resources. The rooms should be designed so that they can be used for a variety of purposes: for small group discussions, viewing and listening activities, and conferences between school librarians and users. Each room should have movable furnishings, provision for using audio-visual equipment and typewriters, and chalkboards and screens. Visual control can be maintained by glass panels.

Office space and administrative area   School librarians need office areas in which to carry out professional library tasks and in which to interview teachers, students and parents. School librarians' offices need to be located so as to provide for visual supervision of the library. There needs to be provision for desk space, files for library records, shelving and a telephone. The office of the head school librarian should be easily accessible from the rest of the school.

Work space   This should be located near the production areas and should have access to a corridor so that materials being delivered to the work room do not have to be moved through the library. Adequate shelving for the storage of items awaiting processing and repair needs to be provided. Benches should be provided for item processing, and a sink is needed in every work room. Adequate power outlets should be provided in this area. Storage areas such as cupboards need to be provided for housing supplies and equipment. In some schools, audio-visual equipment is stored in the workroom but, if at all possible, a separate storage area should be included in the library.

Production area   This area is designed to provide space for teachers and students to produce media items such as films, video tapes, audio tapes, transparency slides and graphics. There needs to be adequate counter and work space, a sink should be provided and the space should be soundproofed with acoustically treated walls for audio productions.

Library furniture   The library needs to be equipped with a wide range of furniture that is aesthetically pleasing as well as functional. All furniture needs to be scaled to the size of the users, and in schools serving a wide age range furniture of different sizes needs to be provided. Although the exact furniture requirements for a school library will vary depending on the nature of the school and its library projects, all school libraries will need to include the following furnishings: circulation desk, card catalogue cabinets, a variety of tables, seating both standard and casual, perhaps including cushions, carrels both 'wet' and 'dry', desks for the library staff, book truck, atlas and dictionary stands, shelving for periodicals, shelving for books and other media, newspaper racks, paperback racks, file cabinets for vertical file materials and office files, and storage cupboards for supplies and equipment.

The Schools Commission has developed a guide for recommended furniture provision for schools based on enrolment.[7] Although each school may need to modify these recommendations in the light of its needs, this guide can be useful to school library planners.

Guide to Furniture Provision for School Libraries, Developed by the Schools Commission[7]

Main Area

Enrolment	Shelving (linear metres)	Periodical stand	Filing cabinet	Catalogue drawers*	Seating of all kinds	Tables and carrels	Circulation desk
1– 100	88	1	1	12	Sufficient seating for planned occupancy of the school library; sufficient tables and carrels to match the formal seating requirements		1
at 200	150	1	1	24			1
" 300	202	1	1	32			1
" 400	247	1	1	36			1
" 500	287	1	2	42			1
" 600	323	1	2	48			1
" 700	357	1	2	52			1
" 800	386	2	3	56			1
" 900	415	2	3	60			1
" 1000	441	2	4	64			1
" 1100	465	3	4	68			1
" 1200	488	3	5	72			1
" 1300	508	3	5	72			1
" 1400	527	3	6	76			1
" 1500	545	3	6	80			1

Small seminar areas   Seating, tables and carrels included above.
* Schools with full dictionary catalogues may require up to 20% more drawers as they approach target collection size.

Services unit

Enrolment	Shelving (linear metres)	Desks and chairs	Chairs or stools for workspace	Visitors' chairs	Filing cabinets	Chairs and tables to seat	Security cupboard	Cloak cupboard
1–100		1	2	2	1		1	1
at 200	9	1	2	2	1	2	1	1
„ 300	18	1	2	2	1	2	1	1
„ 400	24	1	2	2	1	2	1	1
„ 500	27	1	3	2	1	2	1	1
„ 600	27	2	3	2	2	4	1	1
„ 700	27	2	3	2	2	4	1	1
„ 800	27	2	3	2	2	4	1	1
„ 900	36	2	4	2	2	4	1	1
„ 1000	36	2	4	2	2	4	1	1
„ 1100	36	3	4	2	3	4	1	1
„ 1200	36	3	4	2	3	4	1	1
„ 1300	36	3	4	2	3	4	1	1
„ 1400	36	4	5	2	4	4	1	1
„ 1500	36	4	5	2	4	4	1	1

Additional items as appropriate, but at least 2 kickstools, 1 mobile display unit, 3 mobile screens, partitions, 1 vertical chart storage.

Some school librarians have carried out outstanding library programs from inadequate library facilities, and an excellent facility is no guarantee of a successful library program. However, good school library facilities can encourage students and staff to come to the library and make use of its facilities; and inadequate facilities can deter both library staff and library users. If there is inadequate space in the library, if furniture and equipment are not flexible and functional, and if facilities are not arranged so that they can be easily used by the library users, then maximum library service will not be achieved.

School library standards

Published standards for school libraries—that is, the qualitative and quantitative guidelines for planning and evaluating school library programs—have influenced the development of quality school library programs. The Library Association of Australia published its *Standards and Objectives for School Libraries* in 1966; in 1971 a joint committee of the Library Association of Australia and the Australian School Library Association was formed to rewrite the 1966 standards; and in 1975 the Library Association of Australia resolved to make these revised standards available as a discussion paper.[8] In 1977 the Schools Commission published *Books and Beyond: Guidelines for Library Resource Facilities and Services*, and these standards, now in their second edition, have largely replaced the documents produced by the Library Association of Australia.

In recent years many librarians and educators have been questioning the validity of quantitative standards. Many standards are not based on any empirical evidence and have been developed from the collective judgement of a number of librarians. It is not possible to say that one library program is better than another because it has more books or a larger staff. Because schools vary greatly, and therefore school libraries also vary, it is now being accepted that standards are only guidelines which need to be modified to meet local needs, rather than a fixed set of criteria which must be rigidly adhered to. Quantitative standards in areas such as staffing, collection size and physical facilities are useful aids to school librarians when requesting support for the library program and when planning and developing the school library. Some of the quantitative standards published by the Schools Commission in *Books and Beyond* are reproduced in the tables below. The stock figures are only a guideline and the particular needs of each school should determine the size of the collection.

Recommended Staffing Provision[9]

| Enrolment | Professional Staff | | Ancillary staff |
	Head teacher librarian	Other professional	(technical, clerical, aides)
1–100	up to 1		up to 15 hours
101– 200	1		20 hours
201– 300	1		30 hours
301– 400	1		40 hours
401– 500	1		50 hours
501– 600	1	1	60 hours
601– 700	1	1	70 hours
701– 800	1	1	80 hours
801– 900	1	1	90 hours
901–1000	1	1	100 hours
1001–1100	1	2	110 hours
1101–1200	1	2	120 hours
1201–1300	1	2	130 hours
1301–1400	1	3	140 hours
1401–1500	1	3	150 hours

Evaluating the school library

When library programs are being evaluated, qualitative measurements must be included as well as quantitative ones. The school librarian will need to know how well the library is meeting the needs of the school and its community. The students and staff of the school can be surveyed to find out what they want from the library and if the library is providing the required services. The library staff should document just how the library is being integrated into the educational program of the school and find out the barriers that keep the library and its resources from being fully utilised. The opinions of experts in the field can be a useful evaluation tool, and school libraries may wish to bring in an outside expert, or a panel of outside experts, to evaluate the library program and give advice on plans for improved library service. Various techniques have been developed for evaluating library service, by measuring library holdings, user satisfaction rates and response time to users' requests, for example. Some of these techniques are described by writers such as Ernest R. De Prospo and James Liesener, as aids in both the evaluation and the planning of school library programs.

Recommended Space Allocation in Secondary Schools[10]

Adjusted secondary enrolment*	Total area of library/resource facility (including service area)	Service area
1– 99	No separate allocation. Facilities incorporated into existing class areas.	
100– 199	95 m²	Small partitioned area within
200– 299	140 m²	reading room
300– 499	225 m²	59 m²
500– 549	263 m²	68 m²
550– 599	279 m²	68 m²
600– 649	295 m²	68 m²
650– 699	312 m²	68 m²
700– 749	328 m²	68 m²
750– 799	344 m²	68 m²
800– 849	480 m²	86 m²
850– 899	497 m²	86 m²
900– 949	513 m²	86 m²
950– 999	530 m²	86 m²
1000–1049	546 m²	86 m²
1050–1099	563 m²	86 m²
1100–1149	579 m²	86 m²
1150–1199	594 m²	86 m²
1200–1249	610 m²	86 m²
1250–1299	627 m²	86 m²
1300–1349	644 m²	86 m²
1350–1399	660 m²	86 m²
1400–1449	809 m²	114 m²
1450–1499	823 m²	114 m²
1500–1549	840 m²	114 m²
1550–1599	856 m²	114 m²
1600–1649	881 m²	123 m²
1650–1699	898 m²	123 m²
1700–1749	913 m²	123 m²
1750–1799	930 m²	123 m²
1800–1849	1004 m²	152 m²
1850–1899	1024 m²	152 m²
1900–1949	1040 m²	52 m²
1950–2000	1073 m²	152 m²

Enrolment figures refer to actual numbers of students enrolled except in schools with a year 12 enrolment, where the year 12 enrolment is doubled and added to the number of students in the preceding years.

The service area provides spaces for the following: teacher-librarian's office area; workroom area; production area; planning and preparation area; A/V storage area.

Service area is included in total area of library resource facility.

Schools with enrolment 1–99: When a school has room available for a library and therefore no building costs are involved and where the space could function effectively as a library, small grants may be made available for the rooms to be equipped for this purpose.

Recommended Space Allocation in Primary Schools[11]

Enrolment	Total area of library/resource facility (including service area)	Service area
1– 99	No separate allocation. Facilities incorporated into existing class areas.	
100– 199	67 m²	Sink and cupboard only
200–299	128 m²	28 m²
300–399	172 m²	42 m²
400–499	214 m²	56 m²
500–599	256 m²	70 m²
600–699	300 m²	70 m²
700–799	342 m²	84 m²
800–899	381 m²	84 m²

Areas are calculated on the basis of 0.427 m² per person in enrolment gradations of 100. The service area provides space for the following: teacher-librarian's office area; workroom area; production area; planning and preparation area; A/V storage area.

The service area is included in total area of library resource facility.

Schools with enrolments 1–99: When a school has available for a library and therefore no building costs are involved and where the space could function effectively as a library, small grants may be made available for the rooms to be equipped for this purpose.

The library size of 67 m² represents an area which could be converted to other uses when the school population exceeds 200.

Recommended Bookstock in a School Library[12]

Enrolment	Size of collection for adequate library service	Basic funded bookstock
1– 100	3000	*
101– 150	4104	2250
151– 200	5097	2750
201– 250	6008	3250
251– 300	6853	3500
301– 350	7644	3750
351– 400	8388	4000
401– 450	9091	4200
451– 500	9758	4400
501– 550	10392	4600
551– 600	10997	4800
601– 650	11574	5000
651– 700	12126	5200
701– 750	12656	5400
751– 800	13163	5600
801– 850	13650	5800
851– 900	14118	6000
901– 950	14567	6150
951–1000	15000	6300
1001–1050	15416	6450
1051–1100	15817	6600
1101–1150	16203	6750
1151–1200	16575	6900
1201–1250	16933	7050
1251–1300	17278	7200
1301–1350	17611	7350
1351–1400	17931	7500
1401–1450	18240	7650
1451–1500	18538	7800
1501–1550	18825	7950
1551–1600	19101	8100
1601–1650	19367	8250
1651–1700	19624	8400
1701–1750	19870	8550
1751–1800	20100	8700
1801–1850	20336	8850
1851–1900	20556	9000
1901–1950	20767	9150
1951–2000	20969	9300

The figures incorporate both book and non-book items. The ratio of book to non-book items in each collection should be determined by individual schools to meet their particular needs. It is expected that all collections will include a variety of book and non-book media.

It is recommended that schools determine interim targets relative to available funds and ability to expend these.

Enrolment figures refer to actual numbers of students enrolled except in schools with a year 12 enrolment where the year 12 enrolment is doubled and added to the number of students in the preceding years.

For each school with an enrolment in excess of 100, the target collection is calculated by multiplying the enrolment by (60−15 log x) where x is the enrolment.

The figures derived from the above formula are intended to provide a guide. Each school should establish the size of its collection on the basis of its own perceived needs.

*For schools with enrolments of less then 100, the book-stock will be calculated by funding on the basis of 20 volumes per student, but no school will have a book stock of less than 500.

References

1. *Aims of Primary Education in New South Wales* (New South Wales Department of Education, Sydney, 1977), p. 14.
2. *Education for School Librarianship: Proceedings, Findings and Recommendations of a Workshop held in Canberra, 1–4 August 1972* (AGPS, Canberra, 1973), pp. 57–62.
3. LAA/ASLA Working Party on School Library Personnel, School Library Personnel: Types of Staff and Their Educational Requirements (unpublished draft, 1977), pp. 5–6.
4. *Clerical Assistant (Library) Handbook* (Library Services, New South Wales Department of Education, Sydney, 1976) p. 4.
5. LAA/ASLA Working Party on School Library Personnel, p. 12.
6. James W. Liesener, *Planning Instruments for School Library/Media Programs* (University of Maryland, College Park, 1974).
7. Schools Commission, *Books and Beyond: Guidelines for Library Resource Facilities and Services* (2nd edn, AGPS, Canberra, 1979), p. 46.
8. Library Association of Australia, *Discussion Paper: Towards Guidelines for Standards and Objectives for School Libraries* (LAA, Sydney, 1975), preface.
9. Schools Commission, p. 9.
10. Schools Commission, p. 26.
11. Schools Commission, p. 27.
12. Schools Commission, p. 36.

Bibliography

AUSTRALIA. DEPARTMENT OF EDUCATION. *Education for School Librarianship: Proceedings, Findings and Recommendations of a Workshop held in Canberra, 1–4 August 1972.* AGPS, Canberra, 1973.

BROADBENT, MARIANNE. 'Differences of opinion: the school librarian's role—as teachers see it', *Australian Library Journal* 26, 4 (1977), 253-6.

BROADHEAD, MARGARET. 'Staff roles in the organisation of the educational resources centre', *Australian School Librarian* 9, 3 (1972) 5–12.

COMMONWEALTH SECONDARY SCHOOLS LIBRARIES COMMITTEE. *Initial Organization of the School Library.* AGPS, Canberra, 1973.

DE PROSPO, ERNEST R., ALTNAN, ELLEN, AND BEASLEY, KENNETH E. *Performance Measures for Public Libraries.* American Library Association, Chicago, 1973.

DODGSON, MARGARET. 'The teacher-librarian as administrator', *Journal of the School Library Association of Queensland* 6, 3 (1973), 11–14.

LIBRARY ASSOCIATION OF AUSTRALIA. *Discussion Paper: Towards Standards and Objectives for School Libraries.* LAA Sydney, 1975 (mimeo).

LIBRARY ASSOCIATION OF AUSTRALIA. *Standards and Objectives for School Libraries.* Cheshire, Melbourne, for the LAA, 1966.

LIESENER, JAMES W. *Planning Instruments for School Library/ Media Programs.* University of Maryland, College Park, 1974.

LIESENER, JAMES W. *A Systematic Planning Process for School Library/Media Programs.* American Library Association, Chicago, 1974.

LUNDIN, ROY A. 'On establishing standards for school libraries'. *Australian Library Journal* 22, 6 (1973), 221–7.

LUNDIN, ROY A. 'Using a looking glass: some guidelines for self-evaluation of school resource services', *Orana* 13, 4 (1977) 115–24.

MARTIN, BETTY, AND CARSON, BEN. *The Principal's Handbook on the School Library Media Centre.* Gaylord, Syracuse, 1978.

NEW SOUTH WALES. DEPARTMENT OF EDUCATION. *Aims of Primary Education in New South Wales.* NSW Department of Education, Sydney, 1977.

NEW SOUTH WALES. DEPARTMENT OF EDUCATION. LIBRARY SERVICES. *Clerical Assistant (Library) Handbook.* Department of Education, Sydney, 1976.

NEW SOUTH WALES TEACHERS FEDERATION. *Teacher Librarians' Bulletin.* rev. edn, Teachers Federation, Sydney, June 1979.

PEGG, PETER J. (ed.). *Prospects: Proceedings of the Advanced Seminar for Teacher-librarians in Secondary Schools.* School Library Association of Queensland, Brisbane, 1973.

PEGG, PETER J. 'Staffing of school libraries: an approach to standards', *Journal of the School Library Association of Queensland* 5, 3 (1973), 4–7.

SCHOOLS COMMISSION. *Books and Beyond: Guidelines for Library Resource Facilities and Services.* 2nd edn, AGPS, Canberra, 1979.

'SLAV policy on staffing 1979', *Australian School Librarian* 16, 3 (1979), 80–94.

TASMANIA. EDUCATION DEPARTMENT. LIBRARY SERVICES BRANCH. *Procedures Manual: Recommended Practice for Tasmanian School and College Libraries.* Education Department, Hobart, 1978.

TATE, LENORE. 'The teacher librarian as administrator', *Journal of the School Library Association of Queensland* 6, 3 (1977), 4–9.

VICTORIA. DEPARTMENT OF EDUCATION. *Primary School Libraries: Guide I. Objectives and Standards.* Department of Education, Melbourne, 1973.

CHAPTER 10

The School/Community Library

James G. Dwyer

One of the most fascinating studies in the library field is that of joint-use libraries, particularly school/community libraries. Quite apart from the actual facilities and the programs centred on them, much of the fascination lies in the world-wide literature on the topic, a literature that is perhaps clouded by more emotion than any other subject of librarianship.

Nowhere is this more clearly exemplified than in an 'Action Exchange' segment of *American Libraries*[1] in 1978, in which Edward H. Fenner drew conclusions that, at best, can only be described as highly suspect. Having asked for the pros and cons of locating public library branches in school buildings, he received various and conflicting responses. These included the following comments: 'We have found that the combined school/public library concept works.' 'After four years of experience . . . my advice is don't combine.' 'The situation is fluid, and there is more to be done.' 'It is possible to combine school and public libraries and, in doing so, provide the services and programs to meet the needs of all patrons. However, success of a combined facility is subject to certain conditions and circumstances. Fifty-two of the 55 libraries surveyed supported the concept without reservations.' Fenner's conclusion to those responses reads, 'It is interesting that the replies to my question bear out the fact that public library service in a school building is not satisfactory, and this opinion has not changed over the years.'

Terminology

Considerable confusion has been caused by the lack of precise definition of the type of joint-use facility being referred to. The range of shared services and facilities is quite large, and a better understanding of the diversification would perhaps overcome some of the prejudice.

The report of the Committee of Inquiry into Public Libraries states that 'The term Community Library . . . means different things to different people. It may mean a school library open to the public, a public library open to the school, a school library and a public library operating separately in the one building or a combined school and public library building located within the school grounds. A contrasting concept is the community or total library service—a locally based service made up of a number of existing information agencies, including the school and public library, but also agencies such as citizens' advice bureaux, information sections of government departments and other library services within the community such as special and college libraries.'[2] While that statement does not cover the total range of options, it does provide sufficient evidence that confusion in terminology exists. Since each type of service referred to in that statement is a separate concept with some unique features and requirements, it is obviously essential to have a clear understanding of the types of facilities to be considered in this chapter.

Because the variations on a theme are numerous, precise definitions are not really possible. However, essentially the service being referred to in the present context is a joint library service based within or adjacent to a school, serving the school clientele and the public and financed by school and public library authorities; it may operate on separate or integrated collections; it may have a unified or a divided staff structure. This broad range of facilities I will refer to as a school/community library.

Need for dual services

In an editorial comment of May 1979, John Berry, editor of the American *Library Journal*, stated that 'One of the sacred dogmas of librarianship is the belief that America's young people need access to two libraries, one in the school they attend and another in the community. So entrenched is this article of our library faith that the mere mention that it may not be the proper solution to the problem of library service for children and young adults is apt to bring forth violent, emotional and powerful reaction.'[3]

The Australian experience has been a little different. There has existed a similar, almost dogmatic assertion on the need for two libraries; but there has been little evidence of a potentially violent, emotional or powerful reaction to the mention of alternative solutions. No doubt the lack of adverse reaction can be attributed to the paucity of local and national publicity on the issue, the Australian library community preferring to treat school/community libraries as a slight irritant which, if ignored, would disappear. The mid-to-late 1970s, however, brought an upsurge in joint library suggestion and experimentation and a realisation that the irritant might well become a parasite and even an acceptable hybrid.

History

It is sometimes thought that the concept of joint library services is one of recent vintage. Not only is this far from the fact in Europe and the Americas; it is also an inaccurate assessment of the Australian position. There have been many attempts, albeit of a local and minor nature, to make existing school and public library services available to a wider clientele. Such efforts have tended to be unofficial in the sense that they have operated under a local 'gentleman's agreement', ignoring the central bureaucracy and frequently being of limited duration because of changes of personnel or the provision of alternative services. They have also had little publicity and have left scarce documentation.

One of the most interesting attempts at a wide-scale scheme of joint library service occurred in Queensland early this century and has been recently documented by Laurel Clyde.[4] The proposal stemmed from a recommendation of the Conference of Inspectors in 1908 that the Department of Public Instruction should encourage and assist the establishment of school libraries. Appalled at the cost of such a proposal, the Department proposed that the collections of the local Schools of Arts should be expanded to include materials suitable for school children who would then be encouraged to use those central collections, thus eliminating the need for separate school library collections. The proposal received much favourable press publicity but little support from the Schools of Arts. As Clyde points out, 'As early as July 1909 it had become very clear to the Department of Public Instruction that an attempt to build a school/community library service through the School of Arts was not going to succeed, partly because the Department, in approaching the Schools of Arts, was looking for a way of building school libraries cheaply; and partly because the School of Arts libraries had their own problems of accommodation, finances, staffing and bookstock, of which the Department had taken no account. There was much suspicion too on both sides. The Department, while handing over the responsibility for ordering books, preparing them, circulating them and maintaining accounts, wanted to keep firm control over book selection; and the libraries saw the Department trying to reduce their endowments for their adult libraries . . . On 16 July 1909 the Minister informed the Brisbane School of Arts that it was not intended to pursue this matter further at present, and that a small amount had been applied for on the Estimates for 1909–10 to enable the Department to make small grants towards school libraries.'

So much for 1909. Little of significance occurred in subsequent years, apart from isolated, local attempts at co-operation, until the 1970s. In fact, in 1965, when preparing a paper on relationships between school and children's libraries, I sought details from all over Australia on school and public library co-operative projects; there was a totally negative response, and it was dismissed as having little bearing on the national scene at that time.[5] It is surprising to realise just how vastly the situation changed in the next 15 years.

In a survey carried out in December 1973 and January 1974, Roy Lundin was able to ascertain that school/community libraries were once more coming into prominence, at least in the thinking and planning of education and library administrators. He pointed to cautious but definite activity, with four projects in operation or about to commence joint services, and a number of other schemes under discussion. Of particular interest is his comment that 'Generally, such shared use of school facilities is being encouraged by State Education Departments, but teachers and librarians may not be ready for this change, if it is desirable.'[6] One may assume that Lundin regarded the impetus for such experimentation as stemming from education authorities. However, he stated elsewhere that the library profession had the matter under active discussion at various levels. It is of significance that in the intervening years little can be seen from those discussions. While various education authorities have issued statements supporting school/community library projects in certain circumstances, the same categorical approach has not been taken by the library profession. A few of its members, as individuals, have publicly stated a position; the profession has not seen fit to take a stand or offer consistent guidance—although there are signs in the winds of change.

The Boronia experiment

If there is one factor that could be said to have had more influence than any other on school/community library development in Australia, it is the development of the joint facility at Boronia in Victoria. Carefully planned, documented and discussed between all the parties involved, the project has been in operation since 1974. As the first large-scale scheme to be developed in Australia, Boronia had many critical eyes turned towards it. Its Advisory Committee was at pains to emphasise the experimental nature of the project and the fact that it was a new venture in the experience of all the authorities involved; thus it was very much an exercise in understanding and one that could succeed only if it were to respond to the developing needs of its clients, by changing operational procedures as need dictated.

Initial reaction to the Boronia experiment was predominantly adverse. Visits by a large range of interested outsiders and external surveys and reports generally produced an unfavourable picture which highlighted the limited hours the facility was available to the public, the comparatively poor response as reflected in public usage and the real or imagined difficulties arising from joint staffing control.

One cannot but admire the professional integrity of the authorities responsible for the policies and practices at Boronia. Conscious of the widespread adverse criticism levelled at its operation, the Advisory Committee chose not to enter public debate on the issues but to consider such criticism in the light of the library's purpose and to make relevant changes as time and circumstance seemed appropriate and in accordance with the expressed will of the clients. Thus, for instance, the hours of opening to the public went through a series of changes, each more liberal than previously, leading eventually to total availability during operating hours; in other words the school students no longer had exclusive use of the facility at specified times. To many, it seems axiomatic that a school/community library should be available to all clients during opening hours, otherwise one group might be disadvantaged. That attitude, commendable as it appears on the surface, takes no account of the size of community or the number of hours the community would have access to a public library in other circumstances. No doubt these were factors that had some prominence in the deliberations of the Advisory Committee for Boronia.

One of the publicised fears of the opponents of school/community libraries is that authorities responsible for library provision might opt to repeat examples like Boronia in preference to providing a separate public library service, and that such decisions might flow solely from economic motives. There is little evidence, at least in Australia, of such dangers. Projects that have commenced or are at an advanced stage of planning have had a variety of factors as their motivating force. Generally the provision of a necessary service that would otherwise be unavailable has been the major criterion on which decisions have been made, although it cannot be denied that economic motives are also involved even in the most 'worthy' cases.

There is no apparent movement to establish a rash of Boronias. Undoubtedly Boronia created much interest, but the experiment and publicity pointed out dangers and problems as much as offering an alternative library service for consideration. Other projects, whose providers have obviously taken counsel in the light of Boronia, have been developed. There is also ample evidence that other school/community library projects have been under consideration but have been rejected for reasons other than prejudice.

Committee of Inquiry into Public Libraries

In view of the slow but definite increase in interest, experimentation and publicity concerning school/community libraries in Australia, one might reasonably expect a major report on national public library provision and needs to comment meaningfully on the topic, particularly in the area of recommendations for the future. The 1976 report of the Committee of Inquiry into Public Libraries, already referred to, gave scant coverage to the subject. While the Committee acknowledged that 'There will inevitably be circumstances where the school/community library will be justified by the inability to provide otherwise for either a school or municipal library separately'[7], it was of the opinion that schools were generally not well placed to provide the joint function, and action should wait until those libraries were fully developed. No doubt there is wisdom in theory; practice does not always respond. Reaction to the Committee's comment included the obvious question—who would decide when school libraries were fully developed? Needless to say, additional projects have since been set in train, and the issue of the level of development of respective school libraries has been of minor consequence, the authorities taking the attitude that any shortfall in resources or staffing was capable of rectification through the public library input. Practice has proven this to be a naive attitude.

Schools Commission involvement

The growing comment on and interest in the school/community library concept struck a responsive chord in the Schools Commission which, since 1974, had been providing supplementary funding for education, including school library development. The School Libraries Committee of the Commission recognised the growing influence of school/ community libraries on the scene and recommended that the Commission should fund a research study into the matter. The Commission agreed to the request and proposed that the study should be undertaken in late 1977 and that some of its aspects should relate to the report of the Committee of Inquiry into Public Libraries.

The report of the study was produced in 1978 under the title *Co-operation or Compromise*. It covered joint-use library facilities for education and general community purposes, although the majority of projects covered were school/community libraries. Existing and proposed services were included amongst the 21 schemes. Each project was treated separately, under the range of headings: status; type of institution; type of service; local factors; library planning; setting; participation in wider service; financial responsibility; staff and responsibility; collections and arrangement; hours of access; availability of material; technical processing; general comments. Thus comparisons could be made between the provisions and conditions of various services.

The Schools Commission had requested a state-of-the-art, non-evaluative report. Nevertheless some trends could easily be deduced from the survey:

- School/community libraries were more suited to the secondary school than the primary school.
- They lend themselves to and gained ready acceptance in rural areas and rapid growth areas.
- Shared funding arrangements were quite diverse.
- Reasonably satisfactory service may be provided even where an existing library has been extended to cater for additional clientele and a different service.
- The existence of sound personal qualities is the most important factor for the librarian-in-charge.
- Integration of collections was seen as more conducive to good service than separate collections.
- Concern over public use of school material and child access to adult material was virtually of no significance.
- While there was little evidence of restricting the public to after school hours, public use during school hours was frequently slow in developing.[8]

It is pertinent at this stage to refer once again to the Lundin study in 1974.

He claims that the literature points to three basic issues on which there is consensus:

- Neither service to the school nor service to the public should be compromised and in fact in any joint project there should be clear gains (other than economic) on both sides.
- There should be complete integration of facilities, materials, staff and services.
- The major problem to be overcome is the reconciliation of the different roles of the two types of library when an integrated service is being contemplated or provided.[9]

The *Co-operation or Compromise* survey by no means supported those contentions. There was general support in principle for the first two issues, and there is no doubt that the ideal situation calls for such an approach. Since ideal situations appear only in theory, a certain degree of compromise is essential if projects are to reach fruition. Needless to say, levels of service suffer accordingly. Frequently a choice must be made between the provision of a service which falls below the ideal and the continued lack of a service. It would appear that many Australian authorities have opted for the former course.

The third stated issue of consensus proved to be a non-issue. Far from being the greatest problem to overcome, reconciling the different roles of school and public libraries appeared to offer no difficulties when the philosophy of the various joint services was addressed. This is not to say that the role of the school library was considered identical with that of the public library. It would appear that considerable progress has been made in reconciling these different roles. Of significance, however, is the undeniable fact that school libraries have gone through rapid change during the 1970s, broadening their range of materials, services and activities and, while not duplicating the role of the public library, providing a service well beyond the needs of a narrow and formal curriculum.

Levels of support

In a country as large as Australia and with such diverse education systems and levels of public library service, it is not surprising that school/community libraries have received checkered support. In Tasmania, Victoria and South Australia there is some definite commitment and experimentation has proceeded apace, although there are limitations to provision; education, public library and local government authorities have been able to come to agreement for specific cases. Examples exist in New South Wales, but they are limited and there is some difficulty in developing agreement between authorities for further proposed services. Basic support for specific cases exists in the Australian Capital Territory and the Northern Territory, though extensive provision is not contemplated. Neither in Queensland nor in Western Australia is there an example of a school/community library. In each case firm proposals have been made but they have not come to fruition, although on at least two occasions in Western Australia planning had been well advanced.

In examining the situations where school/community libraries have been established and those where they have been resisted, no consistent picture emerges. A pattern does not relate to levels of public library development, to their regionalisation, to density of population, to the size of the area or to school library development. However, the following facts are interesting:

- Tasmania's public library and school library central administrations are under the one umbrella.
- When a ministerial committee was appointed in South Australia to develop guidelines for school/community libraries, the Minister concerned had responsibility for education and public libraries.
- Close liaison has existed in Victoria between the Library Council of Victoria (within the Ministry for the Arts) and the Education Department. Latterly an inter-departmental committee involving those two authorities was established to recommend policy on joint-use libraries.
- South Australia is recognised for its leadership role in innovation in education and, together with Victoria, in parent and community involvement in education.

While these matters may not individually explain reasons for the incidence of school/community libraries in those States, they perhaps have much to do with creating a climate of discussion and awareness which are prerequisites for reasonable understanding and eventual provision.

Guidelines

The inter-departmental committee established to recommend policy on school/community libraries in Victoria presented its report in October 1978.[10] Coverage included a draft policy, draft guidelines and draft agreement between participating authorities. No definite bureaucratic action has emanated from the presentation of the report and there has been some limited criticism of its draft provisions. Nevertheless it is an honest attempt to face the issues involved; and it will be valuable in drawing attention to matters that should be considered by authorities contemplating the provision of a joint service.

The only definitive set of criteria and guidelines for school/community libraries in Australia has been that used in South Australia in the late 1970s.[11] Produced in 1974 by a ministerial committee representing the bodies involved in school/community libraries, they were approved for implementation and subsequently revised in 1976 and again in a minor way in 1977. A number of projects have been instituted under those guidelines, which apply to isolated, rural areas of below 3000 population. One of the unusual features of the guidelines concerned funding arrangements: the Education Department agreed to pay half the cost of building extensions to allow the school library to be used for public purposes and to provide additional staffing and shelving required at the library. Such generosity undoubtedly encouraged local authorities to participate. Some localities with populations larger than that in the guidelines have also managed to gain exception, and, it may be said, have killed the goose that laid the golden egg.

With the advent of economic and staffing restrictions, the Education Department was forced to seek redress. Consequently a halt was called to further projects, while new guidelines were determined, particularly concerning financial provisions. Developments will be watched with considerable interest, especially the reaction of local governments if, as seems certain, a greater share of financial burden is to fall on them.

Community centres

Brief mention should be made of a facility that fits the category stated earlier, though not based in a school. The library is one of a number of services, including a school, within a community centre complex. It serves the whole community, including the school community, and is a joint library in the full sense of being available to any user at any time of opening; there is no suggestion of it being a public library or a school library in a traditional sense. The first project of this type (Parks Community Centre) has been in operation in South Australia since late 1978 but has far from settled the financial, staffing and service difficulties associated with its establishment. Nevertheless, progress has been made towards a satisfactory resolution of early difficulties and at time of writing a new integrated staffing structure was being implemented. Definitive documentation on the project is not yet available but should be an essential guide for similar schemes. Other projects with a related philosophy but of smaller magnitude have been planned for Minto in New South Wales and Wanniassa in Canberra, but there is no expectation of multiple repetition.

Assessment and evaluation

One of the real problems besetting school/community libraries in Australia is the dearth of independent evaluative literature on local projects. There exist some internal evaluations which are interesting and enlightening (for example, of Boronia and Templestowe in Victoria). Recent external evaluation, however, does not exist. Sufficient projects have been established to warrant proper research on their effectiveness and value as an alternative library service in the Australian context; and the research is essential if a professional approach is ever to be given to the matter of joint service.

There is no doubt that school/community libraries in Australia have been through the parturition stage and are in the throes of growing pains. Even though they have made no impact in certain States, their existence is such that a foothold has been attained and a future is assured. That future must be guided by the experience of the past, so that the best elements may be repeated and mistakes avoided. This can happen only through the acceptance of that type of library as a viable alternative in certain circumstances, through the ready exchange of information, and through reasonable discussion. These approaches are being fostered and with some success. But perhaps the greatest obstacle is fear—fear that to give recognition might create an avalanche that would endanger successful levels of service that were achieved through hard-fought battles. Such fear is real and cannot be dismissed lightly. Yet there are favourable signs on the horizon. With the first national seminar on joint-use libraries in 1980 and a policy statement formulated by the Library Association of Australia, there is hope of a more rational approach to the whole question.

References
1. 'Action Exchange', in *American Libraries* 9, 1 (1978), 29–30.
2. *Public Libraries in Australia: Report of the Committee of Inquiry into Public Libraries* (The Horton Report) (AGPS, Canberra, 1976), p. 31.
3. J. Berry, 'School/public library service', *Library Journal* 1 May 1979, 989.

4. L. Clyde, 'The magic casements—1909', *Journal of the School Library Association of Queensland* 10, 3/4 (1978), 15–18.
5. J. G. Dwyer, 'Aims and relationships between school and children's libraries', in *Papers of the 13th Biennial Conference of the Library Association of Australia*, Canberra, 1965. (Sydney, 1965), p. 194.
6. R. Lundin, *School Community Libraries*, (Commonwealth Secondary School Libraries Research Project, Paper no. 5) (Department of Education, University of Queensland, Brisbane, 1974), p. 19.
7. *Public Libraries in Australia*, p. 81.
8. J. G. Dwyer, *Co-operation or Compromise: School/Community Libraries in Australia* (Adelaide, 1978), pp. 67–8.
9. Lundin, pp. 4–6.
10. *Report of the Interdepartmental Committee on Joint-use Libraries* (Library Council of Victoria, Melbourne, 1979).
11. *Community Use of School Libraries*, report of the committee appointed by the Minister of Education (Education Department of South Australia, Adelaide, 1974).

CHAPTER 11

Centralised Services
for School Libraries

James G. Dwyer

In 1963, L. H. McGrath wrote that 'The further development of school libraries in Australia requires the establishment and development in all States of a vital School Library Service, as an integral section of the Education Department, with adequate staff, accommodation, facilities and finance to provide administrative, bibliographical, advisory, supervisory and central ordering, processing, cataloguing and repair services'.[1] He went on to outline the position at that time in each State in Australia. Before proceeding, however, he referred to the scathing comments on school libraries made in the Munn-Pitt report of 1935[2] and then commented, 'Thirty years have passed. Marked development in school library service has been effected. Unfortunately many of the needs so lucidly stated . . . remain unsatisfied today in Australian schools.'[3]

Those comments were largely supported by Sara Fenwick, who visited Australia in 1964 to survey and report on (among other things) conditions in school libraries: 'Library service to children should have passed through its infancy and early growing pains and be emerging into the status of a full grown member of the professional family. That this has not happened is a serious problem worthy of a thoughtful assessment of the climate for future growth and development.'[4] Fenwick also observed that 'More progress in school library development and a higher level of growth is evident in those states where there is direction and co-ordination from an established office charged with this responsibility in the Department of Education.'[5]

Some ten years later, in a paper presented at a UNESCO regional seminar, Ed Parr stated, 'The Fenwick Report proved effective and in 1968 the Commonwealth Government announced a three-year plan for the expenditure of $27 million on secondary school libraries. This was followed by other grants to secondary schools, and to primary schools in 1974. State governments have also become very active and there is now a central school library service in each State. These central services have varying responsibilities and functions, but all have planning and co-ordinating roles within the State education systems and advisory relationships with independent schools . . . Ten years after the Fenwick Report, the situation of school libraries has been transformed.'[6]

The views of Parr, in claiming a transformation in Australian school libraries, were given credence in papers presented to the conference of the International Association of School Librarianship, in Melbourne in 1978.[7] New dimensions then appeared, factors that have had considerable influence on Australian school librarianship. One of these factors was the existence of central school library services not only in each State, but also in the major territories (Australian Capital Territory and Northern Territory). The other factor was the emergence of the Schools Commission as a catalytic and moderating influence in school libraries.

Education systems

In each State in Australia, the education system is autonomous—in funding, in administration, in function and in curriculum. As mentioned above, each government system now maintains its own central school library service. Each service is unique in philosophy and practice, paralleling the autonomy of the government education system of which it is a part. The unique nature of each service is a two-edged sword—it perpetuates expensive duplication, unrelated practices and incompatible organisation patterns across the country; it also permits central library services to schools to be geared to local needs and practices, in keeping with autonomous systems.

One recent feature of government education systems in Australia is the development of regionalisation. In some instances, certain elements of the central authority have service aspects at the regional level. School library authorities in some States have developed regional services, and the incidence of such provision seems likely to increase. Generally the services provided are advisory and bibliographical, with an increasing reliance on regional resource centres, both static and mobile.

Co-operation and rationalisation

While there are major differences in the services offered by each central school library administrative unit, and those differences and the right to them have been vigorously defended, a new climate is beginning to emerge. Co-operative schemes of various types are being espoused; the American influence of networking is being felt; rationalisation of services is being promoted; and the idiocy of unnecessary duplication of effort and resources in a time of financial stringency is being realised. It is unlikely that the early 1980s will bring a marked change in the provision of autonomous services. There is a possibility, however, that more flexible attitudes will prevail and that major barriers to co-operation will be removed.

Perhaps symptomatic of the new attitude is the rationalisation of central services to school and public libraries in Tasmania. These services are now provided through the State Library of Tasmania, a move accomplished not without opposition but yet with much goodwill and common sense. As indicated by W. L. Brown, the State Librarian, 'Special services of the State Library are now freely available to the [School] Library Services Branch and among those where useful and productive interaction have already taken place are reference services, bibliographical services, and technical services, resources development, children's pool stock, systems development, etc.'[8] There is little chance of the integration of aspects of school and public library central services in Tasmania being repeated in other States in the foreseeable future; other systems do not have the geographic and demographic factors or the public library regionalisation features pertinent to the Tasmanian condition. Nevertheless, the development is a major one and provides grounds for soul searching by library and education administrators and for serious inquiry by legislators.

If school libraries in Australia have made the rapid strides that are claimed, one aspect of the central services is perhaps incongruous. Undoubtedly school libraries have developed as multi-media resource centres similar to the American model. Yet at the central departmental administration level, there is little evidence of a unified approach. Of the State administrations, only in Queensland is there a physical and practical development that can claim to be an integrated approach to resource provision and service. The Northern Territory provides an example of an even more unified approach. With those exceptions, however, central services to Australian school libraries do not reflect the integrated policies inculcated at the school level. The reasons are not hard to find—tradition and personalities being difficult task masters.

Schools Commission

The beneficial effects of the Schools Commission on school library development in Australia have not been widely appreciated. In the early years of its existence, the Schools Commission maintained a detailed school library program, specific funds being allocated for library facilities and resources. For state government schools, the funds were provided in bulk with broad guidelines governing their allocation. In recent years, a specific library program has not been part of the Commission's activities; though education funding to State departments still allowed for some expenditure on library facilities and resources.

The massive injection of funds to supplement State efforts in school library development had several effects. Firstly, it provided the necessary impetus and encouragement to the few States in which primary school libraries had not been supported; and the States that previously provided libraries in primary schools were able to upgrade the level of provision. Secondly, training programs for the education of school librarians were given some priority in Commission funding. In consequence, most systems were constrained to employ additional school librarians in schools. Thirdly, central school library authorities in each State required additional staffing to cope with the increased demands from schools. Finally, Commission funding had some influence in the exchange of ideas and cross-fertilisation between systems.

Before the Commission's existence, the State systems had maintained their autonomous practices largely through isolationism. No formal structure existed to allow heads of central services to meet regularly; nor did opportunities arise when they could all be present at one conference. It might be claimed that a feeling of self-sufficiency existed. Then formal committees of the Schools Commission and monitoring groups for its programs, including schemes not specifically library-oriented, brought together representatives from the various systems on a somewhat regular basis. The Commission also sponsored State and national seminars on aspects of school library practice and needs. Thus a high level of respectability for the school library was engendered at a national level, and acceptable avenues for the exchange of ideas and the discussion of policies and practices were established.

As well as influencing State school library central services, the Schools

Commission also succeeded in establishing a responsive attitude in related professional associations, notably the Library Association of Australia and the Australian School Library Association. An awareness by these bodies of the Commission's existence has often led to joint ventures, wider representation and rationalisation of activities.

Non-government schools

Within the Australian education context is a vast array of schools not affiliated with a government system. Most of these are associated with religious denominations; others are quite independent of such affiliations. Because the central library services of government systems were established primarily to serve the schools of the relevant systems, those services are generally not available to non-government schools. Although there are exceptions, they tend to be in the area of advisory services; furthermore, financial constraints are reducing the incidence of such exceptions.

Generally, then, non-government schools receive comparatively little support from the central library services of government systems. The establishment of their own central services, is of course, out of the question for the separate or even small groups of independent schools. Some efforts have been made by the larger groups of church schools to provide central library support, notably in some Catholic dioceses, but the number engaged in such activities is pitifully low. Consequently, even where central library support is available, it tends to be advisory in nature, with little or nothing in the way of bibliographical, ordering, processing or cataloguing services or of back-up collections of materials.

Before 1974, libraries in non-government schools, particularly primary schools, had little to commend them; the exceptions stood out like beacons. Again, the advent of Schools Commission finance and involvement has vastly affected provision and practice. It has influenced the provision of support staffing in the non-government central library systems that exist; it has led to a healthy growth in relationships between government and non-government systems and staff; it has helped develop the exchange of ideas between systems; and even the exchange of staff between government and non-government systems has been undertaken for experimental periods.

These innovative programs have had their critics. There are, of course, those who object to 'tarnishing' a system with outside ideas and personnel. Such minority views, however, have not hindered experimentation. It is also claimed that the government sector is the minor beneficiary in such arrangements. While this is an exorbitant claim in universal terms, few would deny that non-government schools have had their educational goals and achievements markedly extended in some areas. The school library is certainly one such area. However, there can be little doubt that government central library services, in some of their activities, have also gained enormously from the joint sponsorship, combined activities, exchange of staff, influx of ideas and exposure to other systems, which have resulted from Schools Commission programs, from growth in non-government school library activity and increased contact with other government systems.

Central cataloguing

If any one central library service can lay claim to being the most-expressed need of school libraries in Australia, it is a central cataloguing service. Only one State, Western Australia, has had anywhere near a complete service for its government schools; and that has been a manual operation, which has been generally successful with perhaps the exception of some delays. (Many would claim that such an exception constitutes an *unsuccessful* service.) Other government systems have provided a manual service limited to certain materials, a manual service limited to particular schools, or no service at all. Non-government schools have traditionally had no such service, although limited availability was afforded in certain cases in the late 1970s.

For many years, a feature of American librarianship has been the availability of prepared catalogue cards from commercial suppliers. An extension of this practice has been the access to catalogue data banks through computerised systems, thus allowing even greater flexibility and individuality in the supply of prepared catalogue cards, even to the extent of choice in the allocation of classification numbers and subject headings.

With its restricted clientele, Australia has not been similarly favoured. For the past decade the National Library of Australia has been the only local supplier of catalogue cards on a wide, commercial basis. Its success in this role, however, has been limited.

National Library trial
In the early 1970s, the federal government funded a feasibility trial on the suitability of the National Library card service for Australian schools.[9]

The study was an important one, for it pointed out the limited nature of the service. Admittedly some participating schools were sufficiently happy with the scheme to continue as subscribers well beyond the trial period, and others later became users. The overwhelming consensus, however, was that the service was unsatisfactory for school purposes. Major reasons for that conclusion were:

(a) the comparatively poor overall hit rate (cards supplied for requests made);

(b) the surprisingly low success rate for Australian material;

(c) close to nil return for lower-age material, especially picture books;

(d) excessively detailed information on cards, geared more to a research institution;

(e) similar criticism of classification and subject heading usage;

(f) delays in supply.

Other reasons, such as cost, were also cited as inhibiting factors.

The trial provided much useful information and enabled further approaches to be made to National Library authorities with a view to providing a service acceptable to schools. Those negotiations were unsuccessful. It became clear that the provision of a card service would not be given high priority in the allocation of personnel and resources within the National Library. It was also clear that the nation's schools would not accept the service that was available to them.

Cataloguing studies

The matter was not left to rest there. With pressures still coming from various sources, including advisory committees of the Schools Commission, the Commission arranged for further investigations to be undertaken. The studies of Wesley Young and Douglas Down in 1974[10] and 1977[11] on behalf of the Commission pointed to the continued need of Australian schools for a cataloguing service. They also emphasised the need for a responsive service, one that would cater for the expressed needs of a variety of systems and schools with individual requirements.

SAERIS and ASCIS

In the meantime, the central school library service of the South Australian Education Department had been developing and was approaching the implementation of an automated central cataloguing service for all its schools. The scheme, SAERIS (South Australian Education Resources Information System), was a multifaceted resource system which, in its first phase, allowed for a dual approach—copy cataloguing from COM

(Computer Output Microfiche) or the provision of computer produced catalogue cards on demand. Developmental problems delayed its implementation until early 1980.

Realising the potential of a school-based and oriented system, the Schools Commission funded a pilot project, ASCIS (Australian School Catalogue Information Service), based on SAERIS and aimed at testing the feasibility of a national cataloguing service for Australian schools. Some modification of the original project has occurred, aided by the delay in instituting SAERIS.

In essence, ASCIS provides a three-pronged approach. Firstly, in return for constantly updated microfiche output of the total data base, central school library services in the States and Territories provide to SAERIS, in MARC (machine readable) format, cataloguing data for items catalogued locally but not appearing on the data base output. Secondly, non-government schools in South Australia and selected government and non-government schools in Queensland receive constantly updated microfiche copies of the data base and participate (as do SAERIS schools) by copy cataloguing or requesting sets of catalogue cards; these ASCIS schools, however, must pay for cards thus supplied, the cost being subsidised by the Schools Commission. The third approach, as modified, involves the provision of duplicate magnetic tapes of the data base to the State Library of Tasmania (which incorporates the central State school library service); catalogue cards are then made available from the Elizabeth Computer Centre to government and non-government schools in Tasmania as requested.

The Schools Commission clearly indicated that ASCIS was a pilot project, with a feasibility-testing role. Its funded life was limited to 1980. The Commission appointed a representative steering committee to monitor progress and to make recommendations concerning the project. While there were fears that delays in implementing SAERIS may adversely affect the ASCIS experiment, the South Australian commitment to SAERIS, the Tasmanian acceptance (without amendment) of South Australian cataloguing and classification procedures, and the stated intentions for continued involvement from some non-government authorities were sufficient signs that the experiment was worthwhile. The commitment from South Australia to provide, to the data-contributing authorities who desired it, tape copies of the total data base at the conclusion of the ASCIS project gives rise to speculation of further experimentation at the local level and the possible development of compatible systems. Of major import, of course, will be the recommendations of the steering committee and the reaction of the Schools Commission to those recommendations.

Much attention is being focused on the glamorous nature of automated cataloguing procedures. There are other services, however, which are equally important for the central support of school libraries. They may not relieve the school librarian of repetitious tasks in order to concentrate on other activities, but they do provide an important back-up service in the performance of normal tasks.

Advisory services

All government school systems maintain some degree of advisory service, and in certain cases this is regarded as a major support system. Experienced school librarians are given the responsibility of visiting a number of schools to provide advice and guidance. Before the wide employment of trained school librarians, advisory staff frequently found themselves cataloguing and selecting materials for many of the schools under their guidance. Their proper role thus was deposed by the schools' need for practical organisation of the library.

Since the employment of trained school librarians became a more regular practice, advisory personnel have been able to turn their attention to tasks more in keeping with their training and experience. While in most systems advisory personnel have been engaged fully in advisory duties, for many years in Victoria some personnel have had responsibility as school librarians for part of their time and as advisory school librarians for the remainder of their time.

Inservice education

Continuing or inservice education activity for school librarians is recognised and practised as a responsibility of the central service, although recently much of this has been carried out at the regional level. Frequently advisory personnel perform the task as one of their most important duties. While the majority of inservice training courses has been carried out in the traditional method of bringing school librarians to a central point for indoctrination or developmental activity, a more pertinent and satisfactory type of course has sometimes been carried out at the school level by a team of advisory or central office personnel going en masse to a school for inservice activity. On these occasions the library staff and the subject or class teachers undertake a combined activity for some hours, a day or a few days under the guidance of the visiting team. Although this approach brings obvious administrative problems, it is considered a most beneficial practice and has brought excellent results in developing understanding and better teaching and learning methods.

Bibliographic services

A constant need in school libraries is advice on selection of materials. Conscious of this, heads of central services have endeavoured to provide appropriate assistance. In some instances, this consists of full reviewing services for new print and non-print materials carried out at the central service, the reviews being made available to schools at regular intervals. In other instances, materials are assessed at the central level and lists of recommended materials are compiled and forwarded to schools. Both types of operation are of value to schools. The former is a preferable service in giving detailed information about each item and enables an informed decision to be made at the local level, dependent of course upon the level of competence and experience of the reviewers. The latter has a similar dependency and generally has the advantage of a greater range of material included.

Each government central school library service in Australia has built up support collections of materials to assist their school libraries; such collections are often regionally based as well as centrally based. These operate in a variety of ways which include the provision of bulk loans to small schools and to newly established schools, a pre-selection perusal centre, a reference service and the base for an inter-library loan scheme. Many of these collections commenced as model libraries, which contained materials that it was felt schools should provide in their libraries. In most cases, the concept has changed, as school collections became more diverse and school-based curricula developments gained respectability.

A recent alternative to the static support library has been the provision of mobile collections, similar in some respects to the familiar mobile libraries of public library services. Innovation grants from the Schools Commission have enabled some of these to be established by non-government school systems; their services, however, have been made available to both government and non-government schools. In the Northern Territory and in Tasmania, mobile resource vans have been providing major support particularly to outlying schools; while the Victorian Education Department has developed a large network of

Mobile Area Resource Vans covering extensive areas in the country and providing a service that has become a major aspect of its central support.

Publications

Communication between central school library authorities and schools is critical to concerted operations and compatible services. As part of the communication chain, the central services have established publication programs which range from simple advice sheets, through selection lists and cataloguing information, to comprehensive professional journals. While there is much repetition in subject matter and even in coverage, this is frequently defended on the grounds of system autonomy and greater ability to provide locally for individual needs. In purely economic terms, this defence appears untenable; but there are factors that militate against radical change in systems developed individually over many years. These include valid arguments against rigid uniformity and the disruption, rather than improved service, that sudden change would cause in thousands of schools already serviced satisfactorily.

Central purchasing and processing

Australian school library systems do not have extensive examples of central ordering and purchasing of library resources or of central processing procedures. Only in Western Australia have such schemes been in common use. There, because of large discounts applying to bulk ordering, the unit cost of materials to school libraries is less than in other systems. Against that, of course, must be offset the central costs of staffing and handling charges. It may appear surprising that other systems do not follow similar practice, particularly in cases with government contracts for the central purchase of materials for public libraries. Such action has occasionally been proposed and discussed but with no positive outcome as yet. There has been little enthusiasm for the proposal because of additional staffing costs at the central level, implications for local suppliers of materials, and concern by school personnel at the possibility that central purchase could lead to central selection—a practice opposed by most school librarians.

Automation

No doubt automation will play an ever-increasing role in the provision of central services to Australian school libraries. While the first phase of

SAERIS provides for copy cataloguing and an on-demand catalogue card service, later phases make provision for fiche catalogues for the holdings of individual schools, and eventually for on-line access to the central data base. Already many secondary schools in Tasmania have on-line access to their central computing centre and thus to the data bases stored there, including those supplied through the ASCIS project. The National Library's development and gradual extension of AUSINET (the Australian Information Network) and its recent decision to install the Washington Library Network system as the basis for a comprehensive Australian bibliographical network are evidence of other areas in which central school library services are likely to become involved. There is also the rapidly developing field of micrographics, which has considerable implications for educational use and thus for resource organisation and manipulation.

It would, indeed, be shortsighted to ignore the trends and to hide behind the cloak of conjecture. Equally rash would it be to continue the isolationist policies of the past and not to share the technologies devised if they have applicability beyond the immediate area of development. The late 1970s have provided the impetus for a future of mutual exchange and co-operative activity. I hope the lead will be accepted.

References
1. Lawrence H. McGrath, *Central Library Services of the Education Departments of the Australian States* (Libraries Board of South Australia, Adelaide, 1965), p. 1.
2. Ralph Munn and Ernest R. Pitt, *Australian Libraries: A Survey of Conditions and Suggestions for their Improvement* (Australian Council for Educational Research, Melbourne, 1935).
3. McGrath, p. 4.
4. Sara Innis Fenwick, *School and Children's Libraries in Australia: A Report to the Children's Libraries Section of the Library Association of Australia* (Cheshire, Melbourne, for the LAA, 1966), p. 6.
5. Fenwick, p. 20
6. E. Parr, 'An overview of Australian library services', in *Planning and Development of School Library Services: Proceedings of the UNESCO Regional Seminar on School Libraries* (Perth, 1976), p. 26.
7. *The Democratization of Education: Implications for School Libraries*, Conference Papers, International Association of School Librarianship Conference, Melbourne, 26 July–1 August 1978 (Melbourne, 1978).
8. In *Ed. Lib* 5, 4 (1978), 1.
9. J. M. Cronin, Card Service to School Libraries—Pilot Project: An Assessment (unpublished paper, Canberra, 1973).
10. Douglas W. Down and Wesley A. Young, *Cataloguing for Schools: The Feasibility of Catalogue Card Services for All Schools in Australia*. A report to the Australian Schools Commission (Melbourne State College, Carlton, Vic., 1975).
11. Douglas W. Down and Wesley A. Young, *Australian Schools Cataloguing Service*. A report to the Schools Commission (Melbourne State College, Carlton, Vic., 1977).

CHAPTER 12

Education for School Librarianship

Joan Brewer

The dilemma in planning the ideal educational program for a prospective school librarian has in the past been in deciding whether the student is to be primarily a teacher or primarily a librarian. Librarians without teaching qualifications have been appointed to school libraries, as have teachers with little or no library training. It used to be the case in Australia that education for school librarians was a course of varying length and quality added on to a teaching qualification. With the changing concept of the role of the school librarian as an educator, one who must be concerned with and involved in the educational program, came the need for different and more specialised courses. It was some time before it was recognised that a truly professional course, if it was at undergraduate level, had to be carefully planned, with close attention, from the beginning of the first year of study, to the integration of studies in education, in librarianship and in at least one other subject area. Such undergraduate courses, usually of four years of study or longer, have been implemented in countries such as Australia and the United States of America. In addition, there are graduate courses available in the field of school librarianship. Indeed, some library educators insist on the absolute necessity for graduate rather than undergraduate programs, especially in the United States where studies cover five or six years.

A profession

School librarianship is now recognised as a profession in its own right, and its practitioners are usually expected to have dual qualifications. It has taken a long time for teachers to accept the fact that managing a school library is not a task that can be allotted to a member of the staff as an extra responsibility and a relatively unimportant one. It used to be seen as something that could be done in spare time, rather than as an important, full-time occupation. In this view the emphasis was on the techniques of indexing library materials and on organising them for ready access, and it was incorrectly assumed that these were relatively simple tasks. The librarian's role was seen as primarily that of a custodian. But library schools today have to consider the librarian's educational role as well as the increasing importance of the administrative role. The rapidity of change and the impact of technology have introduced new media, computers, library networks and access to school libraries by the community as topics that must be considered, not to mention new curricula and different teaching methods.

In some places, particularly in Great Britain but also in Australia, professional librarians without teaching qualifications are still being appointed to school libraries, particularly in secondary schools. Their background and training are seen as different from the teaching staff and usually they are on a different salary scale. However, increasingly many educational authorities insist that a school librarian must be qualified as both a teacher and a librarian. An official publication of the Australian Schools Commission states that 'The person responsible for resource services in the school should have qualifications and experience in teaching and librarianship and should be regarded as a member of the school teaching team. Such a person is usually known as a teacher-librarian although the term school librarian is also used.'[1] Librarians in government schools in all Australian States must have a teaching qualification. At a symposium held in London a decade ago, the need for expertise in both fields was also recognised: 'Thus whether he is originally a teacher or originally a librarian he will need something more than a superficial knowledge of the technique of the other profession and he will need, probably, continuing in-service training as the educational system and the society in which it is embedded change.'[2]

Type and length of courses

Graduate or undergraduate programs
Discussion as to the best way in which to educate prospective school librarians has been taking place at conferences and in the professional literature in many countries. The initial argument usually centres on the respective claims of undergraduate and graduate programs. The

American Library Association accredits graduate courses only, although there are many undergraduate courses available. In the final assessment of the Knapp School Library Manpower Project, this question was raised. 'As a result of this Project there is now evidence which suggests that at the first professional entry level graduates of an undergraduate program can successfully compete with graduates of an M.A. level program.'[3] The report goes on to discuss what the relationship might be between graduate and undergraduate programs and raises the difficulties associated with trying to cover so much material in one year in a graduate course. This question of increasing the length of graduate courses has been a concern of library educators in general, not just of those who teach school librarianship. 'The trend in North America seems to be toward two or more years of graduate education', stated Andrew Horn at a Colloquium in Western Australia in 1973.[4] In Australia both graduate and undergraduate programs in school librarianship are available, sometimes at the same institution (as is the case at Canberra College of Advanced Education and Melbourne State College). And both kinds of courses have been accredited by the Library Association of Australia. The same argument has been debated in relation to courses for teachers, the advantages and disadvantages of end-on versus concurrent programs. Those who favour graduate librarianship programs urge extension of the program to at least three semesters to allow for additional and essential material to be added to an already overcrowded syllabus. Others suggest that integrated studies over several years are more effective and allow the student to link together the various components of the course. Of course, it will depend not merely on the content of the course but also on the way in which it is taught, which ideally should allow the student to see the relationships between the various parts. There seems to be a need for both types of program.

Entry qualifications

Entry qualifications vary. For graduate courses, a qualification in education is required. Some institutions insist on a certain number of years' teaching experience in schools before admission is granted to graduate programs. The argument is that qualified and experienced teachers are more likely to be successful, provided of course that they have already been successful in the teaching situation. Such graduates may also be more acceptable to other teachers who know that these school librarians understand their problems in using materials effectively in teaching.

Discussion of entry qualifications should give consideration to courses for those who have librarianship training and experience so that they may add the education component. Beswick described ways in which chartered librarians in Great Britain could gain such a qualification.[5] If the double qualification is needed then entry must be possible from either discipline. And of course there is the usual entry examination requirement for school leavers beginning an undergraduate program, as well as special entry examinations for mature-age students. Entry to the profession should be possible for qualified graduate teachers, for professional librarians, for school leavers and for mature-age entrants who have had work experience in other areas, including other professions.

Teaching institutions

Librarianship should, of course, be studied in tertiary institutions. There are courses in librarianship in two universities and in many colleges of advanced education in Australia. All accredited courses in school librarianship are in the colleges, some of which offer graduate programs. Graduate courses are one year in duration, and all undergraduate programs that have been accredited by the Library Association, except one, are four-year programs. In Great Britain there are three-year undergraduate programs in librarianship at both universities and polytechnics, leading to the award of a degree in librarianship. There are also graduate courses in universities. In the United States there are undergraduate and graduate programs at colleges and universities.

Many experts argue that school librarians should be educated alongside teachers. As Doreen Goodman stated in 1970, 'the new concept of the school library emphasizes the close relationship between teachers and school librarians. They are two sides of the one coin. Their education and training covers basically the same ground, any difference being one mainly of emphasis.'[6] This raises the need for the education of teachers in the role of the library in the school and the ways in which they can use the library's resources to improve learning. 'All problems of school library development come back to the crucial question of the nature and quality of teacher training. The training of teachers to use libraries and library materials is as important as the training of librarians.'[7]

In both Great Britain and Australia there have been examination systems conducted by the professional associations by which candidates could gain professional status. This practice ceased in Australia in 1980, but in the past many teachers have gained librarianship qualifications by studying for the examinations conducted by the Library Association of Australia. The Library Association in Great Britain continues its examination system. An attempt to meet the needs of school librarians resulted in the establishment of a special course, leading to the award of the Certificate for Teacher Librarians. This has been superseded by a Certificate in School Library Studies, given on completion of a course in certain colleges. The planning and supervision of these two Certificate courses has been a joint project of the Library Association and the School Library Association.[8]

Academic staff

Obviously most of the academic staff teaching school librarianship should themselves have dual qualifications. There will also be a need for specialists in various aspects of librarianship or education, who do not have a recognised qualification in both areas. For example, experts in educational technology or in children's literature or in computer applications to libraries or in administration might well be chosen to join the academic staff. Certainly academics from other teaching departments or faculties are usually invited to give lectures or to provide special courses for school librarianship students. Visiting lecturers and experienced practitioners are important too. The staff should have the same status as other academic staff in the institution, as well as opportunities for further study and particularly for research. In Australia there has not been enough research on school libraries, apart from the work which was sponsored by the Australian Government. It is interesting to read the regular reports of research carried out in the United States in each issue of *School Media Quarterly*.[9]

Course content

With so many developments in school libraries and with so many skills being required of the school librarian, a great deal of emphasis has been placed on the competencies required to carry out all these tasks. This was the emphasis in the Knapp School Library Manpower Project.

> By electing to follow the guidelines which emerged from Phase 1 of the School Library Manpower Project, the experimental programs chose to pursue the competency-based, field-centered program in their efforts to achieve an efficient and effective educational system for preparing professional school library media personnel. This was dependent upon a systems design or process which would incorporate clear statements of expected behaviours, a task

analysis followed by an ordered sequencing of learning experiences, a systematic assessment of the learner's achievement in the program and a flexible curriculum structure to permit modification of the program.[10]

A compilation of a tasks checklist was also part of the project.[11] This program had a considerable influence on a Canberra workshop mentioned later, in which one of the American documents was included as an appendix in the published proceedings.[12] Chisholm and Ely have also outlined the competencies required of today's professional school librarian.[13] The American Library Association published a booklet, *Certification Model for Professional School Media Personnel*, in an attempt to establish a national standard.

> The educational preparation required of persons in this type of environment is different from that of the traditional librarian, audiovisualist and educational television personnel. A wide variety of media competencies are needed by media professionals so that they may satisfy the demands placed upon the school media program.[14]

The committee identified seven areas of competencies as follows:
1. Relation of media to instructional systems.
2. Administration of media programs.
3. Selection of media.
4. Utilisation of media.
5. Production of media.
6. Research and evaluation.
7. Leadership and professionalism.[15]

Because of the need for competency over a broad area of skills, undergraduate programs in Australia have usually been four years in length, one year longer than courses in librarianship and courses in teaching. Attempts have been made to develop an interdisciplinary approach, linking studies in education, in librarianship and in other academic areas. Students are encouraged to do this in many ways, particularly in the area of curriculum where they are urged to study curriculum content and methodology at various grade levels and in all subject areas and to consider the planning of library facilities, services and programs in relation to curriculum demands. Reading programs, particularly those designed for special groups, and study skills programs are other areas in which the interrelationship between studies in education and studies in librarianship is very obvious. Knowledge of the great variety of formats of materials available, ability to select them, to organize them for easy use and to instruct teachers and students in their use are necessary components of a course for school librarians. In some tertiary institutions, educational technologists may be part of the instructional team for such courses.

The difference in education and training required for primary and secondary school librarians is minimal. There is a difference in emphasis and this can often be achieved by elective units within the program. But the basic program is the same because the educational philosophy is the same. In any case, some graduates in Australia may work in schools that have an enrolment from Year 1 through to Year 12, or they may choose to move from primary to secondary school or vice versa.

General studies

The wider the selection of general studies available to the student the better. Too many school librarians have confined their general academic studies to the humanities and social sciences. The advantage of teaching librarianship in an institution offering a wide variety of professional programs is that it should be easier to offer a wide choice of subjects. That this is not always so is due to rigid structures within institutions that make it unnecessarily difficult for students to take units in schools or faculties other than the one to which they belong. It is usual for students who want to be school librarians to take many subjects with students who will be classroom teachers. It is desirable that they study with students who are preparing for other professions too, if at all possible. In Australia the importance of study in depth in at least one other subject has been generally accepted. At a national workshop in Canberra designed to discuss the planning of suitable educational programs for school librarians, the final statement said 'In addition to the three areas of education, librarianship and administration . . . it is important that tertiary education should be undertaken to the level of a third year major within another academic field.'[16] The Library Association of Australia stresses this point in its Statement on the Recognition of Courses referring both to generalist and specialist courses.[17]

Librarianship

Courses in school librarianship should include those core subjects of which all librarians are expected to have some understanding. The Statement on the Recognition of Courses in Librarianship which appears in the 1980 *Handbook* of the Library Association of Australia states:

> The professional content of any course leading to professional qualifications whether of the undergraduate or of the postgraduate type should include the following studies . . .

(a) the place of the library in society today, together with its historical development;
(b) the library as an agency of communication;
(c) the principles of bibliographic organization;
(d) the principles of collection building;
(e) the principles of library management.
In each case the study of the principles should be illustrated by study of their application, and where appropriate by practical exercises.[18]

In a course for school librarians the emphasis will naturally be on the application of the principles to the school library—for example, in collection building and in management. However, school libraries must be seen as part of a wider library network. It is necessary to study other types of library and the wide variety of information agencies, other than libraries, that are available in the community. School librarians have a responsibility to make pupils and staff aware of these agencies, and to guide them in their effective use. Consequently courses for school librarians should consider the wider library and information network.

Education
Obviously school librarianship courses must include studies in eduction. In Australia such studies will be almost identical to those undertaken by classroom teachers. In both undergraduate and graduate programs there will be courses in such subjects as educational psychology and human development from infancy to young adulthood. The social framework in which the school exists, ethics and education, the different philosophies of education and the history of education will usually be part of the syllabus. The development of language and various learning theories and teaching strategies will be examined. There is a strong emphasis on relating theory to practice in most undergraduate programs, so that experience in schools, both for observation and for practical teaching sessions, is built into the course. The relationship between these studies in education and their application to the school library should be stressed in seminars and tutorials.

However, it cannot be assumed that teachers who have been in the schools for some years have kept up to date with educational developments. Consequently graduate programs in school librarianship usually include some studies in education, not only to update the knowledge of their graduate students but also to make them aware of those changes in educational theory and practice that have had such an important impact on the role of the school library.

Administration

Studies in administration are also increasingly important. Those who are in charge of the management of school libraries must know something of the administrative framework of the school itself, as well as of the outside agencies and institutions, such as School Boards or Regional Centres or central government departments or local government authorities which have some jurisdiction over the school. Suitable courses may be provided by lecturers in business management or in educational administration rather than by lecturers in librarianship. For example, certain units in a course in educational administration may be suitable for inclusion in a librarianship program, perhaps with specially designed assignments. School librarians are responsible for large budgets, they have to assign tasks to other staff members, they may be required to design buildings and, facilities in co-operation with architects, and they must set up systems of management within the library to ensure the selection, acquisition, organisation and use of all kinds of media. Management skills are essential, and Hicks and Tillin give useful advice on this topic.[19]

Computers

Computer applications to libraries must be included in courses. School libraries are increasingly being involved in various computerised networks, such as the well-known Ohio College Library Center in the United States and the Australian School Catalogue Information Service based on a South Australian scheme described by James Dwyer elsewhere in this book. John Balnaves stresses the need for both theory and practice in relation to computers.

> It would be possible to learn about riding a bicycle, to make all the correct responses, yet not to be able to do it . . . Similarly in the present state of the art, learning about some of the concepts embraced by the term library automation is not enough. You have to do it if you are really to understand it. Indeed, especially in the area of information retrieval, students have great difficulty in understanding the literature unless their reading is illuminated by doing.[20]

Media

It goes without saying that a knowledge of non-print materials is essential. Courses of training for teachers have improved in this regard, and there is usually a compulsory unit in both teaching and librarianship courses. This should include some practice in the production and use of materials, because many teachers and librarians are making materials to match the curriculum in their own schools. Students should be encouraged to present assignments in a variety of formats.

Children's literature

Studies of literature for children and young people are included in school librarianship programs. Sometimes these courses are taught by members of the English faculty, at other times by the librarianship teaching staff. In either case, there is a need for a basic course and for several elective units in special areas such as literature for adolescents, traditional literature or story-telling.

Methods of teaching

Methods of teaching should put into practice the theories underlying the school library's development as the learning centre of the school. There should be large- and small-group instruction and discussion, in lectures, tutorials and seminars. All kinds of media should be utilised to aid instruction: blackboards, overhead projectors, sound tapes, videotapes, films, slides, charts, models, etc. Students should be given the opportunity to present assignments in various media too. Individualised programs of study, in which the student follows up a particular interest and studies that topic in depth, are desirable, as are assignments that may be modified by a student to meet his or her particular needs. For example, part-time students who are already working in school libraries benefit from altering the parameters of an assignment to something that is actually applicable to their own situations. The Knapp Project stressed the need for curricula to be occupationally relevant. Case studies are useful too.

Practical workshops are usually included, especially in bibliographic organisation, in computing, in the use and production of various media, and in various library management routines.

Field experience is important, although it is sometimes difficult to arrange. Time constraints in graduate programs limit the amount of practical experience. Union problems can arise too. Adequate supervision of field work is essential, and this may be costly, especially if it has to be undertaken at a school that is some distance from the homes of both student and supervising lecturer. Study tours are also expensive. Sometimes these may be part of an elective course rather than a compulsory component. In other cases the teaching institution may carry the cost of such study tours, if not in total at least a large proportion.

Again, the Knapp Project favoured such field work. 'Internships, practicums, and other fieldwork experiences were part of all six experimental programs. This Project clearly demonstrated the validity of such field experiences. Graduates and faculty alike thought that these aspects of their programs were most effective and useful.'[21]

The teaching methods should stress the links between the various parts of the course. This is much more likely to happen if the teaching of some units is a joint enterprise between lecturers in librarianship and lecturers in other subject departments or faculties. For example, in one college a course on traditional literature, dealing with myths and legends and story-telling, was planned by a children's literature expert, a lecturer in religion studies and a drama lecturer. Similarly co-operation with the experts in the design and production of educational media resulted in a more effective discussion in seminars, based on specially prepared videotapes made in schools, with lecturers from both departments taking part in the seminars. Librarianship lecturers can also establish links by taking part in lectures and tutorials in the education component of the school librarianship course. In this regard the importance of the practical experience in schools cannot be overestimated, particularly if some of that experience involves activities in the classroom as well as in the library. This is not necessarily designed to prepare the students for classroom teaching but it certainly gives students an understanding of the ways in which children learn and helps to develop their confidence in dealing with children. The student also shares this school experience with other students who are preparing to be teachers. Sometimes it happens that the student librarian can assist the student teacher to acquire and organise materials for teaching, which is a small sample of the librarian's future role as a curriculum consultant.

Part-time and external teaching
The question of part-time and external study has been an important issue in Australia, where the majority of the tertiary institutions are in the large coastal cities. Many practising librarians and teachers and former teachers want to study librarianship by part-time study and most tertiary institutions allow this. This usually involves repetition of lectures for evening students or special time-tabling arrangements. Many teachers of librarianship object to part-time study on principle. It is difficult for the student to retain an overview of the whole course when studying units separately. Contact with other students and with the teaching staff is certainly more difficult. However, most institutions teaching librarian-

ship in Australia allow part-time study, particularly to those working in libraries who are at the same time gaining a professional qualification.

External studies are more difficult and only a few tertiary institutions offer courses by this mode. Many factors have to be considered, including careful selection of students; the possibility of students in an area forming a tutorial group; compulsory attendance on campus at certain times; the preparation of course booklets; the use of audio-visual materials, particularly lecture tapes and tapes for communication between students and lecturer; local resources available, such as libraries of various types, which can be a crucial factor inhibiting student progress in isolated areas; and the setting up of a mailing centre to dispatch, receive and record correspondence and assignments. The biggest problem is one of communication. Visits by lecturers to the larger centres can help to alleviate this problem. But the difficulties are not confined to librarianship, although there are particular problems in studying librarianship because the student must have access to major libraries, to a variety of libraries and information centres, and these are usually available only in one or two major cities in each Australian State. On-campus attendance and study tours are essential.

Courses for support staff

It is inappropriate to discuss this topic in detail, but it must be mentioned. Any discussion of what is required in a school library makes it obvious that one person cannot carry out all the tasks. The latest American Standards list media specialists, other media professionals and support staff. 'Preparation for the position of technician or media aide is acquired either by specialized training or on-the-job experience.'[22] The Schools Commission's document lists 'teacher-librarians, specialist teachers, librarians, technical support staff, clerical support staff, aides'.[23] The increase in the number of courses for library technicians in Australia indicates the need for training for support staff, and the Schools Commission recommends the number of support staff required in schools of various enrolments.[24]

The role of professional associations

The professional associations have played an important role not only in accrediting courses but also, in both Great Britain and Australia, in conducting an examination system. The general association of librarians and the special association for school librarians have generally worked together to improve the standard of school libraries. In Australia, for example, the Library Association was active in promoting federal funding for school libraries and for publishing the first set of standards for school libraries.[25] The Australian School Library Association has been responsible for bringing prominent school librarians from the United States to act as advisers on school library developments. Both associations sponsor national conferences as well as workshops and seminars. The accreditation process of the Library Association of Australia through its Board of Education and the Board's statements on school librarianship have been important in establishing professional status.

Continuing education

The professional associations have an important role to play in the continuing education of librarians. That they recognise this is evident in the formation of a Continuing Education Committee by the Library Association of Australia, which attempts to co-ordinate the various programs offered throughout the country and to organise courses. The library schools have an obligation to assist in this area too, because there is continuous change and development and a need for librarians to update their knowledge. Employers, too, must be involved. The various State Departments of Education recognise this by arranging in-service conferences and training programs. Some programs receive financial support from the Schools Commission. Co-operation between the professional associations, the teaching institutions and the employers is desirable to make the most efficient use of available resources.

School librarians should also consider further study programs, not only higher degrees but also study in other areas that are relevant to librarianship, such as educational technology, administration, computer studies and reading, to name a few possibilities.

Conclusion

School librarianship courses have developed to professional status. There is a variety of courses available with emphasis on both librarianship and education so that the school librarian is recognised as a professional by both teachers and librarians. It may be that teaching institutions and the profession will have to consider offering more opportunities for specialisation, because what is expected of a school librarian seems to be increasing rapidly. This specialisation may be achieved through elective units in the first librarianship course or through further study in certain aspects of school librarianship. And librarians must be aware of the place of the school library in the provision of library resources to the community, not only through such specific means as school/community libraries but also through the development of library networks.

References

1. Schools Commission, *Books and Beyond: Guidelines for Library Resource Facilities and Services* (2nd edn, AGPS, Canberra, 1979), p. 7.
2. C. Waite (ed.), *School Libraries in the 1970s: A Symposium including Papers from the Conference on School Libraries in the 1970s held at University College, London, in July 1970* (University of London, London, 1972).
3. R. N. Case and A. M. Lowrey, *Evaluation of Alternative Curricula Approaches to School Library Media Education* (American Library Association, Chicago, 1975), p. 74.
4. A. Horn, 'Reflections on the curriculum: an American approach', in *Curriculum Design in Librarianship: An International Approach: Proceedings of the Colloquium on Education for Librarianship held at the Western Australian Institute of Technology, 28–30 August 1973* (WAIT Press, Perth, 1974), p. 55.
5. N. W. Beswick, *School Resource Centres: The Report of the First Year of the Schools Council Resource Centre Project* (Evans, London, 1972), p. 81.
6. D. M. Goodman, 'Implications of school libraries for the education and training of teachers and librarians', in *The Role of Libraries in Secondary Education: Proceedings of the Australian UNESCO Seminar*, held at University of New South Wales, August 1970 (AGPS, Canberra, 1971), p. 11.
7. *The Role of Libraries in Secondary Education*, p. vii.
8. Note in *School Librarian* 26, 2 (1978), 100.
9. *School Media Quarterly* (American Association of School Librarians, Chicago).
10. R. N. Case and A. M. Lowrey, *Curriculum Alternatives: Experiments in School Library Media Education* (American Library Association, Chicago, 1974), p. 13.
11. R. N. Case and A. M. Lowrey, *Behavioural Requirements Analysis Checklist: A Compilation of Competency-based Job Functions and Task Statements for School Library Media Personnel* (American Library Association, Chicago, 1973).
12. American Library Association, Task analysis survey instrument (American Library Association, Chicago, 1969) Appendix 3 in *Education for School Librarianship: Proceedings, Findings and Recommendations of a Workshop held in Canberra, 1–4 August 1972* (AGPS, Canberra, 1973), pp. 57–62.
13. M. E. Chisholm and D. P. Ely, *Media Personnel in Education: A Competency Approach* (Prentice-Hall, Englewood Cliffs, N.J., 1976).
14. American Association of School Librarians, *Certification Model for Professional School Media Personnel* (American Library Association, Chicago, 1975), p. 1.
15. *Certification Model for Professional School Media Personnel*, p. 9.
16. *Education for School Librarianship*, p. 43.
17. Library Association of Australia, *Handbook* (LAA, Sydney, 1980), p. 71.
18. *Handbook*, p. 71.
19. W. B. Hicks and A. Tillin, *Managing Multimedia Libraries* (Bowker, New York, 1977).

20. J. Balnaves, 'Education for library automation', *LASIE: Information Bulletin of the Library Automated Systems Information Exchange* 9, 2 (1978), 10–17.

21. Case and Lowrey, *Evaluation of Alternative Curricula Approaches to School Library Media Education*, p. 75.

22. American Association of School Librarians and Association for Educational Communications and Technology, *Media Programs: District and School* (Chicago, 1975), pp. 22–3.

23. Schools Commission, *Books and Beyond*, p. 7.

24. Schools Commission, *Books and Beyond*, p. 9.

25. Library Association of Australia, *Standards and Objectives for School Libraries* (Cheshire, Melbourne for the LAA, 1966).

Index

852510502
Pergamon

Indexing by Infotech